TALKS WITH TEACHERS OF YOUNG CHILDREN

TALKS WITH TEACHERS OF YOUNG CHILDREN
A COLLECTION

LILIAN G. KATZ

*UNIVERSITY OF ILLINOIS
URBANA—CHAMPAIGN*

ABLEX PUBLISHING CORPORATION
NORWOOD, NEW JERSEY

ISBN 1-56750-177-X

Printed in the United States of America

Library of Congress Cataloging-in-Publication Data

Katz, Lilian.
    Talks with teachers of young children : a collection / Lilian G. Katz.
       p. cm.
    Includes bibliographical references and index.
    ISBN 1-56750-176-1 (case) — ISBN 1-56750-177-X (paper)
    1. Early childhood education.   I. Title
LB1139.23.K38 1994
372.21—dc20   94-39608
                                                      CIP

Ablex Publishing Corporation
355 Chestnut Street
Norwood, New Jersey 07648

CONTENTS

Father, Father . . .

Father, father
Father me.
Help me set my sails
As far as I can see.

Mother, mother,
Mother me.
Help me when the winds of time
Appear to be
Stronger than the strength I feel
Inside of me.

But who is this who knows that I'm
As far as I set out to see
As strong as I decide to be
As long as I live up to me?

Brother, brother
Sail with me.
Look upon the stars
To guide us faithfully.

Sister, sister
See the shore
Turning from the sea
To land once more
And with an anchor to the rock of our new-found land
We are a family one step closer to our home.

Stephen J. Katz, July, 1978.

INTRODUCTION
TO THE COLLECTION

In 1977, the National Association for the Education of Young Children published a collection of nine of my previously published articles on early childhood care and education and under the title *Talks with Teachers* (Katz, 1977). In 1985, five more previously published articles on similar issues were published in a collection by the ERIC Clearinghouse on Elementary and Early Childhood Education (ERIC/EECE) under the title *More Talks with Teachers* (Katz, 1985). In the collection presented here, five more recent articles have been added to the twelve from the earlier collections that are most often requested and cited.

Presented as chapters in this collection, all have appeared previously in slightly different versions as articles in professional journals, as chapters in books, and as monographs published by ERIC/EECE.

Each chapter was written in response and reaction to particular events or contexts that were provocative. Many of the issues explored were stimulated by experiences with teachers and caregivers of young children, many of whom were also my students, as well as with other professional colleagues around the country and in many other countries. These background experiences and events are described briefly in the introduction to each article. I am deeply indebted to all of these students, colleagues, and co-workers for the challenges and the support they offered, and for many meaningful discussions.

I ask readers to forgive the overlap and repetition of themes, topics, ideas, and examples, inevitable in a collection of papers published over a period of more than twenty years.

Many colleagues too numerous to list contributed helpful critiques and suggestions when these papers were written. I am, however, especially indebted to Professor James D. Raths, now of the University of Delaware, who generously offered the most significant critical feedback and encouragement over a period of more than twenty years.

Special thanks are also due to my co-workers on the ERIC/EECE staff who readily responded to numerous versions and revisions of each article in helpful ways, including the speedy provision of the most up-to-date information. It would be impossible to do justice to the way the ERIC database has been a source of assistance in the work represented in this collection. I want to thank Mima Spencer, Dianne Rothenberg, and Bernard Cesarone for their editorial and critical advice with many of the chapters. Special thanks are due also to Norma Howard for her final editing of the collection.

I know of no way to express my appreciation for the support, encouragement, and inspiration of my husband, Boris, and our three children, Dan, Steve, and Miriam. No matter how great the distances I travel, they are never far away in mind or spirit.

Urbana, Illinois.
April, 1994

PART I

YOUNG CHILDREN AND THEIR EDUCATION

1

WHAT IS BASIC
FOR YOUNG CHILDREN?*

INTRODUCTION

This chapter is based on the opening address presented at the National Conference of the Australian Preschool Association in Melbourne, Australia in 1976.

To determine the most pertinent topics to address in Australia, I asked the conference convener for some suggestions. She replied that I could select any topics I wished, but since I was allowed a total of twenty minutes in which to discuss them, I had better just "stick to the basics."

The conference followed closely on a session with a group of my graduate students, whom I asked to share their views on what absolutely basic requirements have to be met for adequate development for young children. The challenge of a twenty-minute speech seemed an ideal opportunity to address that question for myself in the light of my own understanding of what was basic for young children. As readers can see, many of the propositions listed in the chapter have been developed further in other chapters.

---

*This chapter is based on the Opening Address at the National Conference of the Australian Preschool Association, May, 1976, Melbourne, Australia, and originally published as "What Is Basic for Young Children?" by Lilian G. Katz, October, 1978, *Childhood Education*, 54(1), pp. 16–19. Reprinted by permission.

A group of young and zealous students were discussing their reactions to practice teaching in child care centers. One of them spoke of her experience in deeply disappointed tones. Among her complaints was that the program director refused to let the children have small animals in the center. I listened appreciatively for awhile to the righteous indignation only the young and inexperienced can enjoy. I then asked her as gently as I could: "What do you think are the chances that a child can develop into a competent adult without having had animals to play with in the child care center?" "In other words," I said, "speculate about what is really basic for young children." A lively discussion followed, leading all of us to search our own assumptions for answers to the question: What does each child have to have for optimum development? On this occasion I want to share with you my answer to this question by offering six interrelated propositions. I hope these propositions will be helpful to you as you inspect your own answers to the same question.

The six propositions below rest on the assumption that whatever is good for children is only good for them in the "right" proportions. Just because something is good for children, more of it is not necessarily better for them. This generalization applies to so many influences on children's environments that I refer to it as the *principle of optimum effects*. Among the many examples are attention, affection, stimulation, independence, novelty, choices of activities, and so on. All of these can be thought to be good for children, but only in optimum amounts, frequencies, or intensities. With this principle as backdrop, here is my list of what every child has to have for healthy development.

1. A Sense of Safety   The young child has to have a deep sense of safety. I am referring here to psychological safety, which we usually speak of in terms of feeling secure, that is, the subjective feeling of being strongly connected and deeply attached to one or more others. Experiencing oneself as attached, connected—or safe—comes not just from being loved, but from *feeling* loved, *feeling* wanted, *feeling* significant, to an optimum (not maximum) degree. Note that the emphasis is more on *feeling* loved and wanted than on *being* loved and wanted.

As I understand early development, feeling strongly attached comes not just from the warmth and kindness of parents and caregivers. The feelings are a consequence of children perceiving that what they do or do not do really matters to others—matters so much that others will pick them up, comfort them, get angry, and even scold them. Safety, then, grows out of being able to trust people to respond not just warmly but authentically, intensely, and honestly.

2. *Optimum Self-Esteem* This proposition applies to all children, whether they live in wealthy or poor environments, whether they are at home or at school, whether they have special needs or typical needs, whatever their age, gender, race, ethnic group, or nationality. Every child has to have adequate—not excessive—self-esteem.

One does not acquire self-esteem at a certain moment in childhood and then have it forever. Self-esteem is nurtured by and responsive to significant others—adults, siblings, and other children—throughout the growing years. Even more important to keep in mind here is that one cannot have self-esteem in a vacuum. Self-esteem is the product of our evaluations of ourselves against criteria that we acquire very early in life. We acquire these criteria from our families, neighborhoods, ethnic groups, and later on from peer groups and the larger community. These criteria against which we come to evaluate ourselves as acceptable and worthwhile, and against which we evaluate and experience ourselves as lovable, may vary from family to family. In some families beauty is a criterion; in others, neatness or athletic ability or toughness are criteria against which one's worth is evaluated. Consider for a moment that such personal attributes as being dainty, quiet, garrulous, pious, well-mannered, or academically precocious might constitute the criteria against which young children are evaluated as being lovable, worthy, and acceptable. (See Chapter 2 for further discussion of this issue.)

It is of course the right, if not the duty, of each family to establish what it considers to be the criteria against which each member is judged acceptable and upon which esteem is accorded. The processes and the patterns by which these judgments are implemented are most unlikely to occur at a conscious level in either formulation or expression.

One of our responsibilities as educators is to be sensitive to the criteria of self-esteem children bring with them to the early childhood setting. We may not agree with the family's definition of the "good boy" or the "good girl," but we would be very unwise to downgrade, undermine, or in other ways violate the self-esteem criteria that children bring with them to the early childhood setting. At the same time we must also help children acquire criteria in the setting that serve to protect the welfare of the *whole* group of children for whom we are responsible. I cannot think of any way in which it could be helpful to children to undermine their respect for their own families.

3. *Feeling that Life Is Worth Living* Every child has to feel that life is worth living, reasonably satisfying, interesting, and authentic. This proposition suggests that we involve children in activities, and interactions about activities, that are real and significant to them, and that are intriguing and absorbing to them. I have in mind here the potential hazard inherent in modern industrialized societies of creating environments and experiences for young children that are superficial, phony, frivolous, and trivial. I suggest also that we resist the temptation to settle for activities that merely amuse and titillate children. Thus, criteria for selecting activities might include that they (a) give children opportunities to operate on their own experiences and to reconstruct their own environments and that they (b) give adults opportunities to help children learn what meanings to assign to their own experiences.

Visits to early childhood programs often provoke me to wonder whether we have taken our longstanding emphasis on warmth and kindness, acceptance and love to mean simply "Let's be nice to children." As I watch adults being nice and kind and gentle, I wonder also whether if I were a child in such pleasant environments I would look at the adults and ask myself something like "Everybody is kind and sweet, but inside them is there anybody home?" (See Chapter 9.)

Children should be able to experience their lives throughout their growing years as real, authentic, worth living, and satisfying, whether they are at home, in child care centers, or in schools.

4. *Help with Making Sense of Experience* Young children need adults and others who help them make sense of their own experiences. By the time we meet the young children in our care they have already constructed some understandings of their experiences. Many of their understandings or constructions are likely to be inaccurate or incorrect though developmentally appropriate. As I see it, our major responsibility is to help the young to improve, extend, refine, develop, and deepen their own understandings or constructions of their own worlds. As they grow older and reach primary school age, it is our responsibility to help them develop understandings of other peoples' experi-

ences, people who are distant in time and place. Indeed, increasing refinement and deepening of understandings is ideally a life-long process.

We might ask: What do young children need or want to make sense of? Certainly of people, of what they do, and why they do it, of what and how they feel; and of themselves and other living things around them, how they themselves and other living things grow; where people and things come from, and how things are made and how they work, and so forth.

If we are to help young children improve and develop their understandings of their experiences we must *uncover* what those understandings are. The uncovering that we do, and that occurs as children engage in the activities we provide, helps us to make good decisions about what to *cover* next and what follow-up activities to plan.

5. *Authoritative Adults* Young children have to have adults who accept the authority that is theirs by virtue of their greater experience, knowledge, and wisdom. This proposition is based on the assumption that neither parents nor educators are caught between the extremes of authoritarianism or permissiveness (Baumrind, 1971). Authoritarianism may be defined as the exercise of power without warmth, encouragement, or explanation. Permissiveness may be seen as the abdication of adult authority and power, though it may offer children warmth, encouragement, and support as they seem to need it. I am suggesting that instead of the extremes of authoritarianism and permissiveness, young children have to have around them adults who are authoritative—adults who exercise their very considerable power over the lives of young children *with* warmth, support, encouragement, and adequate explanations of the limits they impose on them. The concept of authoritativeness also includes treating children with respect—treating their opinions, feelings, wishes, and ideas as valid even when we disagree with them. To respect people we agree with is no great problem; respecting those whose ideas, wishes, and feelings are different from ours or troubling to us, may be a mark of wisdom in parents and of genuine professionalism in teachers.

6. *Desirable Role Models* Young children need optimum association with adults and older children who exemplify the personal qualities we want them to acquire. Make your own list of the qualities you want the young children for whom you are responsible to acquire. There may be some differences among us,

but it is very likely that there are some qualities we all want all children to have: the capacity to care for and about others, the disposition to be honest, kind, accepting of those who are different from themselves, to love learning, and so forth.

This proposition suggests that we inspect children's environments and ask: To what extent do our children have contact with people who exhibit these qualities? To what extent do our children observe people who are counterexamples of the qualities we want to foster but who are also presented as glamorous and attractive?

It seems to me that children need neighborhoods and communities which take the steps necessary to protect them from excessive exposure to violence and crime during the early years while their characters are still in formation.

Children need relationships and experience with adults who are willing to take a stand on what is worth doing, worth having, worth knowing, and worth caring about. This proposition seems to belabor the obvious. But in an age of increasing emphasis on pluralism, multiculturalism, and community participation, professionals are increasingly hesitant and apologetic about their own values. It seems to me that such hesitancy to take a stand on what is worthwhile may cause us to give children unclear signals about what is worth knowing and doing and what is expected.

Taking a stand on what we value does not guarantee that our children will accept or agree with us. Nor does it imply that we reject others' versions of the "good life." We must, in fact, cultivate our capacities to respect alternative definitions of the "good life." My point is that when we take a stand, with quiet conviction and courage, we help the young to see us as thinking and caring individuals who have enough self-respect to act on our own values and to give clear signals about what those values are.

In summary, these six propositions are related to our responsibilities for the quality of the daily lives of all of our children—wherever they spend those days, throughout the years of growth and development. We must come to see that the well-being of our own children, of each and every child, is intimately and inextricably linked to the well-being of all children. When one of our own children needs life-saving surgery, someone else's child will perform it. When one of our own children is struck down by violence, someone else's child will have inflicted it. The well-being of our own children can be secured only when the well-being of other people's children is also secure. But to care for and about others' children is not just practical; it is also right.

REFERENCE

Baumrind, D. (1971). Current patterns of parental authority. *Developmental Psychology Monographs, 4,* 1–102.

2

THE DISTINCTION BETWEEN SELF-ESTEEM AND NARCISSISM: IMPLICATIONS FOR PRACTICE*

This chapter is the most recently completed one in the collection. My concern that certain practices that are intended to enhance children's self-esteem might provoke excessive preoccupation with the self—a condition generally called narcissism—were aroused during an intensive study of an elementary school in 1987. Since then I have discussed these concerns with many teachers, students, and colleagues. The resulting chapter is an essay that presents a personal view of the issues and an initial exploration of its implications for early childhood practices.

If my view is correct, then this phenomenon is likely to be much more than an educational phenomenon and is probably part of the larger culture in which schools function. Thus the influence of the larger context must be considered as we work our way through these issues.

In the course of working with early childhood educators in other countries—the Western industrialized countries in particu-

---

* This chapter has also been published as *Distinctions Between Self-Esteem and Narcissism: Implications for Practice*, 1993. Urbana, IL: ERIC Clearinghouse on Elementary and Early Childhood Education; and in summary form as "All About Me." *American Education*, Summer, 1993. pp. 18–23; and as "Reading, Writing & Narcissism." *Op-Ed Page*. New York Times. July 15, 1993. p. 15; all by Lilian G. Katz, and all reprinted by permission.

lar—I find it interesting to note that they do not share our concern about self-esteem and "feeling good" about oneself. To a large extent these colleagues face most of the same problems and address most of the same goals as we do. However, widespread commitment to enhance children's self-esteem and the "self-esteem industry" that has grown up around it seems unique to the United States. Such uniqueness in and of itself does not negate or recommend these efforts. We might be the only country to have grasped an essential responsibility of schools: the belief that good feelings and happiness can be pursued directly! Whatever the causes of our insistence that children should feel good about themselves, I believe it warrants serious discussion among us. This essay is a preliminary attempt to set out the issues and challenge current practices.

INTRODUCTION

A solitary poster in the cafeteria of a small northeastern school recently caught my attention. The top line, written in large letters, read,

DO <u>YOURSELF</u> A FAVOR

with the word "yourself" underlined as above. Just below the top line was written,

COMPLIMENT SOMEONE TODAY!

The center of the poster featured a cartoon depicting a smiling rabbit closely resembling Bugs Bunny, wielding a paint brush and dripping yellow paint on itself while painting a large sunburst. The words issuing from the rabbit's mouth said,

IT'S HARD TO SPREAD SUNSHINE WITHOUT
SPILLING A LITTLE ON YOURSELF!

The feature of this poster that provoked this discussion is that its message specifically urges readers to compliment others as a favor to *themselves*, rather than as an act of kindness and charity toward *others*. The message implies that a major motive for doing good is that such acts spill onto the doer, thus making the person paying the compliment feel good. The poster explicitly turns the attention of cafeteria users inward toward their own feelings, rather than outward to concern for others. Yet the latter would be a more appropriate message, urging altruism rather than narcissism. In this way, the poster exemplifies a wider trend in early childhood and elementary school practices that seem to confuse narcissism and the important goal of strengthening children's self-esteem.

A central argument of this essay is that a characteristic of current early childhood education practices exemplified by the poster provides environments for young children that are at best unreal and at worst phony rather than authentic, fanciful rather than imaginative, and more amusing and entertaining than interesting and intellectually challenging. Commendable as it is for children to have high self-esteem, many of the practices advocated in the service of this goal may inadvertently develop narcissism in the form of excessive preoccupation with oneself instead of a deep and meaningful sense of self-confidence and self-worth. The fact that the poster's message is issued by a cartoon animal character, another common feature of early childhood practices, further undermines the intellectual vitality of early childhood environments.

The major purpose of this essay is to explore contemporary early childhood educational practices related to self-esteem and narcissism. To begin, examples of the practices in question are described, followed by a discussion of definitional problems associated with self-esteem and their implications for practice. Then specific practices are discussed, and some examples of the uses and misuses of enchantment and their implications for practice are suggested.

Brief working definitions of self-esteem and narcissism follow. Self-esteem refers to feelings derived from evaluations of the self. Narcissism is a preoccupation with oneself and how one is seen by others. These terms are discussed in greater detail in a later section.

SELF-ESTEEM AS A GOAL OF EARLY CHILDHOOD EDUCATION

The development and strengthening of the young child's self-esteem is typically listed as a major goal in the guides for state and school district kindergarten curricula. While early childhood education has long been blessed with many curriculum approaches that emphasize and advocate diverse goals and methods, all seem to concur that helping children to "feel good about themselves" is an important goal. The terms applied to this goal are variously designated as self-esteem, self-regard, self-concept, self-worth, and self-confidence. Some sources refer to *high self-concepts*, even though a concept cannot, technically speaking, be high or low. The term self-esteem is preferred because it refers to a calibrated estimation of the value or worthiness of the self.

For example, in a document titled *Early Childhood Education and the Elementary School Principal: Standards for Quality Programs for Young Children,* the National Association of Elementary School Principals (1990) issued "Standards for Quality Programs for Young Children." The first on the list of twelve characteristics of good quality early childhood programs is that participating children "develop a positive self-image" (p. 2).

Numerous books, kits, packets, and newsletters produced for teachers urge them to help children gain "positive self-concepts." A typical example of this view is given by Sandy McDaniel (1986), as quoted in the National Education Association's *NewOptions:*

> [The] basis for *everything we do* is self-esteem. Therefore, if we can do something to give children a stronger sense of themselves, starting in preschool, they'll be [a lot wiser] in the choices they make. (p. 1)

Along similar lines, the prestigious Corporation for Public Broadcasting (no date) issued a twenty-page pamphlet, apparently directed to teenagers, entitled *Celebrate Yourself: Six Steps to Building Your Self-Esteem.* The first major heading in the pamphlet is "Learn to Love Yourself Again." This section asserts that we all loved ourselves as babies, but as we grew up "we found that not everyone liked everything we did" (p. 1), so we "started picking on ourselves." Six steps toward self-celebration are presented. Step 1 is "Spot Your Self-Attacks." Step 2, "See What

Makes You Special," recommends that the reader compile a list of items that relate to "My Character" (such as "awesome"), "My Talents" (such as "playing trivia"), and so forth. The remaining four steps toward self-celebration are "Attack your Self-Attacks," "Make Loving Yourself a Habit," "Go for the Goal," and "Lend a Hand to Others."

Perhaps it is just this kind of literature that accounts for the presence of a large poster in the entrance hall of a suburban school, with the declaration "We applaud ourselves" surrounded by pictures of clapping hands! While the purpose of the poster might have been to help children "feel good about themselves," it does so by directing their attention inward and urging self-congratulation. The poster makes no reference to other ways of deserving applause, for example, by considering the feelings or needs of others; "feeling good" is not linked to "doing good"! Many schools also feature posters listing the Citizen of the Week, Person of the Week, Super Spellers, Handwriting Honors, and similar displays that often seem to encourage showing off. While I am not aware of empirical evidence to suggest that such posters are damaging, I know of none to indicate that they are effective in improving learning or advancing achievement.

Similarly, over the principal's office in an urban elementary school a sign says, "Watch your behavior, you are on display!" While its purpose may be to encourage appropriate conduct, it does so by directing children's attention to how they *appear* to others rather than to any possible functions of appropriate behavior. The examples listed above exemplify practices that may encourage narcissism rather than self-esteem.

Early Childhood Practices: Narcissism versus Self-Esteem

I first became aware of the possibility that practices designed to enhance self-esteem might encourage narcissism while observing a first grade class in an affluent suburban elementary school. Each child had produced a booklet titled "All About Me," consisting of dittoed pages prepared by the teacher, on which the child had provided information about himself or herself. The first page asked for a list of basic information about the child's home and family. The second page was titled "What I like to eat," the third "What I like to watch on TV," the next "What I want for a present," another "Where I want to go on vacation," and so forth. On each page the child's attention was directed toward his or her own inner gratifications. The topic of each page in these identical booklets put the child in the role of consumer: consumer of food, entertainment, gifts, and recreation. No page was included that put the child in the role of producer, investigator, initiator, out-reacher, explorer, experimenter, puzzler, wonderer, or problem solver.

In these booklets, like many others encountered around the country, no page had a title such as "What I want to know more about," or "What I am curious about," or "What I want to explore, find out, solve, figure out," or even "What I want to make." Instead of encouraging children to reach out and understand or investigate phenomena worthy of their attention, the headings of the pages turned their attention toward themselves.

A similar manifestation of practices that are intended to foster self-esteem but may contribute to self-preoccupation was observed in a suburban school kindergarten. Here, displayed on a bulletin board were comments made by the morning and after-noon children about their visit to a dairy farm. Each of the 47 children's sentences listed on the bulletin board began with the words "I liked": "I liked the cows," "I liked the milking machine," "I liked the chicks." But there was no sentence such as "What surprised me was . . . ", "What I am curious about is . . . ", or "What I want know more about is . . . ", "The most important thing about dairy farming is . . . ."

The children's sentences could be analyzed on many levels. For the purposes of this discussion, they point out two character-istics of the particular teaching practice in the suburban kinder-garten: the tendency to encourage children's exclusive focus on gratification, and the missed opportunity to encourage children's disposition to examine worthwhile phenomena around them. Surely there were features of the visit to the dairy farm that aroused some children's curiosity about the real world and that could spark some further investigations. But such responses were not in evidence and were therefore unlikely to have been appreci-ated and strengthened.

Another common example of practices intended to enhance self-esteem but unlikely to do so was a display of kindergartners' work consisting of nine identical, large paper doll-like figures, each with a balloon containing a sentence stem beginning "I am special because." The sentences depicted in the display read "I am special because I can color," " . . . I can ride a bike," " . . . I like to play with my friends," " . . . I know how to play," and so forth. Although there is certainly value in these skills, traits, or activities, is there not some danger in *stressing* that children's specialness is dependent on these comparatively trivial things—traits that many children share—rather than on more enduring skills and traits, such as the ability to persist in the face of difficulty and the desire to help their classmates? The examples described above are not unusual; very similar work can be seen in many schools all over the country.

Why should children's attention be turned so insistently inward toward themselves? Can such superficial flattery boost self-esteem? Can young children's minds be intellectually engaged by such exercises? Can their dispositions to explore and investigate worthwhile topics be strengthened by such activities? Is it possible that the cumulative effect of such practices, when used frequently, is to undermine children's perceptions of their teachers as thoughtful and knowledgeable adults who are worthy of respect?

In discussions with teachers since first encountering the "All About Me" booklets described above, I have learned that the intentions behind the common "All About Me" exercise is to make children "feel good about themselves" and to motivate them by beginning "where they are." However, the same intentions could be satisfied in other ways. Starting "where children are" can be accomplished by providing topics that would encourage curiosity about others *and* themselves, reduce emphasis on consumer activities, and at the same time strengthen the intellectual ethos of the classroom.

Indeed, starting "where the children are" can just as easily be satisfied by pooling the class data in a project entitled "All About *Us*." The individual data could be collected, summarized, graphed, compared, and analyzed in a variety of ways so as to minimize focusing the children's attention exclusively on themselves.

Such a project was observed in a rural British infant school several years ago. A large display on the bulletin board was titled "We Are a Class Full of Bodies." Just below the title was the heading "Here Are the Details." All the display space was taken up with bar graphs and pie charts of their birth and current weights and heights, eye colors, numbers of lost teeth, shoe sizes, and so forth, in which the data for the whole class were pooled. As the children worked in small groups collecting information brought from home, taking measurements, preparing graphs together, helping each other to mount displays of analyses of many individual characteristics, the teacher was able to create an ethos of a community of researchers looking for averages, trends, and ranges. This project began "where the children were" by collecting, pooling, analyzing, and displaying data derived from each child in the class. Projects such as this can foster children's self-esteem without encouraging excessive or exclusive preoccupation with self and self-gratification, and can maintain children's respect for their teachers.

Materials for Teachers

Many books and kits for teachers recommend exercises to help children "feel good about themselves." One typical example, a booklet with tear-out worksheets for easy duplication, is called *Building Self-Esteem with Koala-Roo* (Fendel & Ecker, 1989). One such worksheet (p. 82) is bordered by fourteen repetitions in capital letters of the phrase "YOU ARE SPECIAL!" At the top left-hand corner is a drawing of a smiling koala bear waving its left paw, holding in the other paw a heart saying, "I love you!" The heading on the page is "You Are Special." Below the heading is a line for a child's name followed by the phrase "You Are Special!" again. This is followed by "I am very glad that I have been your X grade teacher," though no space is provided for the teacher's name. This line is followed by more text that includes "There's no one else quite like you," "You're one of a kind," "You're unique," and so forth.

I doubt whether the complete text of the page described above meets the readability index for kindergartners or first graders or other children young enough to be taken in by such excessive coddling. It would be surprising and disappointing if children old enough to read those pages could be inspired by its content. Page 81 of the same book (Fendel & Ecker, 1989) lists other materials available, such as "Can-Do Kid of the Week" certificates, "Can-Do Deliveroo" with a welcome-to-school note on it, and a "Can-Do Kid of the Week" bulletin board design.

Another example of the genre, found in an advertisement in a popular teachers' magazine, is a kit for teachers titled "Excellence in Early Childhood!" The advertisement promotes a unit of activities entitled "I am Special" for three-, four- and five-year-olds. The advertisement lists a kit that includes a Student Activity Book filled with colorful hands-on projects and illustrated stories, and a Teacher Guide for twenty-nine lesson plans, stories, finger plays, and so forth, designed to promote "feeling good about oneself." In answer to the question "What Will Children Learn from the 'I am Special' kit?" the advertisement claims that they "become aware that they are created in a very special and unique way" and "see themselves as good and worthwhile individuals." These illustrations are simply two examples among many (see also Borba & Borba, 1978; Hamilton & Flemming, 1990). Many similar teaching aids have been observed in early childhood classrooms all over the United States .

The concept of specialness expressed in these activities seems, by definition, self-contradictory: if everyone is special, nobody is special. Furthermore, frequent feedback about how special one is might even raise some doubt along the lines of "Methinks thou dost protest too much!" While each individual may indeed be unique, we surely want to cultivate in children the view that while we are unique in some respects, we also have a great deal in common.

Another common practice that some educators believe helps support children's self-esteem is "Show and Tell." It is not clear, however, whether this common feature of early childhood programs (sometimes referred to as "bring and brag") does as much to enhance self-esteem as it does to encourage children to be unduly concerned about the impressions they make on others, and to engage in one-upmanship. Many early childhood specialists justify the practice on the grounds that it provides children with an opportunity to practice an early form of public speaking and thereby to strengthen their verbal expressive skills. Some teachers also hope that children will sharpen their listening skills as they attend to the showing and telling of their peers. However, it is not clear what happens to children who feel that what they have to show and tell cannot compete with their peers' contributions. Furthermore, observations of many such group sessions suggest that more than a few of the children seem to be learning to tune out their peers rather than to listen to them. There are other more meaningful and intellectually defensible ways that children can speak to groups of their peers. For example, children can report the discoveries, ideas and experiences derived from their own efforts, ideas, and real accomplishments to groups of peers and parents (see Katz & Chard, 1989).

The trend toward excessive emphasis on self-esteem and self-congratulation described above may be due to a general desire to correct earlier traditions of eschewing complimenting children for fear of making them conceited. However, the current practices described above seem to be overcorrections of such traditions. The argument presented in this essay that the practices intended to strengthen children's self-esteem may inadvertently foster narcissism is explored below with a brief discussion of the meanings of these two terms.

DISTINCTIONS BETWEEN SELF-ESTEEM AND NARCISSISM

Some of the distinctions between self-esteem and narcissism become evident in the study of children's development of self-esteem, and in the examination of variations among different cultures' conceptions of self-identity, including the general differences between the viewpoints of Eastern and Western cultures.

These topics are discussed in this section, as are other aspects of self-esteem that shed light on the distinction between self-esteem and narcissism. These aspects include the interrelationship between self-esteem and those moods or feelings that accompany high self-esteem, such as cheerfulness, and low self-esteem, such as doubt; criteria of self-esteem; and the effect of the interpersonal context on self-esteem. Following an examination of the distinctions between self-esteem and narcissism, some definitions of narcissism are provided.

Self-Esteem: Definitions

Even though a vast quantity of theory, research, and commentary on the construct of self-concept has been produced since William James first introduced the notion more than one hundred years ago, the construct and its manifestations remain elusive. As Harter (1983) points out, those constructs that are related to the construct of self-concept are, like that term, usually described by hyphenated terms—such as self-worth, self-esteem, self-assurance, and self-regard.

Bednar, Wells, and Peterson (1989) define self-esteem "as a subjective and realistic self-approval" (p. 4). They point out that "self-esteem reflects how the individual views and values the self at the most fundamental levels of psychological experiencing" (p.

4) and that different aspects of the self create a "profile of emotions associated with the various roles in which the person operates . . . and [that self-esteem] is an enduring and affective sense of personal value based on accurate self-perceptions." According to this definition, low self-esteem would be characterized by negative emotions associated with the various roles in which a person operates and by either low personal value or inaccurate self-perceptions.

Furthermore, Bednar et al. describe paradoxical examples of individuals of substantial achievement who report deep feelings of low self-esteem. The authors suggest that a theory of self-esteem must take into account the important role of an individual's "self-talk and self-thoughts" as well as the perceived appraisal of others (p. 11). They conclude that "high or low levels of self-esteem . . . are the result and the reflection of the internal, affective feedback the organism most commonly experiences" (p. 14). They point out that all individuals must experience some negative feedback from their social environment, some of which is bound to be valid. Thus, a significant aspect of the development and maintenance of self-esteem must address how individuals cope with negative feedback.

Bednar et al. suggest that if individuals avoid rather than cope with negative feedback, they have to devote substantial effort to "gain the approval of others by *impression management,* that is, pretending to be what we believe is most acceptable to others" (p. 13; italics theirs). If individuals respond to negative feedback by striving to manage the impressions they make on others to gain their approval, they also have to "render most of the favorable feedback they receive [as] untrustworthy, unbelievable, and psychologically impotent because of their internal awareness of their own facade" (p. 13). This preoccupation with managing the impression one makes on others is a behavior characteristic usually included in definitions of narcissism.

Developmental Considerations

For very young children, self-esteem is probably best characterized as deep feelings of being loved, accepted, and valued by significant others rather than as feelings derived from evaluating themselves against some external criteria, as in the case of older children. Indeed, the only criterion appropriate for accepting and loving a newborn or infant is that he or she has been born. The unconditional love and acceptance experienced in the first year or two of life lay the foundation for later self-esteem, and probably make it possible for the preschooler and older child to withstand occasional criticism and negative evaluations that usually accompany socialization into the larger community.

As children grow beyond the preschool years the larger society imposes criteria and conditions upon love and acceptance. If the very early feelings of love and acceptance are deep enough, the child can most likely weather the rebuffs and scoldings of the later years without undue debilitation. With increasing age, however, children begin to internalize criteria of self-worth and a sense of the standards to be attained on the criteria from the larger community that they observe and in which they are beginning to participate. The issue of criteria of self-esteem is examined more closely below.

Cassidy's (1988) study of the relationship between self-esteem at age five and six years and the quality of early mother–child attachment supports Bowlby's theory that construction of the self is derived from early daily experience with attachment figures. The results of the study support Bowlby's conception of the process through which continuity in development occurs, and of the way early child–mother attachment continues to influence the child's conception and estimation of the self throughout at least the early childhood period, if not longer. The working models of the self derived from early mother–child interaction organize and help mold the child's environment "by seeking particular kinds of people and by eliciting particular behavior from them" (Cassidy, 1988, p. 133). Cassidy points out that very young children have few means of learning about themselves other than through experience with attachment figures. She suggests that if infants are valued and given comfort when required, they come to feel valuable; conversely, if they are neglected or rejected, they come to feel worthless and of little value.

In an examination of developmental considerations, Bednar, Wells, and Peterson (1989) suggest that feelings of competence and the self-esteem associated with them are enhanced in children when their parents provide an optimum mixture of acceptance, affection, rational limits and controls, and high expectations. In a similar way, teachers are likely to engender positive feelings when they provide such a combination of acceptance, limits, and meaningful and realistic expectations concerning behavior and effort (Lamborn, Mounts, Steinberg, & Dornbusch, 1991). Teachers of young children can provide contexts for such an optimum mixture of acceptance, limits, and meaningful effort in the course of project work as described by Katz and Chard (1989).

Many teachers feel compelled to employ the questionable practices at issue in this essay as a way of helping children who seem to them not to have had the kind of strong and healthy attachment experiences that support the development of self-esteem. While such children may not be harmed by exercises that tell them they are special or by constant praise and flattery, the argument here is that they are more likely to achieve real self-esteem from experiences that provide meaningful challenge and opportunities for real effort.

The Cyclic Nature of Self-Esteem

The relationships between self-evaluation, effort, and reevaluation of the self suggest a cyclic aspect to the dynamics of self-esteem. Harter (1983) asserts that the term *self-worth* is frequently used to refer to aspects of motivation and moods. High self-esteem is associated with a mood of cheerfulness, feelings of optimism, and relatively high energy. Low self-esteem is accompanied by feelings of doubt about one's worth and acceptability, and with feeling forlorn, morose, or even sad. Such feelings may be accompanied by relatively low energy and weak motivation, invariably resulting in low effort. In contrast, high self-esteem is associated with high energy, which increases effectiveness and competence, which in turn strengthens feelings of self-esteem and self-worth. In this way, feelings about oneself constitute a *recursive cycle* such that the feelings arising from self-appraisal tend to produce behavior that strengthens those feelings—both positive and negative.

The cyclic formulation of self-esteem is similar to Bandura's (1989) conception of *self-efficacy*—the processes by which perceptions of one's own capacities and effective action "affect each other bidirectionally" (p. 1176). In other words, effective action makes it possible to see oneself as competent, which in turn leads to effective action, and so forth. The same cycle applies to self-perceptions of incompetence. However, Bandura (1989) warns that a sense of personal efficacy [does] not arise simply from the incantation of capability. Saying something should not be confused with believing it to be so. Simply saying that one is capable is not necessarily self-convincing, especially when it contradicts preexisting firm beliefs. No amount of reiteration that I can fly will persuade me that I have the efficacy to get myself airborne and to propel myself through the air. (p. 1179)

This formulation of the dynamics of feelings about the self confirms the view that self-esteem merits the concern of educators and parents. Nevertheless, it also casts some doubt on the frequent assertion that if children are somehow made to "feel good about themselves," success in school will follow. In other words, just because young children need to "feel good about themselves," telling them that they are special (perhaps because they can color) or that they are unique, or providing them with other similar flattery, may not cause them to believe they are so or engender in them good feelings about themselves.

Dunn's (1988) view of the nature of self-esteem is that it is related to the extent to which one sees oneself as the cause of effects. She asserts that "the sense of cause [is] a crucial feature of the sense of self" and the essence of self-confidence is the feeling of having an effect on things and being able to cause or at least affect events and others. On the other hand, feeling loved by the significant others in one's environment involves feeling and knowing that one's behavior and status really matter to them— matter enough to cause them to have real emotion and to provoke action and reaction from them, including anger and stress as well as pride and joy.

Criteria of Self-Esteem

It is reasonable to assume that self-esteem does not exist in a vacuum, but is the product of evaluating oneself against one or more criteria and reaching or exceeding acceptable standards on these criteria. These evaluations are unlikely to be made consciously or deliberately, but by means of preconscious or intuitive thought processes. It is likely that these criteria vary not only between cultures and subcultures, but also within them. The criteria may also vary by gender. Furthermore, the standards within a family, subculture, or culture that have to be met on these criteria may also vary by gender. For example, higher standards on a criterion of assertiveness may be required for self-esteem in males than in females. In addition, the criteria against which the worth and acceptability of an individual are estimated may carry different weights across cultures, subcultures, and families, and for the two sexes. Criteria may have different weighting for different families, some giving more weight in their total self-esteem to physical appearance, and others to personal traits, creativity, or academic achievement, for example.

Criteria for self-esteem frequently employed in American self-concept research include physical appearance, physical ability, achievement, peer acceptance, and a variety of personal traits (Harter, 1983). As will be indicated in the discussion below, Western and Eastern cultures vary in how the self is defined and the criteria against which the self is estimated. These sources of variation imply that some children are likely to have acquired criteria of self-esteem at home and in their immediate community that differ from those assumed valuable in the classroom and in the school.

One of the many challenges teachers face in working with young children of diverse backgrounds is to help them understand and come to terms with the criteria of self-esteem applicable in the class and the school without belittling or disrespecting the criteria advocated and applied at home. While it is not appropriate for schools to challenge the criteria or standards of self-esteem of children's families, careful consideration of those self-esteem criteria advocated within the school is warranted.

To the extent that self-esteem is based on competitive achievement, it can be enhanced by identifying other individuals or groups who can be perceived as inferior to oneself in achievement. If, for example, parents and schools convey to children that their self-esteem is related to academic achievement as indicated by competitive grades and test scores, then a significant proportion of children, *ipso facto,* must have low self-esteem—at least on that criterion. In such a school culture the development of cooperation and intergroup solidarity becomes very problematic. Furthermore, if competitive academic achievement is highly weighted among not only the school's criteria of self-esteem but also the criteria of the culture as a whole, a substantial proportion of schoolchildren may be condemned to feel inadequate. An adaptive response of children at the low end of the distribution of academic achievement might be to distance themselves from that culture and to identify and strive to meet other criteria of self-esteem, such as the criteria of various peer groups, that may or may not enhance participation in the larger society. To avoid these potentially divisive effects of such competitive and comparative self-evaluations, the school should provide contexts in which all participants can contribute to group efforts, albeit in individual ways. A substantial body of research indicates that cooperative learning strategies and cooperative goals are effective ways to address these issues (see Ames, 1992).

The matter of what constitute appropriate criteria of self-esteem cannot be settled empirically by research or even theory. These criteria are deeply imbedded within a culture, promoted and safeguarded by the culture's religious, moral, and philosophical institutions.

Although, as stated earlier, it is important to value an infant simply for the fact that he or she has been born, if criteria for self-esteem that are applied later in the child's life include characteristics that are present and given at birth—such as one's nationality, race or gender—then the ability of all citizens to achieve self-esteem in a society of diverse groups, especially when one group is culturally or otherwise dominant, is problematic. Furthermore, as suggested above, if children learn to base their self-appraisals on favorable comparisons of themselves with others, then the identification of inferior others—whether individuals or groups—may become endemic in a society. When the two tendencies—to base self-esteem on characteristics that are present at birth and to elevate one's self-appraisal by identifying others who are inferior on any given criterion—occur together in a society, conditions develop that are likely to support prejudice and oppression.

If, on the other hand, the criteria address personal attributes that are susceptible to individual effort and intention, such as contributing to one's community, then all citizens have the potential to achieve feelings of self-worth, self-respect, and dignity. Thus, while a person's nationality might not be an appropriate basis of self-esteem, contributing to the welfare of one's nation and accepting responsibility for the conduct of one's nation in the world might be appropriate bases for positive self-appraisal. In any case, the designation of appropriate criteria is not primarily the responsibility of educators, but of the moral institutions of the community and culture at large that educators are duty-bound to support.

This view that nationality in and of itself may be a faulty basis for self-esteem is not to deny the value and desirability of love of country or patriotism, both of which should contribute to involvement in the country's welfare. Nor should this view be interpreted as belittling civic and national pride, which can motivate and mobilize efforts to work on behalf of one's community and country.

A related issue is the role of reflected glory in self-esteem. Should individuals' self-esteem be influenced by the performance of their hometown football team or their country's Olympic teams? According to research on "basking in reflected glory" (BIRGing) reported by Cialdini and colleagues (1974, 1976), Lee (1985), and Kowalski (1991), the tendency to strengthen one's association with those who are visibly successful and distance oneself from obvious failures as a means of self-enhancement is a common phenomenon. Inasmuch as a sports fan makes no real contribution to the team's performance, that performance would seem an inappropriate source of either pride or shame and attendant fluctuations in self-esteem. One the other hand, the capacity to experience reflected glory and reflected shame might provide powerful motivation for community action. Action on behalf of one's community would seem to be a legitimate basis for self-esteem.

While the issues are complex, the main argument here is that if personal attributes that are present by virtue of birth alone, without individual effort and contribution, are a source of self-esteem beyond the first few years of life, individuals born without these attributes must see themselves as lacking or low in self-esteem; therefore, such attributes seem to be inappropriate criteria for self-esteem.

Situational Determinants of Self-Esteem

Bednar, Wells, and Peterson (1989) state that there may be a "situated" as well as a "general" self-identity (p. 39), suggesting that self-esteem may vary from one interpersonal situation to another. In other words, although the overall context of experience may remain constant, changes in interpersonal situations can cause some individuals to reassess themselves. For example, a teacher might have a fairly high estimation of herself in the context of teaching her own class, but when the interpersonal situation changes by the entrance of a colleague or the principal or a parent, she may shift her estimation or self-rating—probably downward! Although the teacher is exactly the same person five minutes before the intrusion as she is five minutes afterwards, the change in self-esteem is created by the teacher herself when she attributes greater significance to the other's (imagined) assessment of herself than to her own assessment. On the other hand, if the other person's assessment is based on greater knowledge, experience, and expertise than the teacher herself has, then she could consider herself *informed* or *instructed* by that assessment rather than allow it to alter her self-esteem.

Shifts in self-estimation based on the assessments of significant others may be developmentally appropriate for young children. In an adult, however, revision of self-estimation based on the perceived or imagined assessments of another adult that is at variance with one's own requires placing oneself in the role of child with respect to the other person. The essence of self-esteem for mature adults is to take seriously the assessments of others, but not to take them more seriously than they take their own self-assessments.

While adults can seek contexts and interpersonal situations that maximize their self-esteem and can strive to avoid those that minimize it, children are at the mercy of the situations in which adults place them. Inasmuch as young children vary in background, abilities, culture, and so forth, a wide rather than a narrow range of interpersonal situations should be provided for them. In other words, an early childhood program is most likely to enhance children's self-esteem and their capacities to deal with inevitable fluctuations in self-esteem when a variety of types of interpersonal situations is available to them.

Rosenholtz and Simpson (1984) addressed this issue in terms of the variety of dimensions of children's behavior to which teachers assign importance in a classroom. They define classes in which a limited range of child behavior is accepted, acknowledged, and rewarded as *unidimensional. Multidimensional* classes are those in which teachers provide a wide range of ways for children to contribute to and participate in the classroom life and in which a range of behavior is accepted, rewarded, and acknowledged. Rosenholtz and Simpson suggest that the unidimensional classroom limits opportunity for self-enhancement, and the multidimensional classroom makes it possible for many if not all pupils to find ways to enhance their feelings of self-esteem and self-worth. Multidimensionality in the classroom can be fostered when teachers include as part of the curriculum the kinds of projects described by Katz and Chard (1989), in which a wide range of activities of intellectual, social, aesthetic, and artistic value is included.

Cultural Variations

Markus and Kitayama (1991) point out that the construal of the self varies among cultures and that Americans and other Westerners typically construe their selves as *independent*, bounded, unitary, stable entities that are internal and private. On the other hand, they assert that in non-Western cultures such as those in Asia and Africa the self is construed as *interdependent*, connected with the social context, flexible, variable, external, and public. Westerners view the self as an autonomous entity consisting of a unique configuration of traits, motives, values, and behaviors. The Asian view is that the self exists primarily in relation to others, and to specific social contexts, and is esteemed to the extent that it can adjust to others, maintain harmony, and exercise the kind of restraint that will minimize social disruption.

According to Markus and Kitayama (1991), these contrasting culture-bound construals of the self have significant consequences for cognition, affect, and motivation. Asian children must learn that positive feelings about the self should derive from fulfilling tasks associated with the well-being of relevant others. On the other hand, Western children have to learn that the self consists of stable dispositions or traits and that "they must try to enhance themselves whenever possible . . . taking credit for success . . . explaining away their failures, and in various ways try to aggrandize themselves" (p. 242). Eventually American children must learn that "maintaining self-esteem requires separating oneself from others and seeing oneself as different from and better than others" (p. 242). According to this formulation, Americans cannot perceive themselves as better than others without describing the others as worse than themselves. When one's own self-esteem is the result of comparison processes, its maintenance may contribute to constant wariness of the risk of coming out poorly in such comparative assessments of self-worth. At worst, such sources of self-esteem may contribute to a need to identify lesser or inferior others—either individuals or groups. At best, they may contribute to excessive competitiveness and may distract individuals from giving their full attention to the tasks at hand, thereby depressing their learning and effectiveness. Developmental studies reviewed by Markus and Kitayama (1991) indicate that self-enhancement and self-promotion are perceived negatively in Japan and that although it is not apparent in the early years, by fifth grade Japanese children have learned that

> it is unwise to gloat over their accomplishments or to express confidence in their own ability. Research indicates that as children are socialized in an interdependent cultural context, they begin to appreciate the cultural value of self-restraint and, furthermore, to believe in a positive association between self-restraint and other favorable attributes of the person not only in the social, emotional domains but also in the domains of ability and competence. (p. 242)

The distinctions between the Western *independent* and the non-Western *interdependent* construal of the self indicate that the sources of self-esteem are also distinctive. For Westerners, independent self-esteem is achieved by actualizing one's own attributes, having one's accomplishments validated by others, and being able to compare oneself favorably to others. In Asian and other non-Western cultures, self-esteem is related to self-restraint, modesty, and connectedness with others. Stevenson and his colleagues (Stevenson, Lee, Chen, Lummis, Stigler, Fan, & Ge, 1990; Stevenson, Lee, Chen, Stigler, Hsu, & Kitamura, 1990) have noted that American children appear to have more positive conceptions of their mathematical abilities than Asian children do, even though the latter actually perform much better than the former. Such findings must be interpreted in light of the cultural differences of the two groups; Asian children apparently learn early that pride in one's strengths is interpreted as gloating and is unacceptable; American children are encouraged to be proud of their accomplishments. Frequent exhortations to "feel good about oneself" and to see oneself as "special" may contribute to the unrealistic self-appraisals reported by Stevenson et al. (as above).

Along similar lines, Trafimow, Triandis, and Goto (1991) distinguish between private and collective aspects of the self, arguing that the private self is emphasized more in individualistic cultures such as those in North America and parts of Europe and that the collective aspects of the self are emphasized more in collectivistic cultures such as those of East Asia. These contrasts suggest that while self-esteem seems to be important in all cultures, it is achieved in diverse ways in different cultures.

The practices described earlier in this discussion that are intended to help children achieve and maintain high self-esteem (for example, "All About Me" books and "I am Special" celebrations) may inadvertently cultivate narcissism—not in its pathological form as the term is used in psychiatric diagnoses, but as a general disposition. These school practices may be symptomatic of our larger culture, described by several observers as having many of the attributes of a narcissistic society (Lasch, 1979; Wallach & Wallach, 1985). Lowen (1985), for example, claims that when success is more important than self-respect, the culture itself overvalues image and is narcissistic, and further, that narcissism denotes a degree of unreality in individuals and the culture.

Our culture seems almost obsessed with the image that a person projects to others. Many of our political leaders use such expressions as not wanting their actions "to *appear* to be improper" rather than not wanting them to *be* improper. At the beginning of the Gulf War crisis, President Bush said, "We have to appear to be strong" rather than that we have to be strong, suggesting that momentous decisions are based as much or more upon appearances than upon actualities. The term *impression management* has indeed entered into the national vocabulary!

A related manifestation of confusing images with reality is explored thoughtfully by Kakutani in the article called "Virtual Confusion: Time for a Reality Check." Kakutani (1992) points out that "ardent soap opera viewers routinely confuse their favorite characters with the actors who play them . . . and send "CARE" packages to actors who play impoverished characters" (p. B2).

Narcissism: Definitions

According to Lowen (1985), narcissism refers to a syndrome characterized by exaggerated investment in one's own image versus one's true self and in how one *appears* versus how one actually feels. Dispositions often mentioned in definitions of narcissism as being characteristic of the condition include dispositions to behave in seductive and manipulative ways, to strive for power, and to sacrifice personal integrity for ego needs. Adults diagnosed as suffering from the narcissism syndrome often complain that their lives are empty or meaningless, and they often show insensitivity to the needs of others. Their behavior patterns suggest that notoriety and attention are more important to them than their own dignity.

According to Emmons (1987), narcissism is characterized by being self-absorbed, self-centered, or selfish, even to the extent that it "may lessen individuals' willingness to pursue common social objectives . . . [and] increase potential for social conflict . . . on a group level" such as occurs with "excessive ethnocentrism" (p. 11). As part of the definition of narcissism in adults, Emmons refers to the tendency to "accept responsibility for successful outcomes and deny blame for failed outcomes" (p. 11). According to some specialists, narcissism includes a preoccupation with fantasies about unlimited success, power, and beauty, plus a grandiose sense of self-importance. Raskin, Novacek, and Hogan (1991) interpret their research findings to mean that

> narcissistic behaviors are defenses against, or defensive expression of, threatening emotions such as anger, anxiety, and fear. Anger, hostility, and rage seem central to the emotional life of the narcissist; consequently, narcissistic behaviors may allow the expression of these emotions in a way that protects a sense of positive self-regard. (p. 917)

Narcissists are also sometimes described as exhibitionistic, requiring constant attention and admiration, often believing that they are entitled to special favors without the need to reciprocate. They tend to exploit others, to be seekers of sensations, experiences, and thrills, and to be highly susceptible to boredom. Many of these characteristics of narcissism seem to apply to our culture in general and to many of our youth in particular.

Wink (1991) suggests that narcissism takes at least two major forms. The classical form is indicated by an excessive need for admiration, frequent exhibitionism, conceit, and a tendency toward open expression of grandiosity—commonly referred to as "being a bit too full of oneself." Wink calls the second form "covert narcissism," in which individuals "appear to be hypersensitive, anxious, timid, and insecure; but on close contact surprise others with their grandiose fantasies" (p. 591). They tend to be exploitative and to overinterpret others' behavior as caused by or directed to themselves rather than to others.

In sum, healthy self-esteem refers to realistic and accurate positive appraisals of the self on significant criteria across a variety of interpersonal situations. It also includes the ability to cope with the inevitability of some negative feedback. By contrast, unhealthy self-esteem, as in narcissism, refers to insensitivity to others, with excessive preoccupation with the self and one's own image and appearance in the eyes of others.

APPROPRIATE PRACTICES

While the definitions of narcissism discussed above refer to adult personality disturbances, the concept of narcissism is discussed here as a caution against many practices that may inadvertently lead to mild forms of the syndrome. Practices that emphasize self-celebration, appearance, and image, and that are characterized by emphasizing trivial criteria for self-appraisal, are unlikely to lead to healthy self-esteem, in part because they fail to provide children with meaningful challenge, effort, and problem solving. Points to consider in developing appropriate practices are discussed below.

Optimum Self-Esteem

The research of Cassidy (1988) suggests that the foundation of self-esteem, whether high or low, is laid very early in the context of interactions with primary caregivers. It continues to be influenced throughout development in the context of relationships with significant adults and peers within a particular culture. The criteria against which estimations of the self are made are learned early within the family and modified in the course of participation in institutions such as schools and the larger society.

In the halls of an elementary school, a large banner was displayed that read, "There's no such thing as too much self-esteem!" Regardless of the fact that the intended recipient of the message was not clear, the message is misleading, if not incorrect. It is useful to keep in mind the general principle that just because something is desirable and good for us, more of it is not necessarily better; rather, its value may be best realized when it is at an *optimum* rather than a minimum or maximum level (See Chapter 1). Thus, a more appropriate suggestion would seem to be that no one needs maximum self-esteem, if indeed such a thing is possible: it would limit a person's ability to read feedback accurately. Rather, it would seem wiser for parents and teachers to help children achieve optimum self-esteem. Given that some ups and downs in behavior, competence, and feedback are bound to occur, self-esteem should fluctuate within a narrow and optimum range.

Esteem for Children

While there is little doubt that many children arrive at the preschool and school doors with less than optimum self-esteem, telling them that they should feel otherwise is unlikely to have much effect. Feelings cannot be learned from direct instruction. Furthermore, constant messages about how wonderful a person is may raise doubts about the credibility of the message and messenger.

Self-esteem is most likely to be fostered when children are esteemed. Esteem is conveyed to them when significant adults and peers treat them respectfully, consult their views and preferences (even if they do not accede to them), and provide opportunities for real decisions and choices about events and things that matter to them. Young children's opinions, views, suggestions, and preferences about relevant activities and events should be respectfully solicited and considered seriously.

For example, a kindergarten teacher watching her pupils build a model schoolbus in her classroom had noted that their efforts were hampered when more than about six children were working on it at the same time. She shared her observations with the children and suggested that they try to work out a schedule so that no more than four or five of them at a time were working on the project. The children accepted her challenge eagerly and developed a schedule that was not very effective. They soon realized this and then sought her advice and fashioned a more workable one, to their great satisfaction. To be sure, on such occasions some children will come up with wild or silly notions, and their peers may quickly tell them so. However, in the course of discussion, teachers can gain insight into how children understand the matters at hand and can make sound decisions about which children need help and what kind of help would be most appropriate. Unless adults treat children as sensible, their dispositions to behave sensibly cannot be strengthened.

Similarly, a first grade teacher reported that during a daily creative writing time in her class, one boy was unable to generate more than half a sentence. She acknowledged his "writer's block" appreciatively and suggested to him that he return to the task later in the day when he might have more ideas. At the end of the afternoon, his ideas flowed into two and a half pages about which he expressed real satisfaction. Adults are likely to have difficulty producing creative stories according to a time schedule. It is therefore surprising that children who have yet to attain real fluency are often expected to produce creative writing during fixed time periods!

Self-esteem is unlikely to be fostered by easy success on a succession of trivial tasks. Young children are more likely to benefit from real challenge and hard work than from frivolous one-shot activities. In a report on the work of her first grade children's weather project, a teacher complained that it took four children three days to create a working anemometer (a horizontal device for measuring windspeed). Their first few attempts were flawed by their having used so much masking tape to attach the four vanes to the center that a gale force wind was needed to make such a heavy instrument revolve. The children refused to give up their attempt even though their persistence interrupted the teacher's plans. Their eventual success was a source of real satisfaction to them, to say nothing of the learning it provided. The device was much appreciated by their classmates, and ultimately by the teacher as well.

This example illustrates not only the benefits of hard work to children's self-esteem, but also the benefits of mutual cooperation. Educational practices that foster cooperation are likely, therefore, to also foster self-esteem. Such a practice is mixed-age grouping, in which the teaching and other kinds of assistance older children can give younger classmates provide opportunities for children to see their *real* contributions to others clearly (Katz, Evangelou, & Hartman, 1990).

Most of the tasks offered to our young children in early childhood classes provide for individual effort and achievement. However, educational practices such as mixed-age grouping, which encourage mutual support and cooperation, recognize that interpersonal processes that foster healthy self-esteem require a good balance of individual work with ample opportunity for group work in which each individual can make a contribution to the total effort through cooperative work.

Praise and Appreciation

Early childhood practitioners are rightfully assiduous about encouraging children by offering frequent positive feedback in the form of praise for their efforts. However, the distinction between praise and flattery is often blurred. Gushing over a child's fingerpainting may be accepted by the child with pleasure, but it is difficult to know at what point praise becomes so frequent that it loses its value and is dismissed by children as empty teacher talk. If children are accustomed to frequent praise, its inevitable occasional absence may be experienced by some children as a rebuke, even though the latter is not intended. It is also difficult for adults to maintain a constant flow of meaningful praise. Furthermore, if a child's sense of self-worth can be raised by simple flattery from one person, it probably can be just as easily deflated by the absence of flattery or criticism from another.

A large body of evidence indicates that children benefit from positive feedback. However, praise and rewards are not the only types of positive feedback. Another kind is *appreciation*. By appreciation I mean positive feedback related explicitly and directly to the *content* of the child's interest and effort. A teacher might, for example, bring a new reference book to class in response to a question raised by a child, or share with the children the ideas generated from her reflections on the problems they had raised concerning procedures to try in a project under way. In this way, the teacher treats the children's questions and concerns with respect, deepening interest in the issues raised and providing positive feedback without deflecting the children from the content and tasks at issue.

The important point here is that the teacher shows in a positive way that she appreciates their concerns *without taking their minds off the subjects at hand or directing their attention inward.* When children see that their concerns and interests are followed up seriously and respectfully, they are more likely to raise their concerns in the next discussion and take their own ideas seriously. In this way, teachers can strengthen children's dispositions to wonder, reflect, raise questions, and generate alternative solutions to practical and intellectual problems. If rewards and trophies are to be effective, the aspirer has to keep at least one eye on them much of the time, thus becoming less able to be absorbed completely and wholeheartedly in the topic, problem, or task itself. Certificates, stars, stickers, and trophies also provide children with positive feedback, but, in contrast, their salience is likely to deflect the children's and the teacher's attention from the content of the work at hand (Kohn, 1993b).

In their eagerness to reinforce cooperative behavior, teachers often praise young children's efforts by saying such things as "I was really glad when you used your words to get your turn," or "It made me happy to see you share your wagon with Robin." Such strategies may be useful when first introducing children to using verbal strategies for conflict resolution. But like all other strategies, they can be overdone, especially as children reach the preschool years. At issue here is the hypothesis that frequent praise of such behavior may be taken by children to mean that the praised behavior is not expected, as though the unspoken end of those kinds of elliptical sentences is " . . . because I never expected you to." It may be that children sense our unspoken expectations of them and, indeed, frequently live up to them. Furthermore, such teacher responses may imply that the rationale for the desirable behavior is merely to please the teachers.

It seems more appropriate for teachers to exercise a quiet and calm authority by stating clearly and respectfully what behavior is expected as occasions arise. When children squabble about toys and equipment, the teacher can calmly and firmly suggest phrases to use if they have not yet acquired them, or remind them in a low-key authoritative manner to use appropriate verbal approaches they already know. Because young children are in the early stages of acquiring interactive and conflict resolution skills, teachers may have to use this strategy patiently for several months.

I have often heard well-meaning teachers urging young, inattentive children to put on their "listening ears" or their "thinking caps," or to "zip their lips," and other similar expressions. I observed a teacher urging a resistant child to assist in cleaning up the housekeeping corner by saying, "Put the puppets in their bed. It will help them. They like to be in their beds." More to the point would have been a simple suggestion to put the items where they belong. Perhaps many children see these common teacher behaviors as fun or cute, or perhaps a game, but some are likely to see it as talking down to them. It is difficult to imagine that such word games can create an intellectually vital ethos in the classroom. It is also difficult to imagine that frequent exposure to such childish and phony talk can engender real respect for teachers. Furthermore, such teacher talk is dishonest. How can children who are spoken to in these ways perceive their teachers as thoughtful and intellectually alert adults? On the other hand, when parents and teachers address children as youngsters with lively intellects, and appeal to their good sense, clearly assuming that they have it, children are more likely to be intellectually engaged and to respond sensibly.

Over many years of working in early childhood classrooms, I have often asked teachers to list adjectives by which their pupils would describe them if I were to solicit the children's views. Invariably the adjective lists relate to their appearance, clothes, voice quality, kindness, firmness, and other nonintellectual characteristics. These lists produced by large numbers of early childhood teachers have rarely included any intellectual qualities such as "she's smart," "knows a lot," "has good ideas." Indeed, several teachers have followed up this exercise by asking their pupils to describe them and have thus become aware of the absence of references to the teachers' knowledge or wisdom! When teachers make their own intellectual attributes evident to their pupils, the children are more likely to benefit from the teacher's appreciation and praise of their efforts. The positive feedback they receive is more likely to be valued by children when they can perceive its source as a person they can look up to and respect.

Children's Own Criteria of Competence

The practice of giving positive feedback to young children in the form of gold stars, smiling faces, and decorative stickers is unlikely to make an enduring contribution to the development of self-esteem, especially if such feedback is very frequent. Rather, children can be helped to develop and apply their own evaluation criteria.

For example, rather than have children take their work home every day, they can be encouraged to collect it in a special folder or portfolio for a week or more. Then at some point the teacher can encourage children to select an item they wish to take home and discuss with them some criteria they might use for selection. The emphasis should not be on whether they like a piece of work, or whether it is good versus bad. Instead, the children can be encouraged to think about whether a piece of work includes all they want it to, or whether they think it is clear or accurate enough, or whether it shows progress compared with the last item they took home, and so forth. At first, parents might be disappointed when the flow of paintings, collages, and worksheets is interrupted. But teachers can help parents to engage in fruitful discussion with their children about the criteria of selection used, thus encouraging the children to take their own evaluations of their work seriously.

Similarly, when children are engaged in project work with others, they can evaluate the extent to which they have answered the questions with which they began. Together, they can assess the work accomplished on criteria developed with their teacher pertaining to the accuracy, completeness, and interest value of their final products (see Katz & Chard, 1989). The children can also be encouraged to discuss what they might do the next time they undertake an investigation, thus strengthening the disposition to vary their strategies and use their own experience as a source of data from which to improve their next undertakings. Applying such criteria to their own efforts also helps children to engage their minds in their work, and in their growing understandings and competence, rather than to draw attention to themselves or to the image they project to others.

Coping with Reverses

When children are engaged in challenging and significant activities and interactions, they are bound to experience some failures, reverses, and rebuffs. Parents and teachers have an important role to play not in avoiding such events, but in helping children cope constructively when they fail to get what they want, whether a turn with a toy or success at a task. In such incidents the teacher can say something like "I know you're disappointed, but there's tomorrow, and you can try again." Children are more likely to be able to cope with rebuffs, disappointments, and failures and learn from these experiences when adults acknowledge and accept their feelings of discouragement and at the same time indicate that they can try again another time.

Another approach is to teach children to use what they have learned from their own previous experience as a source of encouragement. A teacher might, for example, help a child recall an earlier experience when he or she struggled with a task or situation and eventually mastered it.

Worthwhile Activities

Healthy self-esteem is more likely to be developed when children are engaged in activities for which they can make real decisions and contributions than in activities that are frivolous and cute. The danger also exists that some activities that might be worthwhile can also become frivolous if carried to an extreme. For example, in many early childhood classrooms, much time and effort is given to activities related to holidays. While festive occasions alleviate the routine of daily life and can be opportunities to teach children about significant cultural and historical events, if such festivals are celebrated overmuch the learning opportunity becomes lost in triviality and frivolity.

Early childhood educators have traditionally emphasized the fact that play is children's natural way of learning (Isenberg & Quisenberry, 1988). Indeed, a large body of research and years of practical experience attest to the powerful role of play in all facets of learning in the early years. Besides play, however, it is just as natural for young children to learn through investigation. Young children are born natural scientists and social scientists. Like anthropologists, they devote enormous amounts of time and energy to investigating and making sense of the environments into which they are born and in which they are raised. Teachers can capitalize on these inborn dispositions during the preschool and early school years by engaging children in investigations through project work, investigations that are in-depth studies of topics, environments, events, and objects worthy of children's attention and understanding (see Chaille & Britain, 1991; Katz & Chard, 1989; Shores, 1992).

In the course of such undertakings, children negotiate with their teachers to determine the questions to be answered, the studies to be undertaken, and ways of representing their findings in media such as paintings, drawings, and dramatic play. Project work provides children with ample opportunity for real discussion, decision making, choices, cooperation, initiative, joint effort, negotiation, compromise, and evaluation of the outcomes of their own efforts. In this way, children's self-esteem can be based on their contribution to the work of the group, and to the quality of the group's effort and its results.

USES AND MISUSES OF ENCHANTMENT

Just as one of the features of the poster described at the beginning of this essay raised issues about the distinction between practices that foster self-esteem and those that encourage self-preoccupation, another feature of the poster suggested some misuses of enchantment—to modify Bettelheim's phrase (1975). Note that the medium through which the poster's self-centered message was promoted is a cute, smiling, talking animal! Though this common practice is not directly related to those designed to promote self-esteem, it is related to a general tendency to sweeten and amuse children into "feeling good" and having fun rather than being involved, absorbed, and challenged. In particular, to the extent that every learning environment communicates to children what is important and valuable in the eyes of those who provide it, the decor of many early childhood and elementary classrooms emphasizes what is cute, frivolous, and trivial and also misrepresents children's interests. This emphasis is not only questionable on aesthetic and pedagogical grounds—it also may distract children from achieving self-esteem derived from appreciating and interacting with the real world and their real capacities to understand and contribute to it.

In early childhood settings all over the country, one can see pictures of smiling, talking animals conveying messages to children about rules and routines, often in blazing, flashy colors. One example is a large poster depicting a rabbit, a mouse, and a bear sitting around a table. The caption says, "Be a good listener. Help others work and learn. Be thoughtful." Among others are pictures of a chick with a bow tie saying to an elephant and a giraffe, "Let's read a story"; a bear seated at a desk saying, "Be a good student"; a squirrel separating a combatant rabbit and horse, saying, "Talking helps settle differences"; sad-faced animals captioned, "We all have feelings." Another example is a whole wall of a kindergarten classroom covered with a depiction of Humpty Dumpty perched on a wall, saying, "Welcome to School." (Could children make a connection between Humpty Dumpty's fall and their future careers at the school?) Signs indicating the subjects of books in an elementary school library all featured animals reading, and at the entrance was a sign with a cartoon drawing of a cat titled "Purr-fectly quiet please!" These kinds of displays are more fanciful than imaginative.

These and many similar posters and bulletin board displays seem to exemplify misuse of the natural appeal that enchanting creatures have for children and even for many adults. This phrase is used in contrast to the title of Bettelheim's (1975) well-respected book called *The Uses of Enchantment,* in which he presents eloquent arguments that fairy tales and the like provide children with pretexts and contexts for working out the inevitable conflicts and dark feelings experienced by all children. However compelling the logic of his exposition is, he produces no evidence from child development or psychosocial research that supports his assertion that enchanting tales help children. However, I know of no evidence that they are harmful either.

The argument here is that our efforts to make children feel comfortable and cosy by surrounding them with pictures of cuddly creatures are unnecessary and phony. Instead, live animals, and photographs of real ones, would be appropriate and could evoke children's deep interest in them. It seems to me to be more appropriate to support and appreciate children's own capacities for fantasy than to impose adults' fantasies on them. Most of our children have plenty of exposure to cartoons and the like outside of school. It would be interesting to observe children's responses to being surrounded with real art, especially native and folk art in all its variety, including pottery, baskets, macramé, and quilts, as well as in many graphic forms.

The practices described above seem to reflect our culture's dichotomous or conflicting approach to children. On the one hand, we feel compelled to surround them with silly creatures and to justify many activities on the grounds that they are fun, amusing and exciting, rather than interesting and absorbing (see Chapter 6). On the other hand, we introduce children to "stranger danger," instruct them in ways to resist physical and sexual abuse, teach them—if not hound them—about the elements of good nutrition, warn them of dangerous drugs, and—in some classrooms—AIDS, long before they can understand and cope with such serious matters. *Young children need the constant supervision and protection of adults against such hazards.*

The issue underlying the practices described here—namely, those that confuse self-esteem with narcissism and those that misuse enchantment—is *authenticity* versus phoniness. Engaging children in investigations and close observation of their real worlds in ways that respect their lively intellects, and that provide opportunity for effort and real problem solving, is more likely to foster healthy self-esteem than are amusement, flattery, and praise for cheap success at frivolous tasks.

CONCLUSION

The main argument put forward in this essay is that while the development of self-esteem is an important concern for parents and teachers of young children, many of the practices currently intended to enhance it are more likely to foster preoccupation with oneself and with the way one appears to others. I have suggested that practices that engage children's minds in investigating those aspects of their own experiences and environments that are worth knowing more about and that can present challenges can help them develop realistic criteria of self-esteem.

Self-esteem cannot be achieved through direct instruction or exhortations to "feel good" about oneself. Teachers are more likely to foster healthy self-esteem when they help children cope with occasional negative feedback, frustration, and reverses. While is it clear that children need positive feedback about their behavior and their efforts, it is most likely to strengthen their self-esteem when it is provided at an optimum rather than a maximum level, and when the feedback is specific and informative rather than general praise or flattery. Children are more likely to enhance their sense of self-confidence and self-worth when the learning environment provides a wide variety of activities and tasks, when they have opportunities to make meaningful decisions and choices (see Kohn, 1993a) and when optimum challenge rather than quick and easy success is available. Children should also have opportunities to work in groups in which they are encouraged to make and seek suggestions to and from each other, and in which individuals can contribute in their own ways to the group's efforts. As children grow, they can also be encouraged to evaluate their own efforts on realistic and meaningful criteria. Teachers are also most likely to foster healthy self-esteem when they maintain and communicate their respect for the self-esteem criteria children experience at home and in their community, while they help them to adopt the criteria of the classroom environment and the school. Such practices are more likely than trivial practices that engender self-preoccupation to help children develop a deep sense of competence and self-worth that can provide a firm foundation for their entire future.

REFERENCES

Ames, C. (1992). Classrooms: Goals, structures, and student motivation. *Journal of Educational Psychology, 84*(3), 261-271. EJ 452395.

Bandura, A. (1989). Human agency in social cognitive theory. *American Psychologist, 44*(9), 1175-1184.

Bednar, R. L., Wells, M. G., & Peterson, S. R. (1989). *Self-esteem: Paradoxes and innovations in clinical theory and practice.* Washington, DC: American Psychological Assocation.

Bettelheim, B. (1975). *The uses of enchantment: The meaning and importance of fairy tales.* London: Penguin Books.

Borba, M., & Borba, C. (1978). *Self-esteem: A classroom affair: 101 ways to help children like themselves.* Minneapolis: Winston Press.

Cassidy, J. (1988). Child–mother attachment and the self in six-year-olds. *Child Development, 58*(1), 121–134. EJ 367878.

Chaille, C., & Britain, L. (1991). *The young child as scientist.* New York: HarperCollins.

Cialdini, R. B., Borden, R., Walker, M. R., Freeman, S., Shuma, P., Braver, S. L., Ralls, M., Floyd, L., Sloan, L. R., Crandall, R., & Jellison, J. M. (1974). Wearing the warm glow of success: A (football) field study. *Personality and Social Psychology Bulletin, 1*(1), 13 – 15.

Cialdini, R. B., Borden, R. J., Thorne, A., Walker, M. R., Freeman, S., & Sloan, L. R. (1976). Basking in reflected glory: Three (football) field studies. *Journal of Personality and Social Psychology, 34*(3), 366–375.

Corporation for Public Broadcasting (no date). *Celebrate yourself: Six steps to building your self-esteem.* Washington, DC: Author.

Dunn, J. (1988). *The beginnings of social understanding.* Cambridge, MA: Harvard University Press.

Emmons, R. A. (1987). Narcissism: Theory and measurement. *Journal of Personality and Social Psychology, 52*(1), 11–17.

Fendel, L., and Ecker, B. (1989). *Building self-esteem with Koala-Roo.* Glencoe, IL: Scott, Foresman.

Hamilton, D. S., & Flemming, B. M. (1990). *Resources for creative teaching in early childhood education* (2nd Ed.). New York: Harcourt, Brace, Jovanovich.

Harter, S. (1983). Developmental perspectives on the self-system. In E. M. Hetherington (Ed.), *Socialization, personality, and social development*. Vol. 4 of P. Mussen (Ed.), *Handbook of child psychology* (Fourth Ed.). New York: Wiley.

Isenberg, J., & Quisenberry, N. L. (1988). PLAY: A necessity for all children. A position paper of the Association for Childhood Education International. *Childhood Education, 64*(3), 138–145. EJ 367943.

Kakutani, M. (1992, Sept. 25). Virtual confusion: Time for a reality check. *New York Times*, pp. B1-B2.

Katz, L.G., & Chard, S.C. (1989). *Engaging children's minds: The project approach*. Norwood, NJ: Ablex. ED 326302.

Katz, L. G., Evangelou, D., & Hartman, J. A. (1990). *The case for mixed-age grouping in early education*. Washington, DC: National Association for the Education of Young Children. ED 326302.

Kohn, A. (1993a). *Punished by rewards: The trouble with gold stars, incentive plans, A's, praise, and other bribes*. Boston: Houghton Mifflin.

Kohn, A. (1993b). Choices for children: Why and how to let students decide. *Phi Delta Kappan, 75*(1), 9–30.

Kowalski, R. M. (1991). Half-baked idea: Patriotic fervor in the aftermath of operation desert storm: Basking in reflected glory? *Contemporary Social Psychology, 15*(4), 118–120.

Lamborn, S., Mounts, N. S., Steinberg, L., & Dornbusch, S. (1991). Patterns of competence and adjustment among adolescents from authoritative, authoritarian, indulgent and neglectful families. *Child Development, 62*(5), 1049–1065. EJ 436489.

Lasch, C. (1979). *The culture of narcissism: American life in an age of diminishing expectations*. New York: W. W. Norton.

Lee, M. J. (1985). Self-esteem and social identity in basketball fans: A closer look at basking-in-reflected glory. *Journal of Sports Behavior, 8*(4), 210–223.

Lowen, A. (1985). *Narcissism: Denial of the true self*. New York: Macmillan.

Markus, H. R., & Kitayama, S. (1991). Culture and the self: Implications for cognition, emotions, and motivation. *Psychological Review, 98*(2), 224–253.

McDaniel, S. (1986, April 28). Political priority #1: Teaching kids to like themselves. *NewOptions, 27*, 1.

National Association of Elementary School Principals. (1990). *Early childhood education and the elementary school principal: Standards for quality programs for young children*. Arlington, VA: Author.

Raskin, R., Novacek, J., & Hogan, R. (1991). Narcissistic self-esteem management. *Journal of Personality and Social Psychology, 60*(6), 891–918.

Rosenholtz, S. J., & Simpson, C. (1984). Classroom organization and student stratification. *Elementary School Journal, 85*(1), 21–37. EJ 307223.

Shores, E. F. (1992). *Explorers' classrooms. Good practice for kindergarten and the primary grades.* Little Rock, AR: Southern Association on Children Under Six.

Stevenson, H. W., Lee, S., Chen, C., Lummis, M., Stigler, J. W., Fan, L., & Ge, F. (1990). Mathematics achievement of children in China and the United States. *Child Development, 61*(4), 1053–1066. EJ 417114.

Stevenson, H. W., Lee, S., Chen, C., Stigler, J. W., Hsu, C., & Kitamura, S. (1990). *Contexts of achievement.* Monograph of the Society for Research in Child Development, serial 221, vol. 55, nos. 1–2. Chicago: University of Chicago Press. EJ 407444.

Trafimow, D., Triandis, H. C., & Goto, S. G. (1991). Some tests of the distinction between the private self and the collective self. *Journal of Personality and Social Psychology, 60*(5), 649–655.

Wallach, M., & Wallach, L. (1985, July/August). Altruism and the self: How psychology sanctions the cult of the self. *Current,* pp. 13-20.

Wink, P. (1991). Two faces of narcissism. *Journal of Personality and Social Psychology, 61*(4), 590–597.

3

DISPOSITIONS: DEFINITIONS AND IMPLICATIONS FOR EARLY CHILDHOOD PRACTICE*

It is often difficult to know the exact source of an idea. The notion that dispositions may be a useful concept for education first came to mind during a final doctoral examination for which I was a committee member. At the close of the oral examination the candidate was asked to briefly summarize her reflections on her doctoral research and the questions she had set out to answer. Her response was a distinctly unreflective assertion that although her results were negative, her hypotheses were still right, and that she resolved never to do research again! The response indicated clearly that she had successfully completed all the requirements for her degree but had failed to develop a disposition to investigate, reflect, doubt, or to consider alternative explanations of complex human interaction. It seemed to me that the student had acquired worthwhile knowledge and considerable intellectual skills necessary for successful doctoral work. However, in the process of doing so, her disposition to apply them had been either damaged or undeveloped. Since the graduate program had no explicit dispositional requirements, criteria, or standards, she was awarded a degree.

Since then my concern increased about the extent to which knowledge and skills might be learned at the expense of the

---

*This chapter was originally published as "Dispositions: Definitions and Implications for Early Childhood Practices," 1993, by Lilian G. Katz. Urbana, IL: ERIC Clearinghouse on Elementary and Early Childhood Education. Reprinted by permission.

disposition to apply them, and about the inborn dispositions in children that might suffer from inappropriate curriculum or pedagogies.

In the last several years, as indicated in the chapter, the term disposition has become fairly current in educational litera-ture. It remains, however, a very difficult construct to define, and thus to investigate. This chapter is an attempt to provide a work-ing definition to serve in discussions of the important and com-plex issues surrounding motivation and the goals of education.

One of the major questions to be addressed when developing a curriculum is, What should be learned? I have suggested else-where (Katz, 1991; see Chapter 7 in this volume) that one way to answer this question is to adopt at least four types of learning goals: knowledge, skills, dispositions, and feelings. The acquisi-tion of both knowledge and skills is usually taken for granted as a goal for which educational institutions have a special if not a unique responsibility. That is not to say that knowledge and skills are not learned outside of schools. Families, museums, the media, libraries, sports clubs, and many other settings are sources of intentional as well as incidental knowledge and skill learning. However, preschools and schools are deliberately and explicitly designed to enhance knowledge and skill acquisition. Most educators would also readily agree that many feelings (for example, self esteem) are influenced—for better or worse—by school experiences and are worthy of inclusion among curricu-lum goals. However, dispositions are not usually listed among curriculum goals, though they are often implied by the inclusion of attitudes (for instance, toward learning) as goals. The main purpose of this chapter is to examine the construct disposition, and with a working definition explore its relevance to curricu-lum and teaching practices in early childhood education.

Examination of the place of dispositional learning in early childhood education is prompted by recent discussions of school readiness among professionals that have been stimulated by the promotion of the National Educational Goals Panel, renamed *Goals 2000: Educate America.* A case in point is the report of the Goal One Technical Planning Subgroup to the National Educa-tional Goals Panel titled *Report on School Readiness* (1991). The report includes "approaches to learning" as one of five dimen-sions of school readiness to be assessed in national samples of preschoolers. Elaborating on the "approaches to learning" dimension, the Technical Planning Subgroup defines them as "the inclinations, dispositions, or styles—rather than skills—that reflect the myriad ways that children become involved in learning, and develop their inclinations to pursue it." With this report as a point of departure I begin with a discussion of definitional issues.

PART I—DEFINITIONAL ISSUES

Approaches to Learning

In the Technical Subgroup's report to the National Educational Goals Panel (1991), the terms *inclinations*, *dispositions*, and *learning styles* are used as subcategories of "approaches to learning." Examples of traits referred to by the three terms given in the report are "curiosity, creativity, independence, cooperativeness, and persistence." Though all three terms—inclinations, dispositions, and learning styles—may amplify our understanding of school readiness, they are imprecise. None of these three terms appears in the indexes of major comprehensive child development texts. (See, for example, Bee, 1985; Mussen, 1983; Rathus, 1988; Scarr, Weinberg, & Levine, 1986; Sroufe, Cooper, & DeHart, 1992; Yussen & Santrock, 1982.) How then are these terms to be defined?

Inclination Webster's Dictionary defines inclination as a particular disposition of mind or character, liking or preference (Webster's, 1987). Listed as synonyms are: tendency, propensity, proclivity, and predilection (The American College Dictionary, 1948). Because inclination does not appear in the child development literature and its implications can be subsumed under the term disposition, it does not appear to be a useful term in considering curriculum and pedagogical issues.

Cognitive Style The term cognitive style, frequently used in research on adults and children, has been defined as "ways that individuals perceive, think, understand, remember, judge, and solve problems" (Saracho, 1991, p. 22), leaving no clear picture of what is not included in definition. The research on cognitive styles typically assesses children's ways of thinking on a bipolar dimension of field dependence–field independence when approaching a variety of social and cognitive tasks and situations. Shipman (1989) summarizes research on the cognitive style construct as follows:

> Although cognitive styles represent important understandings of how learners respond to materials and communications, I believe that our understanding of the development, operation and malleability of cognitive styles is insufficient for justifying certain educational decisions. (p. 3)

Learning Style The term learning style is increasingly linked to Howard Gardner's theory of multiple intelligences (Gardner, 1985), in which distinctive strength or weakness in one or another of seven hypothesized types of intelligence is associated with a corresponding learning style. Many educators are attempting to apply this formulation of learning styles in curriculum and teaching practices. Assessment of the usefulness of learning styles associated with the theory of multiple intelligences seems premature at this time. However, while learning styles and cognitive styles are being considered by educators, I suggest that they may serve as sub-categories of the larger construct of dispositions.

Dispositions

Formal Definitions of Disposition Though the term disposition is used in some of the psychology literature, definitions of it are rarely offered. To begin with formal definitions, the *Comprehensive Dictionary of Psychological and Psychoanalytical Terms* (English and English, 1958), offers the following definition of the term disposition:

> 2. a general term for any (hypothesized) organized and enduring part of the total psychological or psychophysiological organization in virtue of which a person is likely to respond to certain statable conditions with a certain kind of behavior: his *disposition* is to think before acting . . . 4. a relatively lasting emotional attitude; or the relative predominance in the total personality of a certain emotional

attitude; a stubborn disposition . . . 5. the sum of all innate tendencies or propensities . . . (p. 158; italics in the original.)

In this part of the definition, the dictionary suggests that a disposition is a stable habit of mind and something called an "emotional attitude" with "stubbornness" as an example. The entry continues:

> Although all behavior depends upon a certain dynamic or propulsive readiness of the organism, as well as upon the stimulating conditions, **disposition** gives sharp emphasis to the former. The resulting behavior may then be described, to adapt a distinction made by B. F. Skinner, as **emitted** by the organism rather than **elicited** by the stimulus. (p. 158; bold in the original.)

This part of the definition suggests that a disposition is internal to the actor, and little influenced by the situation or stimuli to which the actor is subjected. The dictionary goes on to amplify the definition as follows:

> The construct of *something to account for sameness of behavior despite variation in the environing situation* is a formal necessity. Thus it is necessarily and formally true that to enjoy a swim whether the water be hot or cold requires that the person have a certain disposition. But it need not be a specific enjoyment of swimming disposition. It may be a more general athleticism, or a relative indifference to temperature, or a combination of personal qualities each of which also plays its part in other situations. We cannot usually go directly from observed fact to a specific disposition to account for the fact. To constitute a useful construct, a disposition must be more general than the fact that led to its being inferred. The logical requirements for inference are not easily met. (p. 158; italics in the original.)

This last part of the formal definition suggests that the disposition construct is used to identify broad rather than specific categories of behavior, or characteristic ways of responding to a variety of situations more determined by characteristics internal to the actor than provoked by the environment.

Buss and Craik (1983, p. 105) propose a formal definition of dispositions as "summaries of act frequencies" that represent trends or frequencies of acts. According to this definition, a person exhibiting a relatively high frequency of behavior such as making donations to charity, giving gifts to family members, and offering loans to needy friends could be said to have the disposition to be generous. Similarly, children who frequently ask questions, often snoop and pry, and generally poke around their environment can be said to have a robust disposition to be curious. However, Buss and Craik do not address the role of motivation or intentions associated with the act frequencies of which dispositions are constituted.

Katz and Raths (1985) applied the disposition construct to teacher education using the definition proposed by Buss and Craik, namely, as acts that may be conscious and deliberate or so habitual and "automatic" that they *seem* intuitive or spontaneous. Thus the disposition to be generous, illustrated in the previous paragraph, though consisting of intentional acts, is present when it is manifested with relatively little analysis or premeditation; if extensive analysis, premeditation, and reflection preceded each generous act, the disposition to be generous could not be inferred; rather, the person might be described as having the disposition to be cautious, deliberate, and perhaps a grudging or reluctant donor.

Dispositions and Other Personal Characteristics   The term disposition appears with increasing frequency in literature related to children's learning (e.g., Ennis, 1987; Katz, 1985; Katz & Chard, 1989; Langer, 1993; Perkins, Jay & Tishman, 1993; Resnick, 1987). Katz and Raths (1985) attempt to clarify the disposition construct by distinguishing it from constructs of other personal characteristics such as traits, skills, attitudes, and habits. Further clarification may also be obtained by attempting to distinguish dispositions from other related constructs such as thought processes, motives, and work inhibition.

1. *Traits and Dispositions.*   The term disposition appears in the literature on personality (e.g., Buss & Craik, 1983; Cantor, 1990; Hoffman & Tchir, 1990). In discussions of personality and its development, disposition is frequently used interchangeably with the term trait. For example, Maccoby (1987) uses the term disposition when she points out that

> most of us believe that other people are characterized by broad personality dispositions, such as aggressiveness, or

conscientiousness, or sensitivity to the moods and needs of others—dispositions that manifest themselves in a variety of situations and with a variety of social partners. (p. 5)

Later in the same text Maccoby speaks of behavioral dispositions, and still later, discussing the stability of behavior patterns, uses the term dispositions without a qualifier. No definition of disposition is offered in the text; it appears to be employed as a synonym for trait and for stable and general characteristics usually associated with aspects of personality.

Wakefield (1989), combining the concepts of habit and motivation, and emphasizing intentionality, uses the term disposition in his definition of traits as:

stable dispositions to have certain kinds of beliefs, desires, and so on. . . . (pp. 336–337)

. . . traits are dispositions specifically of the intentional system. . . . (p. 337)

The trait explains specific motives in terms of a persistent and more general disposition of the intentional system to generate motives. . . . (p. 338)

A trait is a disposition to have a certain kind of intentional state, and the existence of such a disposition calls out for explanation in terms of underlying structures that account for this property of the intentional system (p. 338).

Wakefield asserts that "a proper explanation of behavior must make some reference to the specific meanings and experiences in the form of mental representations—generally known as *intentionality*—that cause an individual's behavior" (p. 333). In this way Wakefield uses the terms trait and disposition interchangeably and adds motivational and intentional components to their meaning. According to Wakefield's definition, curiosity, generosity, and stubbornness could be classified as dispositions, but capabilities such as mastery of reading, arithmetic, or handwriting skills would not be so classified.

Katz and Raths (1985) suggest that the terms trait and disposition differ in at least two major ways. The first is that a disposition implies a trend in a person's actions rather than his or her emotional state that causes behavior, as implied by the term trait. Thus such terms as honesty, ambition, and courage do not fit a definition of a disposition, but describe aspects of a person's character and the management of his or her emotions. Disposition, on the other hand, can be used to designate actions and characterize their frequency. Terms such as *explorer, problem-solver, bully, whiner,* and so forth, which may be accompanied by emotional states, can be used to describe dispositions.

The second way dispositions can be distinguished from traits is that of *intensity.* Katz and Raths explain this distinction as follows:

> When a man is asked, "Which way to the store?" and he responds with an accurate direction, few observers would attribute the trait of honesty to him on that basis alone. To merit the attribution of honesty as a trait, a person would have to be observed in the face of the temptation to lie, having to overcome some adversity and to behave with the level of intensity necessary to overcome it (Katz & Raths, 1985, p. 303).

2. Thought Processes and Dispositions. Resnick (1987) uses the term disposition in a discussion of "cultivating the disposition to higher order thinking" (p. 40) with the following definition:

> The term disposition should not be taken to imply a biological or inherited trait. As used here, it is more akin to a *habit of thought,* one that can be learned and, therefore, taught. (p. 4; italics in the original)

A related discussion is presented in a text by Resnick and Klopfer (1989) in the chapter "Shaping Dispositions for Thinking: The Role Of Social Communities." In this discussion, the authors use the term disposition almost interchangeably with the word trait, as illustrated in the following segment of their discussion:

> the social setting may help to shape a disposition to engage in thinking. There is not much research on how intellectual dispositions are socialized, but we do know how other traits such as aggressiveness, independence or gender identification develop. By analogy with these traits, we can expect intellectual dispositions to arise from long-term participation in social communities that establish expecta-

tions for certain kinds of behavior. (Resnick & Klopfer, 1989, p. 9)

Perkins, Jay and Tishman (1993), discussing new conceptions of thinking, define dispositions as "people's tendencies to put their capabilities into action" (p. 75). They offer as an example research showing that "people can easily generate reasons on the side of an issue opposite their own when prompted to do so (they have the capability) yet generally tend not to do so (they lack the disposition)" (p. 75).

In a related discussion, Langer (1993) introduces the concept of *mindfulness* as distinctly different from attention and vigilance, and defines it as

> a state of mind that results from drawing novel distinctions, examining information from new perspectives, and being sensitive to context. It is an open, creative, probabilistic state of mind in which the individual might be led to finding differences among things thought similar, and similarities among things thought different. To be vigilant, in contrast, one has to have a particular stimulus in mind, and an expectation of what the stimulus is rather than what it could be. To pay attention is to pay attention to something; at the same time something else may go unnoticed. (Langer, 1993, p. 44)

Langer suggests that activity that does not invoke active examination of information and sensitivity to context is mindless, and attributes this quality to conventional formal instruction that emphasizes repetitive study and memorization.

Using Langer's definition of mindfulness (1993), Perkins, Jay, and Tishman (1993) assert that "Mindfulness can be considered a disposition because it has to do with how disposed people are to process information in an alert, flexible way" (p. 75).

The applications of the construct of disposition cited above suggest that though it is very difficult to define precisely, it offers a way of distinguishing capabilities and capacities from their manifestation.

3. *Skills and Dispositions.*   Katz and Raths (1985) suggest that it is possible to have the various skills required to be able to read, but to be without the disposition to use them, that is, to lack the disposition to be a reader. To state that a child *can* read is to

imply that the child has achieved a certain level of mastery of the complex skills involved in reading. However, the term *disposition,* as implied by the Buss and Craik definition cited above, refers to the *frequency with which the act of reading is manifested,* in the absence of coercion or extrinsic rewards. When the act of reading is manifested frequently and voluntarily, it can be assumed that the child has in *mind,* at some level, an intention or goal that can be served by reading, (given that the child has the requisite skills that make the manifestation possible). When the acts of reading are manifested frequently, it can be said that the child has a robust disposition to be a reader; when it is rarely or never observed, then it can be said that the disposition is weak, has been damaged, or has not been acquired.

4. *Attitudes and Dispositions.* The term *attitude* has a long history of use among educators. In recent years, however, the meaning of the attitude construct has been the subject of substantial controversy (Eagly, 1992; Fishbein, 1980). It is usually defined as "a relatively enduring organization of beliefs around an object or situation predisposing one to respond in some preferential manner" (Rokeach, 1968, p. 112) to a given phenomenon, or as "an evaluative tendency that is expressed by evaluating a particular entity with some degree of favor or disfavor" (cited in Eagly, 1992, p. 693). In this sense, attitudes can be thought of as *pre*dispositions to act positively or negatively with respect to a particular phenomenon. According to this definition, it is possible to have an attitude toward something without accompanying behavior. However, the term disposition, according to Buss and Craik (1983), refers to frequently exhibited trends in actions. Thus one could have an attitude toward something in the absence of manifestations of related behavior. It is possible, for example, to have a negative attitude toward a race or nation without having opportunity or occasion to manifest it in actual behavior. In contrast to attitude, a disposition always implies trends in behavior and not merely an evaluation or cluster of beliefs about something.

Although the shaping of attitudes is often listed among the goals of educational programs (for example, acquiring a positive attitude toward learning), the term attitude is not usually applied to *preschool* children, perhaps because they are assumed not to engage in evaluative thinking, but to respond momentarily in terms of largely spontaneous likes and dislikes, or to be somewhat *tabulae rasae* with respect to their larger environment.

5. *Habits and Dispositions.* To describe a pattern of behavior as a habit is to assume that it is performed without conscious attention (Passmore, 1972). However, Katz and Raths (1985) suggest that dispositions are patterns of actions that require some attention to what is occurring in the context of the action, "although with practice and experience the acts may appear to be spontaneous, habitual, or even unconscious" (p. 303). The term *habit* should be used to refer to acts that are neither intentional nor the consequence of thought, reflection and analysis. Disposition, on the other hand, is a term to be used to refer to trends in actions that are intentional on the part of the actor in a particular context and at particular times. Katz and Raths contrast habits and dispositions by suggesting that

> Inasmuch as intentionality is a mental process, we see dispositions as "habits of mind"—not as mindless habits. They are classes of intentional actions in categories of situations, and they can be thought of as "habits of mind" that give rise to the employment of skills and are manifested (ideally) by skillful behavior. (1985, p. 303)

6. *Work Inhibition and Dispositions.* Bruns (1992) introduces the concept of *work inhibition* to address observations of very able children who do not do the work required of them in school, who "do not stay on task, do not complete class assignments, do not finish their homework on their own" (p. 38) even though they clearly have the requisite capacities to do so. Bruns explains work inhibition in terms of three personality characteristics: dependency, self-esteem, and passive aggression. Dependency is shown in those children who exhibit work inhibition but who work very well "if their teacher is standing or sitting right next to them" (p. 40). Some express their poor self-esteem, sometimes through preoccupation with self-doubts, and sometimes with a kind of bravado in which they "declare that much of their school work is beneath them" (p. 41). As to the passive-aggression component of work inhibition, Bruns describes it as "subtle, indirect expressions of anger" (p. 41) accompanied by forgetfulness, arguing, and often taking a long time to complete work.

According to Bruns, case histories of work inhibited children reveal that it begins early and

> Although the manifestations of work inhibitions are not always apparent until the third or fourth grade (the time

when the demand for independent academic work becomes substantial), the origins begin during infancy. (p. 42)

However, Bruns does not report whether work-inhibited children overcome the inhibition when the tasks required of them appeal to their interests or challenge them more than most school tasks. Bruns' choice of the term inhibition may be interpreted to imply that if dependency and passive-aggression were removed and self-esteem raised, these children would exhibit effort and persistence.

I suggest that Bruns' concept of work inhibition may be more usefully categorized as a dispositional issue. By the time children reach the elementary school grades, reluctance to engage in assigned tasks may constitute instances of damaged or very much weakened dispositions to learn, including the elements involved in persistence, effort, and mastery goals as discussed in the next section.

7. Motives and Dispositions. McAdams (1989), citing Murray, suggests that human motivation can be understood in terms of

> a collection of psychogenic needs, each of which was viewed as an enduring underlying disposition which energizes, directs, and selects behavior, though always within an environmental context.

Emmons (1989) contrasts traits and motives suggesting that

> traits [are] broadly defined as stylistic and habitual patterns of cognition, affect, and behavior. Motives can be defined as a disposition to be concerned with and to strive for a certain class of incentives or goals (p. 32).

In these examples, motivation is defined in terms of underlying dispositions; in this way motives are thought to be more general than dispositions and are defined at higher levels of abstraction than dispositions.

School-Age Children In a discussion entitled "Motivation to Learn and Understand: On Taking Charge of One's Own Learning" Anne Brown (1988) asks: "What is the relation between attitude and study? How stable are those dispositions?" (p. 312). Brown goes on to refer to effort in elementary and secondary school-age children as "motivational dispositions that influence learning" (p. 313) and to assert "that we will be hampered in our attempts to devise effective intervention programs unless we consider these dispositions" (p. 313).

Research on motivation related to dispositions comes under the rubric of mastery motivation (see for example Ames, 1992; Corno, 1992; Dweck, 1991; Dweck & Leggett, 1988). Several contrasts are offered by scholars studying this aspect of children's learning. For example, Dweck and Elliott distinguish between *mastery motivation* and *helplessness* to indicate that children of equal ability, when given feedback on their work, may respond in one of two ways: "mastery-oriented children react as though they have been given useful feedback about learning and mastery" whereas the "helpless [children] react as though they have received an indictment of their ability" (Elliott & Dweck, 1988, p. 5).

Dweck (1989) also distinguishes between motivation toward *learning goals* and *performance goals* that are governed by different sets of underlying concerns. Children oriented toward learning goals are interested in their own mastery for its own sake and those oriented toward performance goals are more concerned about others' judgments of their abilities. Learning-oriented children are more likely than performance-oriented children to believe that effort is effective, to vary their strategies in the face of difficulties and to assist peers who are having difficulties.

In a similar way, Nicholls (1984) makes a distinction between *task involvement* and *ego involvement* in children's approaches to their work. Task involvement, similar to mastery motivation and the learning-goal orientation, is characterized by effort directed toward the task and the learning it provides. Ego involvement resembles the performance goal orientation in that it is associated with more concern for the judgments of others than for the task and the learning to be acquired by performing the task.

Ames, adopting the labels *mastery* and *performance goals*, integrates the research just described by distinguishing between achievement and mastery goals, suggesting that

An *achievement goal* concerns the purposes of achievement behavior. It defines an integrated pattern of beliefs, attributions, and affect that produces the intentions of behavior and that is represented by different ways of approaching, engaging in, and responding to achievement activities (Ames, 1992, p. 261; italics in the original).

With a mastery goal, individuals are oriented toward developing new skills, trying to understand their work, improving their level of competence, or achieving a sense of mastery based on self-referenced standards. Compatible with this goal construct is . . . a "motivation to learn" whereby individuals are focused on mastering and understanding content and demonstrating a willingness to engage in the process of learning (Ames, 1992, p. 262.)

Ames states that a performance goal is a focus on one's ability and self esteem based on comparing one's performance with others', "by surpassing normative-based standards, or by achieving success with little effort" (p. 262). Ames describes these contrasting motives as two forms of approach tendencies that are elicited by different environmental or instructional demands and result in qualitatively different motivational patterns that can be called dispositions toward learning.

In a discussion of issues in the assessment of mastery motivation, Linder (1990) points out that

The examination of mastery motivation provides insight into the developmental domains upon which the child is focusing energy. The degree of persistence, approach to problem solving, and effectiveness of efforts in each developmental area can be determined. . . . A reciprocal relationship . . . appears to exist between persistence and competence. (Linder, 1990, p. 116)

While these motivational tendencies are evoked by the way tasks are presented to children, it seems reasonable to assume that a *cumulative effect* of repeated exposure to mastery oriented teaching practices would be the development of a disposition toward mastery and to persevere that could also be called a disposition to learn.

Corno (1992) summarizes this body of research and its significance for successful participation in schooling as follows:

Students who are generally inclined to approach school work from the point of learning and mastering the material (so-called learning/mastery orientations) tend to differ in work styles from students whose goals or intentions generally lead from the other point, that is, to obtain grades or display competence. Specifically, "learning-oriented" students (a) engage in more attentive behavior, (b) use deeper learning and studying strategies (put in more quantity and quality of effort), and (c) feel better about themselves as learners. A "performance/ego orientation" has been linked to less elaborate efforts to learn the material and feelings of inadequacy about learning. (Corno, 1992, p. 71)

Preschool Children   The development and nature of motives in preschool children is highly problematic and cannot be fully addressed in this paper. The references to motivation in very young children in the *Handbook of Child Psychology* (Mussen, 1983) are related to the internalization of extrinsic rewards (see Harter, 1983) and the young child's "motivation to control his or her own behavior in order to please the significant others in his or her life, to garner their approval and avoid their disapproval" (Harter, 1983, p. 364). While observers of young children readily agree that young children are invariably curious and eager to learn, they do not speak of children's curiosity and eagerness to learn as motives in the same way as when speaking of achievement motives in older children.

However, Dweck (1991) reports research on four- and five-year-old children's task persistence/nonpersistence and demonstrates that the mastery and helpless orientations that are significantly related to achievement in school-age children can be observed in preschoolers. She points out that

> it appears that the helpless pattern occurs point for point in an appreciable proportion of young children. These children show a marked lack of persistence in the face of failure, as well as a strong tendency (a) to express spontaneous negative thoughts and affect when they encounter obstacles, (b) to see difficulty as meaning they are incapable of performing a task (as opposed to seeing difficulty as surmountable through effort), and (c) to exhibit low expectancies of success on similar future tasks. (Dweck, 1991, pp. 219–220)

Based on the research on motivation currently available, it is difficult to formulate a clear distinction between motives and dispositions (see also Appley, 1991). It seems useful for educators to assume that mastery motivation, which could be called a general *disposition to learn,* is most likely present in some form at birth in all normal infants. Its manifestation is likely to change with development, to be related to the child's experience, and is likely to be increasingly varied and differentiated with increasing age and experience. It may be manifested (a) in the newborn as an "orienting response," (b) in the toddler as various types of exploration, play, and experimentation, (c) in the preschooler as a disposition to make sense of experience, and (d) in the school-age child more like the patterns of behaviors described by Dweck and Corno cited above.

Summary and Tentative Definition

In sum, usage of the term disposition is ambiguous and inconsistent. The only attempt to define the construct psychologically that has been found was made by Buss and Craik (1983), who described it as act frequencies constituting trends in behavior. Nevertheless, educators (and most likely other observers as well) recognize that it is possible to have skills and lack the taste, wish, or habit of using them. To speak of using and applying knowledge is more problematic. We do not usually speak of using or applying knowledge in the same way as we speak of associating reading skills with the disposition to read, or listening skills with the disposition to listen. Elements of knowledge are usually associated with mental processes such as inference, recall, memory, classification, or construction, though there is a sense in which we describe people as analytical to mean that they have the disposition to process information analytically rather than holistically or impulsively.

A variety of personal attributes including traits, attitudes, habits, work inhibition, and motives are used to describe trends in behavior across situations, in an attempt to distinguish these attributes from knowledge, abilities, capabilities, and skills.

As far as can be determined, the term disposition and its relevance to the education of young children was first introduced by Katz in "Dispositions in Early Childhood Education" (1985) in which dispositions were defined—as proposed above—as "relatively enduring habits of mind or characteristic ways of responding to experience across types of situations" (p. 1), as for example curiosity, humor, creativity, affability, and quarrelsomeness.

On the basis of an examination of the uses of the term in recent psychological and educational literature I propose that the term disposition can be used to distinguish trends in behavior from skills, attitudes, traits, and mindless habits (for example, fastening one's seatbelt), and that these distinctions have useful practical implications even in the absence of desirable precision. For the purposes of exploring these implications the following tentative definition is proposed:

> A disposition is a pattern of behavior exhibited frequently and in the absence of coercion, and constituting a habit of mind under some conscious and voluntary control, and that is intentional and oriented to broad goals.

The term "habit of mind" is used to distinguish dispositions from such mindless and unpremeditated habitual behavior as obeying traffic lights and fastening seat belts. Both such habits can be thought to have some motivational and intentional dimensions in an ultimate sense. However, they are such strong and frequent habits of action that they are typically enacted with little or no conscious engagement of motives or intentions. These habits, however, may be relatively microlevel acts that are part of a general disposition to be obedient, law-abiding, or cautious.

In the case of curiosity, for example, a child can be said to have the disposition to be curious if he or she typically and frequently responds to the environment by exploring, examining, and asking questions about it. Similarly, the disposition to complain or whine would be robust if exhibited frequently, and weak if rarely. Both are examples of dispositions in that they can be assumed to be intentional and mindfully directed toward particular objects and situations in order to achieve goals. It should be emphasized that not all dispositions are desirable, and curriculum and teaching practices must address not only how to strengthen desirable dispositions but how to weaken undesirable ones.

PART II—THE IMPLICATIONS OF DISPOSITIONS FOR EARLY CHILDHOOD EDUCATION PRACTICES

There are at least seven reasons for suggesting that dispositions should be included among the goals (each of which should be stated in terms of strengthening desirable and weakening undesirable dispositions) of early childhood education. The most important reason is that the acquisition of knowledge and skills alone does not guarantee that they will be used and applied. As Cantor (1990) puts it, "having" is not necessarily "doing." For example, it is likely that most children have the capacity to listen, usually referred to as listening skills, but may or may not have the disposition to be listeners. Similarly, there is some suggestion in the research on social development that children with social difficulties often have the skills required for competent peer interaction, but do not employ them with sufficient strength or frequency to build or maintain relationships. Because skills are likely to be improved with use, teaching strategies should take into account ways that the dispositions associated with them can be strengthened.

Second, dispositional considerations are important because the instructional processes by which some knowledge and skills are acquired may themselves damage or undermine the disposition to use them. For example, one risk of early formal instruction in reading skills is that the amount of drill and practice required for successful reading of the English language at an early age may undermine children's dispositions to be readers (Katz, 1992). It is clearly not useful for a child to learn skills if, in the processes of acquiring them, the disposition to use them is damaged. On the other hand, having the disposition to be a reader, for example, without the requisite skills (if such a disposition were possible) would also not be desirable. Thus the acquisition of reading skills and the disposition to be a reader should be *mutually inclusive* goals of early childhood education.

Emphasizing the disposition to be a reader is not simply to suggest that children have to always enjoy or like reading, or have the desire to read. Rather it is to propose that the disposition be a habit associated with intentions and goals that is so robust that one reads even when it is not particularly pleasant or enjoyable to do so—to read serious matters in newspapers, a lengthy election ballot, complex directions for using equipment—to use reading to serve goals other than just pleasure.

Third, some important dispositions relevant to education, such as the disposition to investigate, may be thought of as inborn. When children's experiences support the manifestations of the disposition with appropriate scaffolding or guided participation (see Rogoff, Gauvain, & Ellis, 1990; Rogoff, Mistry, Göncü, & Mosier, 1993) and environmental conditions, it is likely to become robust, and without such supportive experiences it is likely to weaken if not extinguish. Though knowledge and skills not acquired early in life might be acquired later, dispositions are probably less amenable to reacquisition once damaged or extinguished.

Fourth, the processes of selecting curriculum and teaching strategies should include considerations of how desirable dispositions can be strengthened and undesirable dispositions can be weakened. In the case of desirable dispositions, it seems reasonable to assume they are strengthened when opportunity to manifest them is available, and vice versa for undesirable ones. For example, if the disposition to investigate is accepted as worthy of strengthening, then a curriculum and appropriate teaching strategies must be designed accordingly. If the disposition to accept peers of diverse backgrounds is to be strengthened, then, similarly, opportunity to manifest such acceptance must be available.

Fifth, on the basis of the evidence accumulated from research on mastery versus performance motivation, it seems reasonable to suggest that there is an optimum amount of positive feedback for young children above which children may become preoccupied with their performance and the judgments of others rather than involvement in the task, and hence their emphasis on performance would be at the expense of the disposition to learn. What constitutes an optimum level is likely to vary widely in any group of children, and must be determined by close observations of their reactions to adult feedback.

Sixth, if we agree that dispositions are sufficiently important aspects of children's development and education to be among the goals, then they must be included in the evaluation and assessment of an educational program. Inclusion of dispositions as goals requires determination of which dispositions to include and how their manifestation can be assessed.

Seventh, dispositions are not likely to be acquired through didactic processes, but are more likely modeled by young children from the experiences of being around people who exhibit them. Therefore teachers and parents might consider what dispositions can be seen in them by the children for whom they are responsible. If teachers want their young pupils to have robust dispositions to investigate, hypothesize, experiment, conjecture, and so forth, they might consider making their own such intellectual dispositions more visible to the children. In many years of observations in preschool programs I have yet to observe a teacher say something like "I've been wondering whether this is the best time to do so-and-so. What do you think?" Or, "I'm not sure if this is the best place to put this [piece of equipment]. Anybody got any ideas?" Or, "When I thought about [your question], I thought that the answer might be X or Y. It would be interesting to find out what the answer is. . . . " or "I haven't thought about [X] that way before. . . . " and so forth. The list of potential ways that teachers of young children could exhibit the intellectual dispositions to be strengthened and supported in the early years is potentially very long and deserves serious attention in the course of curriculum planning and teacher education.

CONCLUSION

It seems reasonable to assume that dispositions are always more or less influenced by experiences in early childhood education programs, whether by intention or by default. Much work is needed to determine which dispositions merit attention, and how general or specific they should be. If the desirable dispositions listed among the goals are very specific, the list is likely to become unmanageably long. For example, to associate reading skills with the disposition to be a reader, and listening skills with the disposition to be a listener, then we may end up with a list of dispositions as long as any list of specific skills! However, if dispositional goals are too general, they become too difficult to observe and therefore to assess. Ideally, educational goals should include dispositions that strike an optimal balance between generality and specificity.

In the interim, while questions of which dispositions are desirable and how specific they should be are addressed, it seems timely to include them among important outcomes of education at every level. By placing dispositions in the list of educational goals we are likely to pay more deliberate attention to ways in which desirable ones can be strengthened and undesirable ones can be weakened. For the moment I suggest that the most important disposition to be listed in educational goals is the disposition to go on learning. Any educational approach that undermines that disposition is miseducation.

REFERENCES

The American college dictionary. (1948). New York: Harper and Brothers.

Ames, C. (1992). Classrooms: Goals, structures, and student motivation. *Journal of Educational Psychology, 84*(3), 261–271.

Appley, M. H. (1991). Motivation, equilibration, and stress. In R. A. Dienstbier, (Ed.), *Perspectives on motivation. Nebraska symposium on motivation, 1990* (pp. 1–68). Lincoln, NE: University of Nebraska Press.

Bee, H. (1985). *The developing child.* (Fourth Ed.). New York: Harper and Row.

Brown, A. L. (1988). Motivation to learn and understand: On taking charge of one's own learning. *Cognition and Instruction, 5*(4), 311–312.

Bruns, J. H. (1992, Winter). They can but they don't: Helping students overcome work inhibition. *American Educator,* pp. 38–44.

Buss, D. M., & Craik, K. H. (1983). The act frequency approach to personality. *Psychological Review, 84,* 106–126.

Cantor, N. (1990). From thought to behavior: "Having" and "doing" in the study of personality and cognition. *American Psychologist, 45*(6), 735–750.

Corno, L. (1992). Encouraging students to take responsibility for learning and performance. *The Elementary School Journal, 93*(1), 69–84.

Dweck, C. S. (1989). Motivation. In A. Lesgold, and R. Glaser (Eds.), *Foundations for a psychology of education* (pp. 87–136). Hillsdale, NJ: Erlbaum.

Dweck, C. S. (1991). Self-theories and goals: Their role in motivation, personality, and development. In R. A. Dienstbier, (Ed.). *Perspectives on Motivation. Nebraska Symposium on Motivation, 1990* (pp. 199–236). Lincoln, NE: University of Nebraska Press.

Dweck, C. S., & Leggett, E. L. (1988). A social-cognitive approach to motivation and personality. *Psychological Review, 95*(2), 256–273.

Eagly, A. H. (1992). Uneven progress: Social psychology and the study of attitudes. *Journal of Personality and Social Psychology, 63*(5), 693–710.

Elliott, E. S., & Dweck, C. S. (1988). Goals: An approach to motivation and achievement. *Journal of Personality and Social Psychology, 54*(1), 5–12.

Emmons, R. A. (1989). Exploring the relations between motives and traits: The case of narcissism. In D. M. Buss & N. Cantor (Eds.), *Personality psychology: Recent trends and emerging directions* (pp. 32–44). New York: Springer-Verlag.

English, H. B., & English, A. C. (1958). *A comprehensive dictionary of psychological and psychoanalytic terms.* New York: McKay.

Ennis, R. H. (1987). A taxonomy of critical thinking dispositions and abilities. In J. B. Baron & R. S. Sternberg (Eds.), *Teaching thinking skills: Theory and practice* (pp. 9–26). Hillsdale, NJ: Erlbaum.

Fishbein, M. (1980). A theory of reasoned action: Some applications and implications. In H. Howe, Jr. (Ed.), *Nebraska Symposium on Motivation* (Vol. 27) (pp. 65–116). Lincoln, NE: University of Nebraska Press.

Gardner, H. (1985). *Frames of mind: The theory of multiple intelligences.* New York: Basic Books.

Goal One Technical Subgroup of National Educational Goals Panel. *Report to the National Educational Goals Panel.* (1991, September). Unpublished document.

Harter, S. (1983). Developmental perspectives on the self-system. In E. M. Hetherington (Ed.), *Socialization, personality, and social development.* In P. Mussen, (Ed.), *Handbook of Child Psychology: Vol. 4* (4th Ed.). New York: Wiley.

Hoffman, C., & Tchir, M. A. (1990). Interpersonal verbs and dispositional adjectives: The psychology of causality embodied in language. *Journal of Personality and Social Psychology, 58*(5), 765–778.

Katz, L. G. (1985). Dispositions in early childhood education. *ERIC/EECE Bulletin, 18*(2), 1–3.

Katz, L. G. (1987). Early education: What should young children be doing? In S. L. Kagan & E. F. Zigler (Eds.), *Early Schooling. The National Debate* (pp. 151–167). New Haven: Yale University Press.

Katz, L. G. (1991). Pedagogical tssues in early childhood education. In S. L. Kagan (Ed.), *The care and education of America's young children: Obstacles and opportunities* (pp. 50–68). Ninetieth Yearbook of the National Society for the Study of Education. Part I. Chicago: National Society for the Study of Education.

Katz, L. G. (1992). *What should young children be doing?* ERIC Digest. Urbana, IL: ERIC Clearinghouse on Elementary and Early Childhood Education. University of Illinois.

Katz, L. G., & Chard, S. C. (1989). *Engaging children's minds: The project approach.* Norwood, NJ: Ablex.

Katz, L. G., & Raths, J. D. (1985). Dispositions as goals for teacher education. *Teaching & Teacher Education, 1*(4), 301–307.

Langer, E. J. (1993). A mindful education. *Educational Psychology, 28*(1), 43–50.

Linder, T. W. (1990). *Transdisciplinary play-based assessment: A functional approach to working with young children.* Baltimore, MD: Brookes.

Maccoby, E. E. (1987). Person constancy within developmental change. Paper presented at the Annual Meeting of the Society for Research in Child Development, Baltimore, Maryland.

McAdams, D. P. (1989). The development of a narrative Identity. In D. M. Buss & N. Cantor (Eds.), *Personality psychology: Recent trends and emerging directions* (pp. 160–176). New York: Springer-Verlag.

Mussen, P. H. (Ed.). (1983). *Handbook of child psychology.* (Fourth Ed.). New York: Wiley.

Nicholls, J. G. (1984). Achievement motivation: conceptions of ability, subjective experience, task choice, and performance. *Psychological Review, 91,* 328–346.

Passmore, J. (1972). On teaching to be critical. In R. F. Dearden, P. H. Hirst, & R. S. Peters (Eds.), *Education and the development of reason.* London: Routledge & Kegan Paul.

Perkins, D., Jay, E., & Tishman, S. (1993). New conceptions of thinking: From ontology to education. *Educational Psychologist, 28*(1), 67–85.

Rathus, S. A. (1988). *Understanding child development.* New York: Holt Rinehart & Winston.

Resnick, L. B. (1987). *Education and learning to think.* Washington, DC: National Academy Press.

Resnick, L. B., & Klopfer, L. E. (1989). Toward the thinking curriculum: An overview. In L. B. Resnick and L. E. Klopfer (Eds.), *Toward the thinking curriculum: Current cognitive research.* Alexandria, VA: Association for Supervision and Curriculum Development.

Rogoff, B., Gauvain, M., & Ellis, S. (1990). Development viewed in cultural context. In P. Light, S. Sheldon, & M. Woodhead, (Eds.), *Learning to think* (pp. 292–339). London: Routledge.

Rogoff, B., Mistry, J., Göncü, A., & Mosier, C. (1993). Guided participation in cultural activity by toddlers and caregivers. *Monographs of the Society for Research in Child Development, 58*(8) (Serial No. 236).

Rokeach, M. (1968). *Beliefs, attitudes, and values.* San Francisco: Jossey-Bass.

Saracho, O. N. (1991). Cognitive style and social behavior in young Mexican American children. *International Journal of Early Childhood, 23*(2), 3–12.

Scarr, S., Weinberg, R. A., & Levine, A. (1986). *Understanding development.* Orlando, FL: Harcourt Brace Jovanovich.

Shipman, S. L. (1989). Limitations of applying cognitive styles to early childhood education. *Early Child Development and Care, 51,* 13–28.

Sroufe, L. A., Cooper, R. G., & DeHart, G. B. (1992). *Child development: Its nature and course* (Second Ed.). New York: McGraw Hill.

Wakefield, J. C. (1989). Levels of explanation in personality theory. In D. M. Buss & N. Cantor (Eds.), *Personality psychology: Recent trends and emerging directions* (pp. 333–346). New York: Springer Verlag.

Webster's ninth new collegiate dictionary. (1987). Springfield, MA: Merriam-Webster.

Yussen, S. R., & Santrock, J. W. (1982). *Child development: An introduction.* Dubuque, IA: Wm. C. Brown.

4

ASSESSING THE DEVELOPMENT OF PRESCHOOLERS*

This chapter grew out of meetings with groups of parents. Invariably one or two parents would ask how they could be sure their child's development was going well. Teachers also sometimes want a general assessment of how an individual child's development is proceeding—a sort of overview of the child that would help put a particular episode or "bad day" into the larger perspective of a child's typical functioning over a period of a few weeks.

The eleven "indices" nominated for inclusion in assessing a child's progress were based on my understanding of what the research had implied about long-term development at the time. The list outlined is not a scientifically derived evaluation tool. It could be used as a basis for staff discussion and for teacher–parent discussion of what each party sees in the overall pattern of an individual child's growth, development, and learning.

Since the publication of the original paper in the early 1980s, many sophisticated and well developed tools have become available for assessing specific aspects of young children's development, and for detecting cases that warrant follow-up evaluation. Parents and teachers are advised to consult their local specialists when their own evaluations of a child's progress raise concerns that merit a qualified specialist's examination.

* This chapter was originally published as "Assessing Preschooler's Development," by Lilian G. Katz, 1985. In L. G. Katz (Ed.), *More Talks with Teachers*. Urbana, IL: ERIC Clearinghouse on Elementary and Early Childhood Education. Reprinted with permission.

It is only natural that from time to time parents wonder whether their children's development is going well. Parents often ask such questions as, "Is my child doing what he or she is supposed to do at this age?" and "Do all children of this age behave this way in the same situations?" Numerous other questions parents raise reflect a desire to know whether the child's development is normal. Preschool teachers also look for ways to assess their pupils' progress and to determine whether there is something in particular that they should be doing to aid the child at a particular time.

Normative scales tend to focus on development as though it were some kind of product, outcome, or end point. Such scales are used to indicate where an individual child stands with respect to all others of a given age or population. They are used primarily for comparing individuals or subgroups to larger groups with respect to specific behaviors or achievements. However, this chapter addresses the question of whether a child's development is *going well* at a given moment in terms of ongoing or continuous developmental processes. Together, the behavioral dimensions outlined below indicate whether or not a child is thriving at the moment of observation. As we look at each child in a given preprimary setting and consider the following items, we can begin to formulate answers to the question, What aspects of a particular child's development need encouragement, support, or intervention right now?

For children whose physical and mental endowments are normal, ups and downs in the long course of development inevitably occur and occasionally require special attention. In order to assess whether or not a child's development is going well, or whether it is in a "down" period requiring intervention, the following categories of behavior can be observed. Difficulties in any single one of these categories should not cause alarm. Indeed, difficulties in several of the categories do not imply irreversible problems. Rather, these difficulties help us notice those periods when the child's own life or situation, for a wide variety of possible reasons, is out of adjustment with his or her emerging needs.

The judgment as to whether or not special and specific interventions are necessary should not be based on one or two days of observations. For children three years of age, a picture of their functioning on these behavioral criteria over a period of approximately three weeks should provide a sufficient sample on which to make an assessment. For four-year-olds, four weeks give a sufficiently reliable picture of the quality of the child's life. At five years, add another week, and so forth.

1. Sleeping Habits. Does the child fall asleep easily and wake up rested, ready to get on with life? Occasional restless nights, nightmares, or grouchy mornings are all right. The average pattern of deep sleep resulting in morning eagerness is a good sign that the child experiences life as satisfying. More than occasional insomnia or morning grouchiness may indicate that a child is currently facing excessive stress, and a modification in life style might be tried.

2. Eating Habits. Does the child eat with appetite? Occasional skipping of meals or refusal of food is all right. Sometimes a child is too busy with activities more absorbing than mealtime to be concerned with food. Or perhaps the child is more thirsty than hungry and thus resists the parents' anxious pleading over vitamins and other nutritional abstractions. A child who, over a period of weeks, eats compulsively or obsessively as though famine were around the corner, or who constantly fusses about the menu or picks at the food, is likely to have "gotten on the wrong foot."

The function of food is to fuel the system adequately in order to be able to get on with the important business of life. It should not become a central part of the content of adult–child interaction. However, it is wise to keep in mind that children, like many adults, may eat a lot at one meal and hardly anything at all the next. These fluctuations do not warrant comment or concern as long as there is reasonable balance in the nutrition obtained.

3. Toilet Habits. On the average, over a period of three or four weeks, does the child have bowel and bladder control, especially during the day? Occasional "accidents" are all right, especially if there are obvious mitigating circumstances such as excessive intake of liquids, intestinal upset, or simply being too absorbed with ongoing activity to attend to such "irrelevancies." Children who sleep well often take longer to stay continent at night.

4. Range of Affect. Does the child exhibit a range of emotions? Over a period of a few weeks, does the child show the capacity for joy, anger, sorrow, grief, enthusiasm, excitement, frustration, love and affection, and so forth? (Not all in one day, of course!) A child whose affect is "flat" or unfluctuating—always angry, always sour, always jolly or enthusiastic—may be in trouble. The capacity for sadness indicates the presence of its correlates, attachment and the capacity to really care about another person. These emotions are important signs of healthy development. Low intensity of feeling, or unvaried or flat affect, may signal the beginning of depression.

5. *Variations in Play.*   Does the child's play vary over a period of time? Does the child add elements to the play, even though he or she plays with the same toys or materials? If the child always ritualistically or stereotypically engages in the same sequence of play, using the same elements in the same way, he or she may be emotionally "stuck in neutral," so to speak, and in need of some temporary special help. Increasing elaboration of the same play or optimum varieties of play indicate sufficient inner security to "play with the environment."

6. *Curiosity.*   Does the child occasionally exhibit curiosity, adventure, and even mischief? If these behaviors are constantly displayed, they may signal a search for boundaries. If the child never pokes at the environment or never snoops where forbidden, then he or she may not be pushing against perceived boundaries enough for healthy development, perhaps due to fear of punishment or to an overdeveloped conscience.

7. *Responses to Authority.*   Does the child usually accept adult authority? Occasional resistance, self-assertion of a point of view or desires, protest and objections, followed by ultimate yielding to the adult, indicate healthy socialization processes. Unfailing acceptance of adult demands and restrictions without a peep suggests excessive anxiety, fear, or perhaps a weakening of self-confidence or curiosity.

8. *Friendship.*   Can the child initiate, maintain, and enjoy a relationship with one or more other children? The evidence is now persuasive that the preschool years are a period of rapid learning of social interactive competence and that lack of such competence can have long term negative consequences for development (see Katz & McClellan, 1990).

A child who often plays alone is not in trouble as long as he or she is not doing so due to excessive fear of peer interaction or insufficient social interactive competence. Similarly, a child who frequently makes great claims concerning his or her own superiority to others may be seeking reassurance, may feel in danger of losing some privileged status or of failing to meet parents' lofty expectations. Such behavior may create difficulties in the development of social competence or ability to build relationships later on, and calls for some kind of intervention. The social and cognitive skills and knowledge required for making and keeping friends are considerable, and experience in the company of other children in and of itself does not ensure optimum learning. Some children need coaching from the sidelines (Asher, Oden, & Gottman, 1977).

9. Interest. Is the child capable of sustained involvement, absorption, and interest in something outside of himself or herself? Does the child's capacity for interest seem to be increasing to longer intervals of involvement in activities, games, or play? The emphasis here is on sustained involvement in activities rather than in such passivities as television. The child's increasing and sustained involvement in television or other passive pursuits may signal difficulties requiring adult intervention. In addition, the child who cannot become absorbed in an activity, who rarely stays with it or rarely sees a project through to completion, may need help.

10. Spontaneous Affection. Does the child express spontaneous affection for one or more of those who is responsible for his or her care? This expression is not the required goodnight kiss but an impulsive declaration of love. Demonstrations of affection vary from family to family and among cultures and subcultures, and such variations must be taken into account when considering this aspect of behavior. Nevertheless, in ways that are culturally appropriate, a child whose development is going well is likely from time to time to let significant others know that he or she loves them, deeply enjoys being with them and near them, and at the same time is experiencing the world and life as gratifying and satisfying. Excessive expressions of this kind, however, may signal doubts about the strength of major attachments and may call for assessment of the child's interpersonal environment to determine whether intervention is necessary.

11. Enjoyment of the Good Things of Life. Is the child capable of enjoying the potentially good things of life? For young children, playing with others, going on picnics or to parks and parties, family gatherings or festivals, and exploring new places, new materials, and new toys are the potentially good things. If a child does have a problem (for example, shyness, fear of insects, food dislikes), but the problem does not prevent him or her from participating in and enjoying these goodies, then it is reasonable to assume that with a little help the problem will be outgrown. This view should reduce the probability of overinterpreting children's behavior and assuming great difficulties or abnormal development on the basis of momentary setbacks. If, however, problems do get in the way of enjoyment or prevent participation in events, then an adult should intervene with appropriate help.

SUGGESTIONS FOR INTERVENTION

The first three criteria of well-being and development on this proposed list—sleeping, eating, and toilet habits—are particularly sensitive indicators of the child's well-being since they are behaviors that only the child has control of and that no other person can perform for the child.

The other criteria are somewhat more culture-bound and more situationally determined. However, they are likely to represent preschool teachers' most important goals for their pupils, and they are generally aspects of behavior that teachers can observe or obtain information about from parents.

It is generally a good idea to survey children in the class periodically and make an assessment of their status on each of the criteria. When the pattern of the child's functioning on as many as half of the criteria seems less than optimum over a period of about a month, some remedial action should be taken. Not all cases of less-than-optimum functioning can be satisfactorily solved by the teacher. For example, difficulties in sleeping, eating, and toileting probably require parental action more than teacher intervention. Nevertheless, much can be gained by parents and teachers working together, and other manifestations of "downturns" in development can be greatly alleviated by teachers' interventions.

While each individual case will require its own special intervention, some general approaches are worth trying right away. For example, no matter what the underlying cause, virtually all young children respond well to spending time alone with an adult who is important to them. The important adult may be a teacher, parent, relative, caregiver, or anyone else with whom the child has a significant relationship. The time can be spent walking around the block, helping out with tidying up a closet, gardening, baking a cake, or anything else the child *really enjoys*. The activity itself should be simple; it need not be an expensive or exotic trip to a faraway place. The idea is that having someone special all to oneself for fifteen minutes a day is often more convincing to the child than anything else that he or she is cared for and important to the adult. A few minutes a day for a few weeks will invariably help alleviate whatever stresses the child has encountered. Once the level of stress is reduced and the child is more relaxed, he or she may then become more responsive to a teacher's or parent's guidance and suggestions about how to cope with the problem at hand.

Another approach many find helpful is to try to imagine what the child would be like without his or her problem, whatever it is (see Katz & McClellan, 1990). Ask yourself, How would the child walk, talk, interact without the problem he or she seems to be struggling with? What might the child say or do if in fact he or she were rid of whatever the problem appears to be? In other words, build a picture in your imagination of the child's potential. Make the picture as detailed as you can. Once the picture is clear, treat the child as you have imagined him or her. While this powerful technique is not magical, its effect comes from the fact that it tends to cause the adult to see more clearly than before the child's attempts to deal with the problem constructively. Perhaps the child's positive attempts were too feeble, or the adult's expectation of negative behavior did not allow him or her to notice the positive strategies before.

Furthermore, the exercise of imagining what a child might be like without the particular problems of the moment helps the parent or teacher to adjust his or her own attitudes and behavior toward the child. Perhaps the adults' attempts to deal with the situation have been a source of anxiety or tension, even reaching the point where the teacher wishes the child would be absent—but he or she never is! The imaginary picture of the problem-free child, created in the laboratory of the adult's mind, can play a significant role in helping him or her to respond more positively. Even adults tend to meet the positive or negative expectations others have of them; imagine how much power such adult expectations can have over children!

Whatever interventions are appropriate for a particular child in a given situation, if the overall and average picture of the child's functioning, obtained from a sampling of the behavioral criteria described above, indicates a low point in development, preschool teachers are in an ideal position to do something to help the child get back on the right foot.

REFERENCES

Asher, S., Oden, S., & Gottman, J. M. (1977). Children's friendships in school settings. In L.G. Katz (Ed.), *Current topics in early childhood education* (Vol. 1). Norwood, NJ: Ablex.

Katz, L. G., & McClellan, D. (1990). *The teacher's role in the social development of young children.* Urbana, IL: ERIC Clearinghouse on Elementary and Early Childhood Education.

5

CONDITION WITH CAUTION*

The first glimmer of the ideas in this article emerged in the late 1960s during my graduate student days at Stanford University. I began graduate study after having been a participating parent in three parent cooperative nursery schools and a teacher in a fourth one, all in Northern California. I often think of the ideological Zeitgeist among nursery school teachers during the 1960s as the Anna Freudian period! At that time and place nursery school teachers seemed greatly concerned about the inner conflicts and inherent creativity of young children and ignored or disdained the growing rumblings of operant conditioning and behaviorism.

When I subsequently became a graduate student at Stanford University, I was introduced to social learning theory. I clearly recall complaining to my doctoral advisor, the late Pauline S. Sears, that when I had been a nursery school teacher I "knew what was right!" Having to come to grips with the central concepts of stimulus-response learning and primary and secondary and intermittent reinforcement, my previous certainties were shaken. Professor Sears's response to my complaint was "Don't decide now! Stay open to all the ideas around!" I admit that I accepted that mentoring grudgingly.

In a subsequent educational psychology course I wrote a paper suggesting that the contrasting theories of development we had to study were probably all valid; they just addressed different aspects of learning and development, and were not necessarily mutually exclusive explanations of the phenomena in question. That paper, well received by the professor, grew into the chapter presented here.

---

*This chapter was originally published as "Condition with Caution," by Lilian G. Katz, June 1972, in *Young Children* 2(1), pp. 20–23. Reprinted by permission.

Behavior modification techniques[1] have frequently been adopted for use in programs for normal young children. A large body of empirical studies support widespread faith in the power of behavior modification techniques to produce desirable changes in behavior. It seems reasonable to summarize the extensive testing of behavior modification techniques to say that when they are properly applied, they "work." The very fact that they do work does not mean they should be applied slavishly. Indeed, precisely because they work, their application must be thought through very carefully. In principle, the more powerful a technique, the more carefully it must be considered and evaluated before it is adopted.

I find it helpful to think about the appropriateness of applying behavior modification in terms of the meaning of the behavior in question. A general principle of relevance here is that the essential thing about behavior is what it *means*—especially to the behaver. For the purpose of discussion let us use the example of disruptive behavior—a favorite topic of behavior modifiers (Becker, Thomas, & Carnine. 1969).

PHENOTYPES AND GENOTYPES

Let us imagine three four-year-old children, each exhibiting the same disruptive behavior, perhaps throwing blocks or toys. All three children look the same. We could say that these three children exhibit the same *phenotype;* that is to say that the surface features of the *phenomena* we observe appear to be the same in all three children.

Now let us consider three such cases in terms of their *genotypes*. The term genotype refers to the *genesis* of the behavior, that is, how the children acquired the disruptive behavior pattern observed, or the motivation that produced the behavior. The main argument in this chapter is that though the behavior may look the same in the three cases, the behavior may have at least three genotypes, although there may be many more. In addition, I am proposing that the genotype of the behavior must be con-

---

[1] These techniques are sometimes called operant conditioning or behavior analysis.

sidered when making decisions about how to respond to the behavior.

Genotype I—Conditioning

The first genotype (G-I) we could call the *conditioning* type. This child's disruptive behavior—no matter how it first began—has been strengthened by the consequences of his or her behavior. He or she learned to be disruptive because on most occasions when he or she behaved this way, at home or at school, he or she received attention or some other type of positive reinforcement or reward. Perhaps the child's mother distracted him or her from disruptive activity by offering a cookie at such a time; or perhaps teachers responded to the undesirable behavior by guiding the child to a favorite activity, ostensibly to distract him or her. We could say that this child has *learned* the undesired behavior according to the principles of behavior modification; unwittingly, the undesirable behavior has been reinforced.

Genotype II—Emotional

The second genotype (G-II) we could call the *emotional* or perhaps in some cases a neurotic type. This child's disruptiveness expresses some kind of emotional distress. Perhaps the child is trying to cope with anxieties or fears that have a long but unknown history. It may be that the child's home environment is emotionally tense or confusing, or that her approach toward school includes some apprehension or expectation of rejection. For Genotype II, as for Genotype I, the disruptive behavior might have been reinforced following its initial expression. It might be reinforced by success in intimidating other children, or by the release of tension; but the major stimulant or genesis of the behavior is some kind of internal emotional pain.

Genotype III—Socialization

A third genotype (G-III) we might call the *socialization* type. In this case, the child's behavior could be caused by the fact that he or she lacks relevant verbal or social skills or knowledge of alternative ways of responding to the situation in which he or she is involved. For whatever reason, no one has socialized or taught the child more appropriate behaviors for the situation.

STRATEGIES FOR TREATMENT

First, it should be acknowledged that for all three genotypes, behavior modification is likely to work. Behavior modifiers have been successful with many varieties of persistent and recalcitrant behavior patterns. However, the approach proposed here is that the treatment is appropriate *if it corresponds to the genotype* (Table 5–1).

For G-I, the conditioning type, behavior modification seems to be highly appropriate. In the case of this child, the reinforcing events that have typically followed disruptive behavior could be consciously withheld. Suppose, for example, that a child has typically been distracted with a favorite activity or a cookie whenever the undesirable behavior has been exhibited. Parents and teachers can evaluate their own responses (see Becker et al., 1969) and begin to carefully extinguish this behavior by ignoring it, while reinforcing more desirable behavior. It should be noted that in most such cases, it is possible to stop acting-out behavior of this kind by firmly restraining the child without giving him or her attention. The child's behavior could then be expected to change quite rapidly.

For G-II, emotional distress, although behavior modification is likely to work, and the behavior disappear, the distress or

TABLE 5–1 POSSIBLE PHENOTYPE/GENOTYPE/TREATMENT RELATIONSHIPS

Phenotype		Genotype		Treatment
Disruptive Behavior	Child I	G-I	Conditioning	Behavior Modification
	Child II	G-II	Emotional Stress	Therapeutic Response
	Child III	G-III	Inadequate Socialization	Teaching

emotional injury may still be present within the child; perhaps a new manifestation would appear and the injury or distress take its toll some other way. For this genotype, a suitable cathartic experience seems called for, *and the disruptive behavior must also be stopped.* Opportunities to work out or express unmanageable fears and tensions may have to be provided while, at the same time, the child acquires new skills and confidence. Parents and teachers can use a *therapeutic response,* sometimes called *reflection of feelings,* with this child. Such adult responses help the child by acknowledging his or her feelings, by offering reassurance that the feelings underlying the behavior are understood though the behavior is not accepted, and at the same time teaching alternative response patterns (see Axline, 1964).

The great danger in applying behavior modification to the G-II—emotional distress phenotype is that the behavior may indeed be extinguished, but so may the capacity to feel. Feelings of anguish and distress are normal and healthy reactions to unpleasant and stressful life events, and to unmet needs for protection and acceptance. It would be inappropriate to cause a child to lose the capacity to feel anguish and distress; they are ways that children signal to their caregivers that their environment or situation must be modified.

For the G-III genotype, inadequate socialization, the treatment needed seems to be straightforward teaching. Certainly behavior modification is likely to work, but it seems unnecessary and, in fact, inefficient to shape the child's behavior surreptitiously— while he or she is not looking, so to speak! This child can be helped by the adults when they inform, clarify, and suggest to the child simple courses of action, or explain, *in situ,* simple alternative strategies for solving the problem at hand. Adults can engage the child's own social intelligence in analyzing the problem at hand (for example, wanting to join a group at play). The child's own intelligence can be relied on to weigh the alternative suggestions for more appropriate and functional behaviors with which to solve the problem at hand.

It would seem inappropriate to offer either the G-III or the G-I (conditioning type) child the therapeutic responses appropriate for G-II, the emotional distress genotype. Not all children need to let off steam—some are taught to be disruptive (G-I) and some are simply not taught how to behave constructively (G-III). The indiscriminate application of conditioning techniques runs the risk of leaving injuries unassuaged and instruction unsupplied. On the other hand, the indiscriminate use of psychotherapeutic techniques, appropriate for the G-II emotional distress pheno-type, runs the risk of protracting a pattern of behavior that expresses no deep mysterious tension or anxiety, but perhaps a faulty conditioning history.

IDENTIFICATION OF GENOTYPES

How can parents and teachers tell which type of child is which? After all, we have said that these three genotypes have the same appearance, or phenotype. It does not help much to say that accurate diagnosis comes with experience! Such behaviors, no matter their geneses, require adult intervention of some kind.

Perhaps it helps to suggest that undesirable behavior of the G-I, *conditioning* type is more likely than the other two types to be out in the open, often flagrant. To be rewarded, the undesirable behavior has to be seen by potential rewarders. The G-II, *emotional* type is probably more stealthy and furtive and perhaps more persistent. The distress is very likely to show in the intensity and seriousness of the behavior. Experienced mothers and teachers often comment that they can tell much about internal stress by the way a child moves his or her body, by his or her stance and characteristic facial expression. But we are often mistaken, of course.

Perhaps the soundest strategy is to begin the treatment of such behavior with the socialization treatment, teaching the child alternative ways of solving the problem at hand. If direct teaching does not work well or reasonably reliably, then careful analyses of the contexts in which the behavior occurs may help the adult to decide which of the other two genotypes might account for the behavior in question.

CONCLUSION

The major purpose of this chapter is to suggest that behavior that often looks alike may have a variety of causes. The three genotypes outlined above are exploratory, and many more types may be useful. One possible explanation for disruptive behavior or any other unwelcome phenotype might be that the curriculum is inappropriate, or that a child is irritable due to an organic disturbance—a developing illness. It should be noted that the contrasting explanations and causes of behavior are not necessarily mutually exclusive. For some children there may be a mix of causes. The child may have begun the pattern through inadequate socialization, Genotype III, and because of that behavior been frequently rejected by peers and/or adults, which in turn could lead to emotional distress. It is reasonable to assume, furthermore, that some children's emotional distress prevents them from the spontaneous learning of social skills in the course of experience with peers.

The paradigm presented above is a general one, and it is intended to suggest that many kinds of behavior (phenotypes) may be understood in terms of contrasting genotypes. For example, children who cling to adults may do so because such behavior has a history of positive reinforcement (G-I), or because they are seeking emotional support (G-II). The treatment offered to these two children should correspond to their genesis. Or suppose, for example, that we are interested in helping so-called permissive parents and teachers. Without going into much detail, we could readily propose at least three genotypes for permissiveness: one might be *fear* of upsetting the child, another might be a *value* or philosophical position, and yet another, simple *neglect* or laziness or parental preoccupation with urgent matters other than the child's behavior. Thus we have three possible genotypes: fear, value orientation, and neglect. These adults may appear to be alike, and the consequences of their parenting may be similar, but their behaviors have different geneses and meanings. Those who wish to help such adults may find that consideration of these alternative genotypes will be helpful in determining effective intervention strategies.

Finally, it is useful to note again that people, young or old, rarely if ever come in pure types. There are many complex mixtures and dynamics in the causes of behavior. We safeguard the quality of children's experiences when we do justice to these complexities. Knowing the children we work with, as well as knowing about them, is probably a prerequisite to discovering the underlying meanings of their behavior. We should remember that behavior modification is a powerful and useful tool for adults who work with children. However, behavior modification theory does not adequately address the issue of feelings, and those of us who work with children must take feelings into full account at all times.

REFERENCES

Axline, V. (1964). *Dibs: In search of self.* Boston: Houghton Mifflin.
Becker, W. C., Thomas, D. C., & Carnine, D. (1969). *Reducing behavior problems: An operant conditioning guide for teachers.* Urbana, IL: ERIC Clearinghouse in Early Childhood Education, University of Illinois.

6

EDUCATION OR
EXCITEMENT?*

This chapter grew out of a graduate class discussion about how to decide what to teach young children. I asked the students—most of them teachers of young children—to talk about what they had taught their pupils the day before. A first-year kindergarten teacher described to the class some activities she had offered her pupils. As she concluded, I was struck by the paucity of intellectual content offered by her to the children. When I asked why she had chosen those particular activities she spoke with great enthusiasm about how much excitement and fun the children had in her class. I then asked her why it mattered for the children to have excitement and fun. She explained that during training she had been taught to make lesson plans and to indicate on each plan how the children would be motivated to engage in the lesson. To her this meant that she was to create excitement and make sure the children had fun.

I noted subsequently how often teachers at all levels of education qualified a curriculum or activity or lesson as successful by reporting how excited the pupils were by it. As suggested in the chapter, the confusion between excitement and interest seems to me to have important consequences for curriculum decisions. Though the original paper was written more than eighteen years ago, it seems to me to remain an important issue in the field of early and elementary education.

*This chapter was originally published as "Education or Excitement," by Lilian G. Katz, 1977. In L. G. Katz (Ed.), *Talks with teachers* (pp. 107–114). Washington, DC: National Association for the Education of Young Children. Reprinted by permission.

During a recent visit to an early childhood classroom a list of pointers for teachers posted on the classroom bulletin board caught my attention. One item high on the list was: "Keep it fun. Make it exciting for both you and the children!" This injunction to keep children excited, or to "make learning exciting," seems to represent a common confusion between what is educative and what is exciting.

WHAT IS EXCITEMENT?

Though most of us know what we mean when we describe something as exciting, it is difficult to pin down a precise definition for it. For the purpose of this discussion, let us assume that each individual has a consistent level of activity or responsiveness to stimuli that is typical for him or her. Some specialists refer to this responsiveness as *level of activation* (Nowlis, 1970), or as *arousal* (Ellis, 1969). Others refer to this characteristic responsiveness as the "rate of stimulation or neural firing" (Tomkins, 1970). For this discussion we are referring to the typical day-to-day responsiveness, activity, and involvement that may characterize an individual who is neither excited nor depressed. In Figure 6–1, this normal level of activity for any given individual is represented by line A. Now let us introduce into the environment an event that this individual experiences as exciting (indicated at point B in Figure 6–1). At this point the level of responsiveness goes up, and when it has reached point C, we say the person is excited. Now let us consider some of the implications of exciting or "turning on" children and adults.

IMPLICATIONS OF EXCITEMENT FOR CHILDREN

By definition, excitement is an extraordinary level of responsiveness, activity, or arousal. Therefore, it cannot be maintained without becoming in turn the new ordinary level. It seems reasonable to assume that the high level of responsiveness must subside or "come down." How long the excitement period lasts or

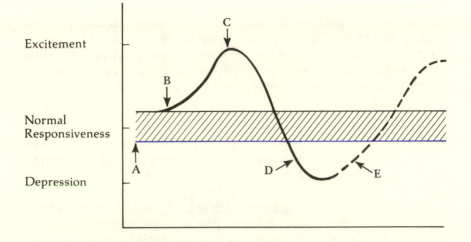

Excitement

Normal
Responsiveness

Depression

FIGURE 6-1

how quickly individuals return to their normal level of responsiveness probably varies widely among and within individuals as well as from one situation to another.

My hunch is that individuals—whether children or adults—may not just simply come down to their normal state, but that they may fall below their own normal level of responsiveness. Although it is difficult to know for sure, I am hypothesizing that in this period (indicated by point D on Figure 6–1), some children may become depressed, and some may withdraw from interaction completely. Other children may appear to fall apart and others to be satiated. On such occasions we are likely to define children's irritability or behavior disorganization as overtiredness.

It may be that when given sufficient rest from an exciting environment children spontaneously recover their own normal level of responsiveness. But another possibility is that adult-induced excitement teaches children to expect and/or depend upon having repeated doses of excitement administered to them in their classrooms. Point E in Figure 6–1 indicates the administration of another dose—perhaps necessarily a stronger dose than what was delivered at point B. In this sense, teachers' belief that their pupils should be excited or turned on leads to an addiction pattern: When the first effect wears off, another, possibly stronger dose must be introduced. Such an addiction pattern could lock both teachers and their pupils into exhausting pat-

terns of activities and relationships. A more important consequence of this pattern is that it may deprive children of the
opportunity to develop and strengthen their capacities for generating interesting, productive, or stimulating activities on their
own. In other words, they may acquire a need to be stimulated,
entertained, or turned on by others.

IMPLICATIONS OF EXCITEMENT FOR TEACHING

It seems to me that if teachers believe that they must keep their
pupils excited, they feel obliged to develop activities that are not
much more than cheap gimmicks of superficial or fleeting interest and value. In so many classrooms one sees the products of
one-shot, one-time activities displayed on bulletin boards. These
activities may have been fun and exciting for their brief duration, but a major index of good quality—that it be *educative*—in a
program for young children is work and play that *invites* or
requires the children's sustained interest and involvement.
Educative activities for young children are those that require
some planning, problem solving, or construction at developmentally appropriate levels that can be sources of satisfaction and
pleasure rather than excitement and fun.

Certainly some educative activities are fun and exciting as
well. "Sesame Street" is an example of an entertainment program that may be instructive as well as exciting and fun for
young children. Many of the standard activities of nursery
schools are also fun: finger painting, lotto games, and climbing
on outdoor equipment. But these are all activities of a relatively
momentary quality. The kind of sustained involvement and
interest that seem to be educative can be illustrated in these
activities seen—all in progress on the same morning—in a nursery school for four-year-old children:

A small group of children who had started playing one day
with doctors' and nurses' dress-up clothes decided to add a
hospital bed, several doctors' instruments, and doll patients. Then they sewed a burlap stretcher and constructed
and painted an ambulance large enough for two children to
sit in the driver's cabin (complete with an old steering

wheel), and for one or two children to attend the patients in the back. This activity developed over a period of a few weeks.

On the same morning, in the same class I saw a complex activity centered around a cement truck the children had constructed from old lumber. The truck was large enough for four children to ride in, climb in and out of, and use to deliver sacks of cement to other children who were building a structure also large enough to enter. This building was constructed with bricks the children made from pairs of egg cartons glued together so that their flat sides were exposed.

A group of children worked for several days on sewing stuffed dolls. Some were painting portraits of the dolls they had made. Two children were constructing replicas of their respective cats and dogs from cartons larger than themselves. The cat was painted orange and white; the head moved from side to side and displayed ample whiskers; and the young artist proudly informed the observer that she had also made the cat food resting at his feet. Several children were adding details to the row houses they had constructed from small cartons. Their houses reflected the typical construction of their own neighborhoods; some included windows, doors, chimneys, and furniture. Some children had added trays of dirt as front gardens and in these gardens were paper trees and one swing set made from popsicle sticks.

Many other activities, which involve planning, problem solving, and construction and invited children's sustained involvement were also seen during that one morning. These children did not seem to be overly excited or turned on. They did seem to be deeply involved and interested in reconstructing salient aspects of their own experiences and environments. The children's involvement seemed to provide deep *satisfaction* rather than excitement.

In their analysis of the open education approach used by the Education Development Center in Newton, Massachusetts, Bussis and Chittenden (1970) point out that:

EDC advisors are less impressed with the teacher who understands and can capture interest for periods of time than they are with the teacher who brings out in children the sort of interests that underlie sustained involvement in learning. In a good classroom the observer would undoubtedly see both the "captured" and the sustaining interests, but the emphasis would be on the latter. (pp. 16–17)

My main argument here is that the selection of activities should be based on whether they are interesting rather than whether they are exciting. But the term *interest*[1] is as fraught with semantic pitfalls as are the terms *excitement* and *education* (Peters, 1966, pp. 91-102). Getzels defined an interest as "a characteristic disposition, organized through experience, which impels an individual to seek out particular objects, activities, skills, understandings, or goals for attention and acquisition" (1969, p. 470). Activities that foster and strengthen this disposition seem to be educative; activities that strengthen children's dependence on adult-induced excitement may undermine or inhibit the development of this disposition. It may be that teacher-imposed or television-induced excitement, or the ubiquitous one-shot, short-term activities so frequently offered young children, encourage the disposition to be a consumer or spectator, at best; a thrill seeker or psychological dropout, at worst.

Another way of looking at the problem is that while excitement may originally have been thought of as a means by which to launch children into educative activities, it has inadvertently become an end in itself. Relatively trivial skills and facts can be learned quickly. The acquisition of significant skills, ideas, and concepts takes time. Perhaps the length of time required for learning is related to resistance to extinction of the same learning. Excitement and the "learnings" associated with it may be rapid in both acquisition and extinction. The learning gained from sustained involvement and effort over extended periods of time may be more enduring.

In discussions with teachers concerning the distinction between what is educative and what is exciting, it is often assumed that giving children practice in boredom is recommended! Far from it! All children inevitably get some practice at coping with boredom; to provide such practice as a matter of policy would be not only unnecessary, but perhaps sadistic as well.

---

[1] I suggest that a useful definition of the term interest is the capacity to lose oneself over a relatively extended period of time in an endeavor outside of oneself.

It may be useful to note that there are two variables involved in this discussion. One variable is the level of responsiveness, defined by excitement at one extreme and depression at the other. Another variable may be called interest, with involvement or absorption at one extreme and boredom or apathy at the other. Teachers are not really caught between providing activities that might lead to the extremes of excitement and depression. Sustained interest, involvement, or absorption—with occasional fluctuations in terms of satisfaction and pleasure—are qualitatively different from excitement and depression.

A useful analogy may be made by drawing a distinction between the music of Tchaikovsky and Bach. The former is delightful and moving from time to time. The "Nutcracker Suite," once or twice a year, is enjoyable. More often than that, it might lose its charm and ability to move us. But good Bach may be heard frequently; on each occasion pleasure is enhanced, fresh nuances and meanings may be enjoyed; a quality of constrained passion is among its many assets.

IMPLICATIONS FOR EDUCATIONAL CHANGE

Like many other problems in education, the confusion between what is educative and what is exciting reflects a pervasive problem in the wider culture and society. We seem to live in an excitement and cheap-thrill oriented culture. Note how often one hears the "exciting" descriptor in advertising pitches and ordinary daily conversations. To a large extent, strategies for educational change, reform, and innovation are also aimed at getting decision makers as well as practitioners excited about new ideas, programs, technologies, and materials. Much pressure is exerted on teachers to adopt new, exciting practices and procedures. My hunch is that this hard selling (typically overselling) is followed (at point D in Figure 6–1) by both disillusionment and mistrust among oversold adopters. It sometimes seems that in order to overcome the disillusionment and mistrust generated by previous disappointments, the change agents make bigger and bigger promises and more and more frequently omit precautions and contraindicators.

If educational practitioners are treated as consumers (perhaps as the proverbial suckers), they may learn to expect to be sold solutions and gimmicks or bags of tricks! Such an expectation may block teachers' alternative learnings to be resourceful, thoughtful, patient, and persistent in the face of education problems. The two dispositions, to be consumers of others' solutions and to be originators of solutions, may be incompatible with each other in the search for effective teaching strategies.

Too many articles in recent publications give educational reform and innovation a kind of soap opera quality (Katz & Krasnow, 1975). My hunch is that the spectacular success stories offered in educational dissemination material are often misleading. They are reminiscent of the television shows and soap operas in which doctors and lawyers are portrayed as living from one peak experience to another—from opening hearts to breaking hearts! Yet the health of a real community is actually maintained by the physician who administers vaccinations and booster shots and looks at sore throats—perhaps a hundred a week. Surely that kind of patient care is not exciting. Perhaps a relevant factor to consider here is that such routine procedures as looking at sore throats must be performed alertly on each occasion in order not to miss potentially significant signs of serious illness.

The ability to perform routine procedures alertly suggests that a part of the distinction I am trying to make between what is educative and what is exciting concerns the pattern of mobilization of energy. Excitement connotes high bursts of energy release with rapid depletion, whereas any task or study involving complex ideas, concepts, or lines of inquiry requires steady energy output over long periods of time. The opportunity to cultivate the ability to manage energy in this steady and sustained way probably should be provided early in childhood.

THE CHALLENGE TO TEACHERS

I have suggested that educators of young children are often both the perpetrators and the victims of a culture-wide confusion between what is educative and what is exciting. It seems to me that teachers who feel pressured to keep children excited have to fail in the long run. I believe that when we bombard children with too many exciting activities and television programs (plus elaborate and gimmicky toys), we teach them to expect if not to *need* to be excited. At the same time, however, we cheat them of the opportunity to learn to gain real and deep satisfaction from sustained involvement and effort. The great challenge to teachers, as I see it, is to develop activities that children will find satisfying over a long period of time rather than momentarily exciting—the kinds of activities that invite genuine and appropriate problem solving, mastery of what is at first difficult, and concentration or absorption, and that even include some routine elements.

REFERENCES

Bussis, A. M., & Chittenden, E. A. (1970). *Analysis of an approach to open education.* Princeton, NJ: Educational Testing Service.

Ellis, M. M., (1969). Sensorhesis as a motive for play and stereotyped behavior. Urbana, IL: University of Illinois Children's Research Center. (Mimeographed.)

Getzels, M. J. (1969). A social psychology of education. In G. Lindzey & E. Aronson (Eds.), *Handbook of Social Psychology: Vol. 5* (2nd Ed.). Reading, MA: Addison-Wesley.

Katz, L. G., & Krasnow, R. (1975). Teachers as consumers of information. In L. G. Katz, (Ed.), *Second collection of papers for teachers.* Urbana, IL: ERIC Clearinghouse on Early Childhood Education.

Nowlis, V. (1970). Mood: Behavior and experience. In M. Arnold (Ed.), *Feelings and emotions.* New York: Academic Press.

Peters, R. S. (1966). *Ethics and education.* Glenview, IL: Scott, Foresman.

Tomkins, S. S. (1970). Affect as the primary motivational system. In M. Arnold (Ed.), *Feelings and emotions.* New York: Academic Press.

7

PEDAGOGICAL ISSUES IN EARLY CHILDHOOD EDUCATION*

This chapter was written in response to an invitation extended to me in 1989 by Dr. Sharon L. Kagan of the Bush Center in Child Development and Social Policy at Yale University, to contribute a chapter on pedagogy to the Ninetieth Yearbook of the National Society for the Study of Education, of which she was the editor.

The invitation came just as the National Educational Goals, now called Goals 2000: Educate America, *were issued by President Bush and the fifty governors. Early childhood educators became preoccupied with the significance of the first of the six goals: "By the year 2000 all American children will come to school ready to learn." This first goal provoked discussion about the meaning and nature of "readiness for school" and a variety of related issues. The chapter that follows was my attempt to address some of these issues, especially as they relate to the nature of teaching and curriculum in the early years.*

To confront a child with tasks for which he is not ready, with the implication that he should succeed, gives him a feeling of failure, undermines his security. Instead, we must guide him into those learning situations that he can attack

---

* This chapter was originally published as "Pedagogical Issues in Early Childhood Education," by Lilian G. Katz. In S. L. Kagan (Ed.), *The Care and Education of America's Young Children: Obstacles and Opportunities.* Ninetieth Yearbook of the National Society for the Study of Education. Part I. (pp. 50–68). Chicago: National Society for the Study of Education. Reprinted by permission.

effectively and with sufficient success to yield satisfaction, encouragement, and growth.

Carleton Washburne (1939, p. 3)

Washburne's admonition, directed primarily at elementary education, is more than fifty years old! For more than twice that length of time, the field of early childhood education has been marked by unrelenting dissension concerning appropriate pedagogical practices. Lazerson (1972) points out that early in this century, controversy in the field raged over such issues as the relative emphasis on symbolism versus realism, the extent of free play versus teacher direction, and the nature and importance of creativity. In the 1930s, Gardner (1948) attempted to put the continuing controversies to rest once and for all with a comparative study of two schools: School A, characterized by practices known in the United States as open or informal methods, and School B, characterized by formal didactic methods of educating young children. Despite findings in favor of School A, the debate resumed barely a generation later.

During the expansion of early childhood programs in the 1960s, Winsor (1977) noted that it was ironic to find the "very nursery movement which had its beginnings in progressive education described as 'traditional'" in contrast with the new academic curricula advocated for compensatory early childhood education (p. 33). The advocates of formal didactic pedagogical practices in this period frequently implied that traditional nursery and kindergarten pedagogy was merely laissez-faire, offering little more than free play and some socialization experiences (Powell, 1987).

Since the 1960s, the issues in early childhood practices have been cast in terms of polar dimensions such as child- versus adult-centered, structured versus unstructured, didactic versus nondidactic, child- versus teacher-initiated, play versus instruction, socialization versus academics, and several variations of each (Powell, 1987). In actual implementation, these dimensions are likely to overlap considerably. Powell points out that it is difficult to determine the extent to which content, activities, materials, and teaching techniques are confounded in actual implementation and that "it is not possible to manipulate teaching technique without modifying program content" (Powell, 1987, p. 195).

A number of factors may account for the length and persistence of the debates over pedagogical practices in the field. It has often been noted that educational ideologies swing back and forth in pendulum fashion. A particular approach to early childhood education that is enthusiastically embraced at a given time is followed within a few years by a countermovement, which in turn is followed by overcorrections for the preceding swing, and then by another zealous movement to correct previous overcorrections, *ad infinitum!* The curriculum developed by Bereiter and Engelmann (1966) in the 1960s (now known as DISTAR) can be seen as an overcorrection of the authors' perception of the traditional preschool and kindergarten curriculum and its apparent ineffectiveness, especially in the case of children of low-income families. However, a clear pattern of overcorrections of DISTAR and other formal academic approaches is not yet clear, though some implementations of a developmentally appropriate curriculum may be cases of overcorrection.

Ideally, dissension between rival schools of thought on early childhood pedagogical principles could be settled by referring to pertinent empirical data. Although many studies bearing on the comparative effects of alternative practices have been reported in the last twenty years, their findings and conclusions are interpreted in many different ways (Powell, 1989). Numerous methodological, measurement, and logistical problems are inherent in longitudinal studies of alternative approaches to early childhood pedagogy. A robust design for such a comparative study would almost certainly pose daunting ethical problems as well.

As we enter the last decade of the century, the controversy centers primarily on the accelerating "downward shift of what were next-grade expectations into lower grades" (Shepard & Smith, 1988). Since next-grade expectations are typically academic and narrow rather than intellectual and open, their appropriateness for younger children has become a major issue for all who have a stake in early childhood education. Indeed, the controversy over the push-down of the primary curriculum became sufficiently acute in the 1980s to prompt the largest membership association of early childhood practitioners, the National Association for the Education of Young Children (NAEYC), to issue a substantial position statement against it in 1986, and to recommend a set of appropriate practices for children from birth through the age of eight years (Bredekamp, 1987).

The NAEYC position statement on appropriate curriculum for young children argues that practices are acceptable to the extent that they take into account what is known about children's development; the position taken assumes that such knowledge can provide a basis upon which curriculum and pedagogy appropriate to the age and maturity of both the group and the individual learners can be generated. However, the relationship between the body of knowledge called child development and pedagogical practices is not a simple or direct one (Spodek, 1986). Indeed, it is difficult to determine just where knowledge and principles of child development fit into the processes of determining appropriate practices. The matter is further complicated by the fact that there are other criteria by which the appropriateness of pedagogical practices might be judged, including cultural, psychological, social, political, ethical, logistical, or even financial criteria, to name a few.

The number of factors that account for the actual nature of early childhood educational practices is potentially very large. It seems reasonable to hypothesize that the major factors fall roughly into three large categories. One is the body of knowledge and principles of child development. Another is characteristics of the parents served, such as their goals, expectations, and aspirations, and their understandings and preferences with respect to appropriate experiences for their children. A third category of factors includes what teachers are willing or able to do. Teachers may be willing to implement some practices, but for a variety of reasons may be unable to do so and vice versa.

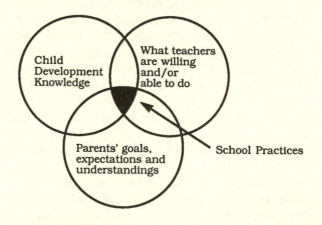

FIGURE 7–1 SCHEMATIC REPRESENTATION OF MAJOR FACTORS THAT ACCOUNT FOR SCHOOL PRACTICES

The Venn diagram in Figure 7-1 is a schematic representation of how the three categories of factors might intersect. It may be that in some situations none of the three categories intersect with each other, and in some only two of them do (for example, child development knowledge and the teacher factors). Furthermore, the extent to which the categories intersect may vary greatly. Nevertheless, the goal of specialists in the field is to enlarge the area of overlap of all three of the categories as much as possible.

In the meantime, those in decision-making roles must proceed to plan and implement programs for young children in the absence of clear empirically derived conclusions and guidelines. The aim of this chapter is to discuss the main issues that have to be addressed in determining the appropriateness of pedagogical practices, and to suggest some principles applicable to the processes involved.

IDENTIFYING APPROPRIATE PEDAGOGICAL PRACTICES

In view of the longstanding tradition of diverse approaches to pedagogy in the field, how can those responsible for planning and implementing programs for young children select the best one for their own communities? Are decision makers faced with either/or choices between opposing camps? Is a compromise or eclectic position feasible so that a community can have the best of all pedagogical worlds? Is there an optimum mix of several approaches? Responses to these questions are proposed by beginning with three interrelated *a priori* questions: (a) What should be learned? (b) When should it be learned? (c) How is it best learned?

Responses to the first question provide the *goals* of the program for which pedagogical practices are to be adopted. The second question is the *developmental* one in that it draws upon what is known about the development of the learner. In other words, child development helps to address the when questions of program design. The third question turns specifically to matters of appropriate *pedagogy* itself; it includes consideration of all aspects of implementing a program by which the program's goals can be achieved.

It is apparent, however, that responses to one of the three questions are inextricably linked to responses to the other two. Thus *what* should be learned and *how* it is best learned depends on *when* the learning it is to occur. Similarly, *how* something is learned depends upon *what* it is, as well as upon the developmental characteristics of the learner. For example, virtually all stakeholders in early childhood education would place literacy high on the list of answers to the question, What should be learned? However, they are likely to diverge considerably upon the question of *when* as well as *how* it should be learned—the latter considerations being related to each other. Terms such as *emergent literacy* and *preliteracy* have recently appeared in the early childhood literature, partly in order to address the confounding of the when and how questions. The confounding of the three questions is acknowledged; however, for the sake of discussion, they are taken up separately below.

What Should Be Learned?

The values and preferences of the parents served by the program would seem to have first claim among criteria for determining what should be learned. However, parents are rarely a homogeneous or monolithic group with a clear consensus about the goals of their children's education. Divergent answers to the question of what should be learned are as likely to be offered within school boards, parent groups, and school faculties as among them. Furthermore, since the answers are based on values, ideals, and assumptions about the future needs of the learners, they cannot be determined empirically; they thus inevitably become the subject of dispute (Clark, 1988). While the community and parents' preferences determine the goals, the special expertise of professional educators should be brought to bear on addressing the questions of when and how the goals can best be implemented.

Four Types of Learning Goals Whatever specific learning objectives are identified by clients and educators, they are all likely to fit into each of four types of learning goals: knowledge, skills, dispositions, and feelings, defined as follows:

1. *Knowledge* during the preschool period can be broadly defined as ideas, concepts, constructions, schemas, facts, information, stories, customs, myths, songs, and other such contents of mind that come under the heading of what is to

be learned. Three Piagetian categories of knowledge—social, physical and logicomathematical—are often used in discussions of the knowledge goals in early childhood education (Williams & Kamii, 1986).

2. *Skills* are defined as small, discrete, and relatively brief units of behavior that are easily observed or inferred from behavior (for example, skills such as cutting, drawing, counting a group of objects, adding, subtracting, friendship-making, problem-solving skills, and so on).

3. *Dispositions* are broadly defined as relatively enduring "habits of mind," or characteristic ways of responding to experience across types of situations (including persistence at a task, curiosity, generosity, meanness, the tendency to read or to solve problems. See Chapter 3 in this volume.). Unlike an item of knowledge or a skill, a disposition is not an end state to be mastered once and for all. It is a trend or consistent pattern of behavior and its possession is established only if its manifestation is observed repeatedly. Thus a person's disposition to be a reader, for example, can only be ascertained if he or she is observed to read spontaneously, frequently, and without external coercion.

4. *Feelings* are subjective emotional or affective states, such as belonging, self-esteem, confidence, adequacy and inadequacy, competence and incompetence, and so forth. Feelings about or toward significant phenomena may range from transitory to enduring, intense to weak, or perhaps ambivalent. In early childhood education attitudes and values can also be included in this category; in education for older children they merit separate categories.[1]

In principle, pedagogical practices are appropriate if they address all four categories of learning goals equally and simultaneously. Pedagogical practices are not appropriate if they emphasize the acquisition of knowledge and the mastery of skills without ensuring that the dispositions to use the knowledge and skills so learned are also strengthened. Similarly, if the desired knowledge and skills are mastered in such a way that

---

[1] In the case of young children, undesirable attitudes and values are assumed to be a function of faulty developmental progress rather than of general institutional socialization. For example, dishonesty or greed in a five-year-old is more likely to be interpreted as a symptom of poor child-rearing or psychosocial environmental influences rather than as a problem of attitudes and values *per se*.

feelings of distaste for or rejection of them or of the school environment itself accumulate throughout the learning process, then the pedagogy may be judged inappropriate. Similarly, if a pedagogical approach succeeds in generating feelings of joy, pleasure, amusement, or excitement, but fails to bring about the acquisition of desirable knowledge and skills, it cannot be judged appropriate.

Most stakeholders in early childhood education are likely to agree on broad goals in all four categories of learning. For example, most state and school district curriculum guides list such goals as knowledge and skills related to literacy and numeracy and various items of cultural knowledge, plus such dispositions as the desire to learn, creativity, cooperativeness, and so forth; the list of goals related to feelings usually includes "positive feelings about themselves" or "self-confidence."[2] Once the knowledge, skills, dispositions, and feelings to be learned have been agreed upon, the next question is *when* they should be learned.

When Is It Best Learned?

In the introductory chapter of the thirty-eighth yearbook of the National Society for the Study of Education, published more than fifty years ago, entitled *Child Development and the Curriculum,* Carleton Washburne states that

> before education can be really effective we must understand child nature. We must know better than we now do what the developing organism is reaching out for at each successive stage. We must know much more than we now do about the experiences, knowledge, and concepts of the child at each level of development. We must learn how to measure at successive levels the child's capacity for adding to his experiences and interpreting them. We must measure the assimilability of new experiences to which the developing organism is to be exposed. At present we are in the first crude beginnings of this stage of scientific approach to our problem. (1939, p. 3)

---

[2] See, for example, Oklahoma State Department of Education (1986); Roberts (1989); State of Connecticut (1988); State of Iowa (1983).

In the fifty years since Washburne's observation, much has been learned about children's development that can help to address the issues in early childhood pedagogy. Indeed, early childhood education has traditionally drawn heavily on studies of children's development. The study of development is typically a major component of early childhood teacher preparation. It is widely assumed that mastery of the knowledge and principles of child development can form a basis for pedagogical decisions most likely to enhance growth and learning and to minimize potential harm to young children.

Usually discussions of curriculum and pedagogical practices use the concept of development to refer to what is known about the typical characteristics of children at each age. Many curriculum guides, for instance, include sections describing typical characteristics of four-year-olds, five-year-olds, six-year-olds, and on and on. However, characteristics of children at particular ages are only one aspect of their development—the *normative* one. The concept of development can be seen as having two distinctive but related dimensions: the normative and the *dynamic* (Maccoby, 1984), each of which should be taken into account when deciding what and how children should learn. Each dimension is defined briefly below.

Normative Dimension of Development Common use of the concept of development draws on the normative dimension. This dimension addresses matters such as what most children can and cannot do at a given age or stage. For example, what is typical and what is most frequently observed in children at two and three and five and nine years of age? We apply the normative dimension when we discuss how many words most children know at a particular age, and the average age at which they can be expected to take their first step, to understand time, to conserve volume, and so forth. When we say that an activity is developmentally appropriate, cite grade level achievement standards, or apply Gesell-type measures to children's behavior, we employ the normative dimension of the concept of development.

Dynamic Dimension of Development The other major dimension is the dynamic one. Rather than compare behaviors across a group of children of the same age, the dynamic dimension addresses within-individual growth through time. The dynamic dimension can be further analyzed into three interrelated subcategories. One deals with the ways that individual human beings *change* over time and with experience. This subcategory addresses the sequence of learning, the transformations that occur in capabilities from one age or time period to another, and the order in which the stages of development and learning occur. Thus some specialists study the progressive, sequential changes, stages, or transitions involved in going from babbling babyhood to becoming a competent speaker of a language by age four or five.

Another subcategory of the dynamic dimension of development is *delayed impact.* This concerns the way early experience may affect later functioning, particularly with respect to affective and personality development. It attends to determinants of behavior that may be unconscious but caused by early experiences that are no longer easily accessible to conscious attention. It is this aspect of development, for example, that leads to widespread concern among early childhood specialists about possible delayed effects of early separation of an infant from his or her mother on later mental health. Delayed impacts may be both positive or negative. For example, a new parent's loving or abusive behavior toward his or her infant may result in delayed impacts on mature behavior based on these no-longer-recalled early experiences.

A third subcategory of the dynamic dimension is the long-term *cumulative effect* of repeated or frequent experiences. An experience might have no effect or a benign one on a child's development if it occurs only once in a while, but might be harmful if experienced repeatedly or frequently over a long period of time. A teacher might not become concerned if the directions for completing school tasks confuse a child once in a while; but the repeated or frequent experience of being confused may have strong cumulative effects on the child's self-confidence and self-perceptions as a learner, and thus become a source of concern to the teacher. Similarly, occasional exposure to horror movies might not affect a child; but the cumulative effects of frequent exposure to them might cause long-term deleterious effects.

In a similar way, an activity might seem to have little positive effect on a child's development if it occurs only occasionally but may yield substantial benefits cumulatively. For example, some parents and educators might question the value of block play or dramatic play to a child's development. If this kind of play is available only occasionally, it may produce few if any positive effects; however, the cumulative effect of repeated opportunities to engage in such peer-interactive, open-ended, expressive, cre-

ative, child-governed activities may be both positive and substantial.

Taking into account both the normative and dynamic dimensions of development suggests, in principle, that just because
children *can* do something does not mean that they *should.* The
determination of what most children of a given age *can* do is a
normative assessment; the determination of what the same
group *should* do depends upon the anticipated dynamic *long-term*
consequences of an experience for each individual. For example,
though it is likely that most young children can learn phonics at
age four—normatively speaking—it does not follow that they
should do so. This issue centers on the potential long term
dynamic consequences of such a practice in terms of its possible
cumulative effect. The distinction between what children *can do*
and what they *should do* is especially serious in early childhood
education because most young children are eager to please their
teachers and appear willing to do almost anything asked of them.
Most even enjoy the activities offered, at least until their novelty
wears off. However, children's willingness and enjoyment are
potentially misleading criteria for judging the appropriateness
of pedagogical practices. Instead, estimates of the possible
delayed impacts and cumulative effects of practices must be considered.

The two dimensions of development, and especially the subcategories of the dynamic dimension—change, delayed impact,
and cumulative effects—provide a framework for considering the
appropriateness of the learning goals derived from answering the
question What should be learned? For example, from a normative perspective, extensive studies of young children suggest that
in principle, pedagogical practices should address helping them
to make better, deeper, and more accurate sense of their own
environments and experiences. As children's age and experience
increase, it is the responsibility of educators to help them to
make better, deeper and more accurate sense of others' environments and experiences: those distant in time and place. Similarly, the view taken of children's intellectual development by
contemporary developmentalists suggests that in principle, the
younger they are, the more likely knowledge is to be acquired if it
is context- or situation-bound (Brown, Collins, & Duguid, 1989).
Furthermore, many Piagetians have made the case that children's intellectual development progresses in fairly predictable
and invariant sequences or stages. Thus both the normative and
stage/sequence aspects of development deserve consideration in

selecting what knowledge is to be acquired in an early childhood program. Similarly, normative and stage/sequence considerations are appropriate in identifying the skills to be included among the goals of a curriculum or program.

When it comes to identifying the dispositions and feelings to be fostered or weakened by a pedagogical approach, the other two subcategories of the dynamic dimension—delayed impacts and cumulative effects—merit consideration. For example, the introduction of formal instruction in phonics at age four or five may be acceptable on normative grounds; but in view of its timing and the amount of instruction likely to be required when starting such instruction so early, the potential delayed or cumulative effects—positive or negative—of adopting this practice must be considered. Opponents of the practice argue that even if the knowledge and skill involved in reading is acquired, the cumulative effects of an early start may be to damage the disposition to read, and that it may engender feelings surrounding literacy and literature that are undesirable (including boredom or dislike). Advocates of early reading instruction, on the other hand, assert that postponing its introduction unnecessarily deprives the learner of whatever knowledge and experiences can be acquired through reading (Carnine, Carnine, Karp, & Weisberg, 1988).

In principle, then, an appropriate pedagogy is one that takes into account the acquisition of knowledge and skills in such a way that the disposition to use them and positive feelings towards them are also strengthened. Some might argue that given the vulnerability of children, it may be that the younger the child, the more consideration should be given to goals in the dispositions and feelings categories of learning than the other two categories. However, because neither of these two types of learning—dispositions and feelings—can be addressed directly, but are byproducts of interactions involving the other two categories, knowledge and skills, they cannot easily be given priority in curriculum planning. It is reasonable to assume that dispositions and feelings are always being strengthened or weakened, either intentionally or by default; they do not wait upon particular lessons or instructions.

How Is It Best Learned?

This question takes us directly to matters of pedagogy; they include consideration of teaching methods, activities, materials, and all other practical matters designed to achieve the learning goals, and to take into account what is known about learners' development. Thus answers to the what and when questions are blended to yield principles of practice that constitute a general pedagogical approach to early childhood education.

Learning in the four categories of goals is facilitated in different ways. In the case of both knowledge and skills, learning can be aided by instruction as well as by other processes, but dispositions and feelings cannot be learned from direct instruction. Dispositions appear to be acquired from models, to be strengthened by being manifested and appreciated, and to be weakened when unacknowledged or ineffective.

Feelings related to school experiences are likely to be learned as a byproduct of experiences rather than from instruction. Both dispositions and feelings can be thought of as incidental learnings in that they are incidental to the processes by which knowledge and skills are acquired. To label feelings as incidental is not to belittle them, or to devalue the role of pedagogy in their development; rather, it is to emphasize that they cannot be taught didactically. Children cannot be instructed in what feelings to have.

We consider first the principles of pedagogical practice applicable to each of the four categories of learning goals and follow with a discussion of pedagogical principles generally applicable to most of the goals of an early childhood program.

PRINCIPLES RELATED TO THE ACQUISITION OF KNOWLEDGE

Recent insights into children's development suggest that in principle, the younger the child, the more readily knowledge is acquired through active and interactive processes; conversely, with increasing age children become more able to profit from reactive, passive-receptive pedagogical approaches or instructional processes. This developmental principle suggests that pedagogical practices are appropriate when the knowledge to be learned is relatively easily accessible to the child's own firsthand, direct experiences and when it is accessible from primary sources (Brice-Heath, 1987). This is not to say that children do not acquire knowledge and information from such secondary sources as stories, books, and film. The extent to which they do so is related to whether young children can connect the material within the secondary sources to the images and knowledge they already possess (Egan, 1986). With increasing age and experience children become more able to profit from secondhand, indirect experiences and secondary sources. This principle is consistent with the concept of *situated cognition* that has recently been proposed to account for the nature of learning at all ages. As Brown, Collins, and Duguid explain,

> To explore the idea that concepts are both situated and progressively developed through activity, we should abandon any notion that they are abstract, self-contained entities. Instead, it may be more useful to consider conceptual knowledge as, in some ways, similar to a set of tools. Tools . . . can only be interpreted in the context of their use (1989, p. 33).

Thus pedagogical practices are appropriate if they provide young children with ample opportunity to interact with adults and children who are like and unlike themselves, with materials, and directly with real objects and real environments. However, interactions cannot occur in a vacuum; they have to have content. Interactions must be *about* something—ideally something that interests the interactors.

What criteria can be used to determine what knowledge or content is appropriate for young children? For example, should young children spend up to ten minutes per day in a calendar exercise? Should young children in southern Florida be making snowflake crystals out of styrofoam in January? Should substantial amounts of time be allocated to observance of public holidays and festivals? Why? And why not? What factors, data, or other matters should be taken into account in answering these questions such as these? One way to approach these questions is to derive principles of practice from what is known about the nature of children's intellectual development.

In principle, a substantial proportion of the content of interaction should be related to matters of actual or potential interest to the children served by the program. Since not all of children's interests are equally deserving of attention, some selection of which interests are the most worthy of promotion is required. Current views of children's learning and their active construction of knowledge suggests that those interests most likely to extend, deepen, and improve their understandings of their own environments and experiences are most worth strengthening.

Child development data suggest furthermore that in principle, the younger the learner, the more integrated the curriculum should be; conversely, as children's age and experience increase, their capacities to profit from subject- or discipline-based study increases. Young children do not differentiate their ideas, thoughts, and interests into categories such as science, language, and math. They are more likely to gain knowledge and understanding by pursuing a topic to which scientific, linguistic, mathematical, and other discipline-related concepts can be applied.

Principles Related to the Acquisition of Skills

Skills can be acquired and strengthened through a variety of processes—including observation, imitation, trial and error, coaching, and instruction—and they can be improved with optimum drill and practice. Contemporary views of the nature of learning also suggest that like physical and social skills, intellectual skills are best learned when they occur in a meaningful situation (Brown et al., 1989). In principle, the younger the child, the more likely it is that skillfulness is strengthened by *application* in meaningful contexts. As children increase in age and experience, and are more able to grasp the relationship between skillfulness and drill, they can more easily understand and accept the need for practice and exercise of disembedded or decontextualized skills—even if they do so reluctantly.

Principles Related to Both Knowledge and Skills

Consideration of both the knowledge and the skills to be learned in the light of what is known about children's development suggests that in principle, the younger the children, the more important it is that what they are to learn about (knowledge) and learn to do (skills) should have *horizontal* rather than *vertical* relevance. Vertical relevance is that which prepares the pupils for the next school experience rather than for the one in which it is occurring; it is a type of "education for the next life." Horizontal relevance means that what the children are learning about (knowledge) and learning to do (skills) are applicable and meaningful to them on the same day, on the way home, and in their contemporary lives outside of the educational setting. As children increase in age and experience they become more able to acquire knowledge and skills that have no immediate application or meaning for them.

Social Competence   Current research suggests that the first six or seven years of development are a critical period in the development of social competence, and that failure to achieve at least a minimum level of peer interactive competence can have long-term negative consequences (Parker & Asher, 1987). Social competence requires such social knowledge as understanding others' points of view and feelings, and such skills as turn-taking, negotiating, devising and carrying out approach strategies, and many more. Data from child development research suggest that in principle, an appropriate pedagogy for young children is one that provides ample opportunity for them to be engaged in activities in which cooperation and coordination of effort are functional and consequential.

Strengthening Desirable Dispositions

The goals listed among the objectives of most early childhood programs invariably include dispositional outcomes. Among them are: having the desire to learn, being cooperative, being creative, having an eagerness to approach and solve problems, and other such desirable dispositions. The assumption underlying these goals is that mastery of knowledge and skills must be accompanied by robust dispositions to employ them.

As suggested earlier, dispositions cannot be taught directly. Dispositions appear to be learned or strengthened to the extent that they are observed by children in significant models, that they are manifested, and that their manifestations are appreciated rather than rewarded. This suggests that desirable dispositions must be observable by the learners in the adults around them. It also implies that in principle, if dispositions are to be strengthened, ample opportunity for their exercise must be available. For example, if childrens' dispositions to be problem-solvers are to be strengthened, they must have real and meaningful problems to solve in the course of their daily activities.

A distinction is drawn here between rewarding and appreciating a dispositional behavior. Although these two types of responses to children's behavior probably overlap, they differ more in manner and in what they communicate to the children than in actual form or content. Let us take the example of a teacher who follows up a question raised by a child a day or two earlier by saying something like, "Remember when you asked about X? I found out that it is such-and-such and found a book about it too. . . . " In this example, the teacher's comment is positive and appreciative without distracting the child from his or her original interest. By contrast, research in child development indicates that rewards tend to distract children from the content of the problem at hand. After all, rewards can only work if children are aware of them! (See Katz & Chard, 1989, especially Chapter 2.) This kind of teacher response also provides children with a model of the disposition to look things up, to seek answers, and to pursue a topic. Given the cumulative negative effects of rewards on children's dispositions related to learning, a pedagogy is appropriate if it strengthens intrinsic motivation by appreciating children's efforts and by encouraging them to evaluate their own work. Furthermore, unless young children have sufficient early experience of acquiring in-depth understanding of a topic, it will be difficult for them to acquire a taste for or disposition to seek deep understanding.

Contemporary research on children's dispositions to learn indicates that excessive emphasis on skilled performance on academic tasks has cumulative negative effects on their mastery, effort and challenge-seeking dispositions (Katz & Chard, 1989). The findings of the research in this area suggest that in principle, pedagogical practices that offer open-ended tasks aimed at learning goals rather than at specific performance goals are more likely to strengthen dispositions toward mastery, effort, and challenge-seeking.

Feelings Related to School Experiences

One of the most typical learning goals found in curriculum guides is that children should learn to "feel good about themselves." Others include feelings of confidence, competence, and acceptance by others.

Like dispositions, feelings cannot be taught directly; they are experienced and strengthened in the context of the ongoing relationships and activities that give rise to them. One of the issues in the dispute over developmentally appropriate practices is that when they focus on a narrow range of academic tasks (such as workbooks, lessons in phonics, and so on) a substantial proportion of the learners is likely to be unable to respond to the work effectively. Indeed, there is some evidence to suggest that when a single instructional approach is employed with any group of children that is diverse in background, ability, and development, about one third is likely to feel left out and to develop feelings of incompetence or inadequacy. Thus, in principle, a pedagogical approach is appropriate if it adopts a variety of methods of teaching and makes a wide variety and range of activities available to the children (Rosenholtz & Simpson, 1984).

GENERAL DEVELOPMENT AND APPROPRIATE PEDAGOGY

Current understandings of development suggest that, in principle, the younger the learner, the larger proportion of time should be allocated to informal activities. However, there are at least three kinds of informal activities: (a) spontaneous dramatic play, (b) arts and craft activities, and (c) cooperative work on extended group investigations or similar exploratory and constructive projects in which the teacher's role is consultative rather than didactic. Some time can also be allocated to varieties of music and literature-related activities that may occur in small or whole group teacher guided activities.

Based on current research on children's learning, it is reasonable to assume that between twenty and thirty percent of all children will need some systematic help from an adult in learning some of the skills among the goals in the first few years of schooling. However, there is a distinction between systematic individual instruction and common use of the term direct instruction. Systematic instruction is given to an individual, or sometimes a pair or trio, planned by a teacher for the particular individuals based on extensive observation and analysis of their needs. This individual or very small group systematic instruction can be provided within the classroom and minimize both the stigma and the logistical problems associated with "pull-out" programs. The individual instruction that some children require from time to time can be offered while others are engaged in spontaneous play or busy with cooperative and individual work on worthwhile topics.

SUMMARY

The main argument in this chapter is that considerations of what young children should learn, and when and how they should do so, have to be addressed together in order to formulate an appropriate pedagogical approach for any of them. In the light of current research related to these questions, it is suggested that such a pedagogy for young children should be largely informal in structure and should attend to the children's dispositional and emotional development as well as to the acquisition of appropriate knowledge and skills. Such a pedagogy is appropriate for young children also if it is primarily *intellectual* rather than *academic* in focus, if it provides a balance of opportunities for both individual and cooperative group work on intellectually engaging tasks, and if systematic instruction is available to individual children as needed periodically.

The pedagogical approach proposed here would bring pedagogical practices into line with what is known about young children's development and learning. A remaining challenge to early childhood educators is to bring parents' understandings, expectations, and preferences into closer agreement with these recommended practices.

REFERENCES

Bereiter, C., & Engelmann, S. (1966). *Teaching disadvantaged children in the preschool.* Englewood Cliffs, NJ: Prentice Hall.

Bredekamp, S. (Ed.). (1987). *Developmentally appropriate practice in early childhood programs serving children from birth through age 8.* Washington, DC: National Association for the Education of Young Children.

Brice-Heath, S. (1987). *Redefining culture: Society, anthropology, and education.* Paper presented at the Annual Meeting of the American Educational Research Association, Washington, DC. April, 1987.

Brown, J. S., Collins, A., & Duguid, P. (1989). Situated cognition and the culture of learning. *Educational Researcher, 18*(1), 32–42.

Carnine, D., Carnine, L., Karp, J., & Weisberg, P. (1988). Kindergarten for economically disadvantaged children: The direct instruction component. In C. Warger, (Ed.), *Resource guide to public school early childhood programs.* Alexandria, VA: Association for Supervision and Curriculum Development.

Clark, R. W. (1988). Who decides? In L. N. Tanner (Ed.), *Critical issues in curriculum: 87th yearbook of the National Society for the Study of Education, part 1* (pp. 175–204). Chicago: University of Chicago Press.

Egan, K. (1986). *Teaching as story telling: An alternative approach to teaching and curriculum in the elementary school.* Chicago: University of Chicago Press.

Gardner, D. E. M. (1948). *Testing results in the infant schools.* (2nd Ed.). London: Methuen.

Katz, L. G., & Chard, S. C. (1989). *Engaging children's minds: The project approach.* Norwood, NJ: Ablex.

Lazerson, M. (1972). The historical antecedents of early childhood education. In I. J. Gordon (Ed.), *Early childhood education: 71st yearbook of the National Society for the Study of Education, part 2* (pp. 33–54). Chicago: University of Chicago Press.

Maccoby, E. M. (1984). Socialization and developmental change. *Child Development, 55*(2), 317–328.

Oklahoma State Department of Education. (1986). *Beginnings: Early childhood education in Oklahoma (3rd ed.).* Oklahoma City: Oklahoma State Department of Education.

Parker, J., & Asher, S. (1987). Peer relations and later personal adjustment: Are low-accepted children at risk? *Psychological Bulletin, 102,* 358–389.

Powell, D. R. (1987). Comparing preschool curricula. In S. L. Kagan & E. F. Zigler (Eds.), *Early schooling: The national debate* (pp. 190–211). New Haven, CT: Yale University Press.

Roberts, P. M. (Ed.). (1989). *Growing together: Early childhood education in Pennsylvania.* Harrisburg, PA: Pennsylvania Department of Education.

Rosenholtz, S. J., & Simpson, C. (1984). Classroom organization and student stratification. *Elementary School Journal, 85*(1), 21–37.

Shepard, L. A. & Smith, M. L. (1988). Escalating academic demand in kindergarten: Counterproductive policies. *Elementary School Journal, 89,* pp. 135–145.

State of Connecticut. (1988). *A guide to program development for kindergarten, part 1.* Hartford, CT: State Board of Education.

State of Iowa. (1983). *Kindergarten: A year of beginnings.* Des Moines, IA.

Spodek, B. (1986). Development, values, and knowledge in the kindergarten curriculum. In B. Spodek (Ed.), *Today's kindergarten: Exploring the knowledge base, expanding the curriculum.* New York:
Teachers College Press.

Washburne, C. (1939). Introduction. In G. M. Whipple (Ed.), *Child development and the curriculum: Yearbook of the National Society for
the Study of Education, part 1.* Bloomington, IL: Public School
Publishing.

Williams, C. K., & Kamii, C. (1986). How do children learn by handling
objects? *Young Children, 42,* 23–26.

Winsor, C. (1977). The progressive movement. In B. D. Boegehold, H. K.
Coffer, W. H. Hooks, & G. J. Klopf (Eds.), *Education before five* (pp.
33–44). New York: Bank Street College of Education.

8

FIVE PERSPECTIVES ON THE QUALITY OF EARLY CHILDHOOD PROGRAMS*

This chapter was developed from an address given at a conference on the theme of quality programs for young children. At that time my aim was to compare two views of quality. One view is from the top down, from the perspective of adults. The other view is from the bottom up, as experienced by the children themselves. In the chapter that follows, the ideas eventually developed to include three more perspectives on the quality of early childhood programs and a brief discussion of their implications.

Today, the issue of how to raise the quality of programs for young children in the United States and most other countries remains high on early childhood conference agendas. The research available to date strongly suggests that any early childhood program in any context that is less than top quality represents a missed opportunity to make a substantial contribution to the quality of children's lives, and to their entire futures.

The quality of programs for young children is one of the most salient issues of the day in the United States. Questions about what criteria and assessment procedures should be used to deter-

* This chapter was originally published as "Five Perspectives on the Quality of Early Childhood Programs," by Lilian G. Katz, 1993. Urbana, IL: ERIC Clearinghouse on Elementary and Early Childhood Education. Reprinted with permission. Based on a paper prepared for the Second European Conference on the Quality of Early Childhood Education (Worcester College of Higher Education, Worcester, England. August, 1992.)

mine quality are as complex for early childhood programs as for other professional services.

Most of the available literature on the quality of early childhood programs suggests that it can be assessed by identifying selected characteristics of the program, the setting, the equipment, and other features, as seen from above by adults in charge of the program, or responsible for licensing it. Such an approach can be called an assessment of quality from a *top-down* perspective. Another approach is to take what might be called a *bottom-up* perspective by attempting to determine how the program is actually experienced by the participating children. A third approach, which could be called an *inside-outside* perspective, is to assess how the program is experienced by the families it serves. A fourth perspective is from the *inside*, which considers how the program is experienced by the staff who work in it. A fifth perspective takes into account how the community and the larger society is served by a program. This can be called the *outside* or, in some sense, the *ultimate* perspective on program quality.

The thesis of this paper is that criteria representing all five perspectives merit consideration in determining the quality of provisions for the care and education of young children. This multiple perspectives approach to quality assessment raises complex issues concerning the causes of poor quality and how accountability for it should be defined.

TOP-DOWN PERSPECTIVE ON QUALITY

The top-down perspective on quality typically takes into account such program features as:

- ratio of adults to children;
- qualifications and stability of the staff;
- characteristics of adult-child relationships;
- quality and quantity of equipment and materials;
- quality and quantity of space per child;
- aspects of staff working conditions;

- health, hygiene and fire safety provisions, and so forth.

According to Fiene (1992), program features such as those listed above, which typically are included in licensing guidelines, are useful as a basis for regulatory strategies for ensuring the quality of child care, in that they are directly observable and enforceable ways by which providers can "set the stage for desirable interaction . . . " (p. 2). They are also program features that are relatively easy to quantify and require relatively little inference on the part of the assessor.

A briefing paper titled *Child Care: Quality is the Issue*, prepared by the Child Care Action Campaign and produced by the National Association for the Education of Young Children (Ehrlich, n. d.), acknowledges that there is no single definition of quality for the variety of types of child care settings in the United States. However, the briefing paper does list the following basic components of quality: the ratio of children to adults, the size of groups, the availability of staff training, and staff turnover rates (p. 4).

There is substantial evidence to suggest that the program and setting features listed above and commonly included in top-down criteria of quality do indeed predict some effects of an early childhood program (Beardsley, 1990; Harms & Clifford, 1980; Howes, Phillips, & Whitebook, 1992; Love, 1993; Phillips, 1987).

THE BOTTOM-UP PERSPECTIVE ON QUALITY

It seems reasonable to assume that the significant and lasting effects of a program depend primarily on how it is experienced from below. In other words, the actual or true predictor of a program's effects is the quality of life experienced by each participating child on a day-to-day basis.

Bottom-up Criteria

If the child's subjective experience of a program is the true determinant of its effects, meaningful assessment of program quality requires answers to the central question, What does it feel like to be a child in this environment?[1] This approach requires making inferences about how each child would—so to speak—answer questions like the following:

- Do I usually feel welcome rather than captured?
- Do I usually feel that I am someone who belongs rather than someone who is just part of the crowd?
- Do I usually feel accepted, understood, and protected by the adults, rather than scolded or neglected by them?
- Am I usually accepted by some of my peers rather than isolated or rejected by them?
- Am I usually addressed seriously and respectfully, rather than as someone who is "precious" or "cute"?
- Do I find most of the activities engaging, absorbing, and challenging, rather than just amusing, fun, entertaining, or exciting?
- Do I find most of the experiences interesting, rather than frivolous or boring?
- Do I find most of the activities meaningful, rather than mindless or trivial?
- Do I find most of my experiences satisfying, rather than frustrating or confusing?
- Am I usually glad to be here, rather than reluctant to come and eager to leave?

The criteria of quality implied in these questions are based on my interpretation of what is known about significant influences on children's long-term growth, development, and learning. Those responsible for programs might make their own list of such questions, based on their own interpretations of appropriate experiences for young children.

It is generally agreed that on most days, each child in an early childhood program should feel welcome in the setting, should feel that he or she belongs in the group, and should feel accepted, understood, and protected by those in charge. Questions concerning other aspects of the child's experiences are included to emphasize the importance of addressing young children's real need to feel intellectually engaged and respected, and to encour-

---

[1] The inferred answers to this question should reflect the nature of experience over a given period of time, depending upon the age of the child. Hence the term *usually* is repeated in most of the questions in the list.

age all responsible for them to do more than just keep them busy and happy or even excited (see Chapters 6 & 7).

The last question on the criteria list reflects the assumption that when the intellectual vitality of a program is strong, most children, on most days, will be eager to participate and reluctant to leave the program. Their eagerness will be based on more than just the "fun" aspects of their participation. Of course, there are potentially many other factors that influence children's eagerness to participate in a program. Any program and any child can have an "off" day or two.

Experience Sampling

The older the children served by a program, the longer the time period required for a reliable bottom-up assessment. Three to four weeks of assessment for preschoolers and slightly longer periods of assessment for older children may provide a sufficient sampling to make reliable predictions of significant developmental outcomes. Occasional exciting events experienced in early childhood programs are unlikely to affect long-term development.

I propose that the quality of a program is good if it is experienced from the bottom-up perspective as intellectually and socially engaging and satisfying on most days and is not dependent on occasional exciting special events.

Cumulative Effects

Assessment of the quality of experience over appropriate time periods helps address the potential *cumulative effects* of experience. My assumption here is that some childhood experiences, if rare, may be benign or inconsequential, but if experienced frequently may be harmful or beneficial (see Chapter 7). For example, being rebuffed by peers once in a while should not be a debilitating experience for a preschooler; but the cumulative effects of frequent rebuffs may undermine long-term social development substantially. Similarly, block play, project work, and other developmentally appropriate activities may not support long-term development if they are rare or occasional, but can do so if they are frequent.

When most of the answers to the questions posed are at the positive end of the continua implied in them, we can assume that the quality of the program is worthy of the children. However, the question of how positive a response should be to meet a standard of good quality remains to be determined.

Needless to say, there are many possible explanations for any of the answers children might give—if they could—to the questions listed above. A program should not automatically be faulted for every negative response. In other words, the causes of children's negative subjective experiences cannot be always or solely attributed to the staff. For what, then, can the staff be appropriately held accountable? I suggest that while they cannot be held accountable for all possible cases of negative experiences, they are accountable for applying all practices acknowledged and accepted by the profession to be relevant and appropriate to the situation at hand.

THE OUTSIDE-INSIDE PERSPECTIVE ON QUALITY

Ideally, assessment of the quality of a program should include the quality of the characteristics of parent-teacher relationships (See NAEYC, 1991a, pp. 26–29, & 1991b, pp. 101–110). Such assessments depend on how each parent would answer such questions as:

In my relationships with the staff, are they:

- primarily respectful, rather than patronizing or controlling?
- accepting, open, inclusive, and tolerant, rather than rejecting, blaming, and prejudiced?
- respectful of my goals and values for my child?[2]
- welcoming contacts that are ongoing and frequent rather than rare and distant?

The positive attributes of parent–teacher relationships suggested above are relatively easy to develop when teachers and parents have the same backgrounds, speak the same languages,

---

[2] The concept of respect does not imply agreement or compliance with the wishes of the other.

share values and goals for children, and in general like each other. Parents are also more likely to relate to their children's caregivers and teachers in positive ways when they understand the complex nature of their jobs, when they appreciate what teachers are striving to accomplish, and when they are aware of the conditions under which the staff is working.

Of course, it is possible that negative responses of some parents to some of the questions listed above cannot be attributed directly to the program and the staff, but have causes that staff may or may not be aware of or able to determine.

THE INSIDE PERSPECTIVE ON QUALITY

The quality of an early childhood program as perceived from the inside, that is, by the staff, includes three dimensions: (a) colleague relationships, (b) staff–parent relationships, and (c) relationships with the sponsoring agency.

Colleague Relationships

It is highly unlikely that an early childhood program can be of high quality on the criteria thus far suggested unless the staff relationships within it are also of good quality. An assessment of this aspect of quality would be based on how each member of the staff might answer such questions as:

On the whole, are relationships with my colleagues:

- supportive rather than contentious?
- cooperative rather than competitive?
- accepting rather than adversarial?
- trusting rather than suspicious?
- respectful rather than controlling?

In principle, good quality environments cannot be created for children (in the bottom-up sense) unless the environments are also good for the adults who work in them. Of course, there may be some days when the experiences provided have been "good" for the children at the expense of the staff (for example, Halloween celebrations), and some days when the reverse is the case; but on the average, a good quality program is one in which both children and the adults responsible for them find the quality of their lives together satisfying and interesting.

Staff–Parent Relationships

It seems reasonable to assume that the relationships between the staff and the parents of the children they serve can have a substantial effect on many of the criteria of quality already proposed. In addition, I suggest that the same set of criteria implied by the questions listed under the outside-inside perspective apply equally to the experience of staff members. Thus assessment of quality from the staff's perspective would require their answers to the question, Are my relationships with parents primarily respectful rather than patronizing or controlling, and so forth.

Certainly parents are more likely to approach teachers positively when teachers themselves initiate respectful and accepting relationships. However, in a country such as the United States, with its highly mobile and diverse population, it is unlikely that all the families served by a single program, or by an individual teacher, are in complete agreement on the program's goals and methods. This lack of agreement inevitably leads to some parental dissatisfaction and parent–staff friction.

The development of positive, respectful, and supportive relations between staff and parents of diverse backgrounds usually requires staff professionalism based on a combination of experience, training, and education, as well as on personal values.

Staff–Sponsor Relationships

One potential indirect influence on the quality of a program is the nature of the relationships of staff members with those to whom they are responsible. It seems reasonable to suggest that in principle, teachers and caregivers treat children very much the way they themselves are treated by those to whom they report. To be sure, some caregivers and teachers rise above poor treatment, and some fall below good treatment. But one can assume that in principle, good environments for children are more likely to be created when the adults who staff them are treated appropriately on the criteria implied by the questions listed above. A recent study by Howes and Hamilton (1993) calls attention to the potentially serious effects of staff turnover on children's subjective experiences of the program. Thus, the extent to which program sponsors provide contexts that are hospitable and supportive of staff should be given serious attention in assessing program quality. Assessment of quality in terms of the inside perspective would be based on the staff's answers to the following questions:

- Are working conditions adequate to encourage me to enhance my knowledge, skills, and career commitment?
- Is the job description and career advancement plan appropriate?
- Am I usually treated with respect and understanding?

Once again, not all negative responses are necessarily and directly attributable to the sponsors or administrators of a program, and the extent to which they are so would have to be determined as part of an assessment procedure.

THE OUTSIDE PERSPECTIVE

The community and the society-at-large that sponsor a program also have a stake in its quality. There is a sense in which posterity itself eventually reaps the benefits to be derived from high quality early experience for its young children, and in which all society suffers social and other costs when early childhood program quality is poor.[3]

All early childhood programs, whether sponsored by private or public agencies, are influenced intentionally or by default, by a variety of policies, laws, and regulations that govern them. Assessment of quality from the perspective of the larger society should be based on how citizens and those who make decisions on their behalf might be expected to answer the following kinds of questions:

---

[3] One aspect of the impressive preprimary schools of Reggio Emilia in Italy is the extensiveness and depth of the involvement of the whole community in all aspects of their functioning. For an interesting description of community partnerships and early childhood programming, see Spaggiari (1993).

- Am I sure that community resources are appropriately allocated to the protection, care, and education of our children?

- Am I confident that those who make decisions on our community's behalf adopt policies, laws, and regulations that enhance rather than jeopardize children's experiences in early childhood programs?

- Am I confident that the resources currently available to early childhood programs in our community are sufficient to yield long-term as well as short-term benefits to children and their families?

- Are high quality programs affordable to all families in our communities who need the service?

- Are the working conditions (salary, benefits, insurance, and so on) of the community's programs sufficiently good that the staff turnover rate is low enough to permit the development of stable adult-child and parent–staff relationships, and to permit staff training to be cost-effective?

- Are the staff members appropriately trained, qualified, and supervised for their responsibilities?

Since programs for young children are offered under a wide variety of auspices, each program can generate its own list of appropriate criteria for assessment from the outside perspective.

IMPLICATIONS OF MULTIPLE PERSPECTIVES ON QUALITY

Four implications are suggested by this formulation of quality assessment for early childhood programs.

Discrepancies Between Perspectives

It is theoretically possible for a program for young children to meet satisfactory standards on the quality criteria from a top-down perspective, but fall below them on the bottom-up or on the outside-inside criteria. For example, a program might meet high standards on the top-down criteria of space, equipment, or child/staff ratio, and yet fail to meet adequate standards of quality of life for some of the children according to the criteria listed for the bottom-up perspective.

The important aspect of experience is the meaning given to it by the one who undergoes it. In much the same way that the meaning of a particular word is a function of the sentence in which it appears and the paragraph in which it is embedded, human beings tend to attribute and assign meanings to their experience in one situation based on their experiences in all other contexts. This being the case, the bottom-up perspective needs to take into account the likelihood that the stimulus potential of a preschool program for a particular child is a function of the stimulus level of the environment he or she experiences outside the program (Katz, 1989).

For example, a child whose home environment includes a wide variety of play materials, television and video shows, computer games, outdoor play equipment, frequent trips to playgrounds, and so forth, may find a preschool program boring that another child whose home environment lacks the same degree of variety finds engaging. Such individual differences in the experiences of children in early childhood programs—that is, in the range of bottom-up perspectives—should be taken into account in assessing the quality of a program, and be considered in weighing the importance of the top down criteria.

In theory, a program could fall below acceptable standards on the top-down criteria (for example, it could have insufficient space or poor equipment) and yet be experienced as satisfactory by most of the participating children. Since I am suggesting, however, that it is the view from the bottom up that determines the ultimate impact of a program, some flexibility in applying the top-down criteria of quality might be appropriate.

It is also conceivable that the staff might have appropriate relationships with parents but few of the children. Or it could be that children are thriving, but parents do not feel respected or welcomed by the staff.

On the other hand, it could be that the bottom-up assessments are low, but the program is rated high in quality from an outside-inside parental perspective, or vice versa. For example, a staff may feel obliged to engage children in academic exercises in order to satisfy parental preferences even though the children's lives might be experienced as more satisfying if informal and more intellectually meaningful experiences were offered. In such instances, the bottom-up assessment of quality is less positive than the one from outside.

Thus, it is theoretically possible that from these multiple perspectives, levels of satisfaction on the criteria proposed could vary significantly. This raises the question: Should one perspective be given more weight than another in assessing the quality of a program? If so, whose perspective has the first claim to determining program quality?

Issues of Accountability

As suggested above, program providers can hardly be held accountable for all negative responses on the criteria listed for each perspective. Some children come to a program with problems of long standing that originated outside of it. Similarly, parents and staff may register low satisfaction on one or more of the criteria due to factors not attributable to the program itself. Some families may be struggling with the vicissitudes of their own lives in ways that influence their responses to the program but are not necessarily attributable to it.

Problems of attributing the causes of clients' perspectives on a program raise the difficult question of establishing the limits to which the staff can be fairly held accountable. As suggested above, the staff of a program is not obliged to keep everyone happy as much as it is required to apply the professionally accepted procedures as appropriate for each case. This suggestion implies that the profession has adopted a set of criteria and standards of appropriate practice. The view of the limits of staff accountability proposed here implies that at least one essential condition for high-quality programs is that all staff members are qualified and trained to employ the accepted practices, accumulated knowledge, and wisdom of the profession. To be able to respond professionally to each negative response from the bottom-up or outside-inside perspectives requires well-trained and qualified staff with ample professional experience—and this is especially true for the program director.

The view of the limits of staff accountability also emphasizes the urgency for the profession to continue the development of a clear consensus on professional standards of practice below which no practitioner can be allowed to fall.

The field of early childhood education has already taken important steps in the direction of establishing consensus on criteria and standards of practice through professional associations' position papers on major issues. The most comprehensive document currently available is the National Association for the Education of Young Children's (NAEYC) *Developmentally Appropriate Practice in Early Childhood Programs Serving Children from Birth Through Age 8* (Bredekamp, 1987). In addition, the accreditation procedures and standards of NAEYC's National Academy of Early Childhood Programs (NAEYC, 1991a) covers most of the items implied by the criteria listed above. Position statements on curriculum content and assessment (Bredekamp & Rosegrant, 1992; NAEYC, 1991b) have also been issued by NAEYC. NAEYC's new National Institute for Early Childhood Professional Education is designed to address professional development, qualifications, and other issues directly and indirectly related to staff accountability for implementing professionally accepted practices.

In the case of child care programs in particular, the high rate of staff turnover, related largely to appallingly low compensation and poor working conditions in the United States (see Whitebook, Phillips, & Howes, 1993) and many other countries, exacerbates the problems of retaining staff with the requisite qualifications and experience required for good quality programs.

Criteria and Standards

Any kind of assessment requires the selection of criteria and the adoption of standards at which the criteria must be met to satisfy judgments of good quality. As suggested above, each question in each of the lists above implies a criterion of quality. For the purposes of this discussion, a *criterion* is a dimension of experience thought to determine the quality of experience. A *standard* is a particular level of quality on the criterion. Thus, for example, for the top-down criterion of ratio of adults to children, the standard of quality might be set at 1:5, 1:10, or 2:25, depending on the age of the children.

Similarly, for the first criterion listed for the bottom-up perspective: "Do I usually feel welcome rather than captured?" a standard would have to be set as to how intense, constant, or enduring such feelings would have to be to meet a standard of acceptable quality. A four- or five-point scale on each criterion continuum is likely to be sufficient for most purposes. However, agreement concerning the point at which a standard of quality has been satisfied must be determined by the assessors. Furthermore, whether standards of quality would have to be met on all or most or particular criteria would also have to be determined by those undertaking the assessment.

High and Low Inference Variables

Assessments based on such variables as the amount of space per child, qualifications of staff, observable characteristics of staff–child interaction, and other commonly used top-down indices of quality require relatively little or low inference on the part of the assessor. However, the multiple perspectives approach involves the use of high inference variables, including inferring the deep feelings of participants and staff, and the thoughts of citizens.

It would be neither ethical nor practical to interview children directly with the questions posed for the bottom-up perspective. It would be ethically unacceptable to put children in situations that might encourage them to criticize their caretakers and teachers. Furthermore, from a practical standpoint, young children's verbal descriptions of their experiences are unlikely to be reliable. Thus, assessing the quality of bottom-up experience requires making inferences about the subjective states of the children. Ideally these inferences would be based on extensive contact, frequent observation, and information gathering from participants over extended periods of time. In addition, reliable unobtrusive indices of children's subjective experiences are also required to assess quality from the bottom-up (see Goodwin & Goodwin, 1982).

CONCLUSION

Answers to the questions posed on the criteria proposed for each perspective can be used as a basis for decisions about the kinds of modifications to be made in the services offered each individual child and the whole group of children enrolled, and all of their families. In this way, each of the five perspectives outlined above contributes in a different way to an overall assessment of program quality as experienced by all who have a stake in the quality of a program. But because not all responses can be directly attributable to characteristics of a program, the early childhood profession must continue current efforts to develop, adopt, and apply an accepted set of professional standards of practice for which practitioners can fairly be held accountable. Any approach to the assessment of quality requires not only a set of criteria to apply to each program, but some consensus on the minimum standards that must be satisfied for acceptable quality on each criterion. A start has been made on the development of consensus about appropriate practices. Further discussion of these matters among practitioners, program sponsors, regulatory agencies, and membership associations in the field is urgently needed.

REFERENCES

Beardsley, L. (1990). *Good day bad day: The child's experience of day care.* New York: Teachers College Press.

Bredekamp, S. (Ed.). (1987). *Developmentally appropriate practice in early childhood programs serving children from birth through age 8.* Washington, DC: National Association for the Education of Young Children.

Bredekamp, S., & Rosegrant, T. (1992). *Reaching potentials: Appropriate curriculum and assessment for young children.* Washington, DC: National Association for the Education of Young Children.

Ehrlich, E. (n.d.). *Child care: Quality is the issue.* Washington, DC: National Association for the Education of Young Children.

Fiene, R. (1992). Measuring child care quality. Paper presented at the International Conference on Child Day Care Health: Science, Prevention and Practice, June, 1992, Atlanta, Georgia.

Goodwin, W. L., & Goodwin, L. D. (1982). Measuring young children. In B. Spodek (Ed.), *Handbook of research in early childhood education* (pp. 523–563). New York: The Free Press.

Harms, T., & Clifford, R. M. (1980). *The early childhood environment rating scale.* New York: Teachers College Press.

Howes, C., & Hamilton, C. E. (1993). The changing experience of child care: Changes in teachers and in teacher-child relationships and children's social competence with peers. *Early Childhood Research Quarterly, 8*(1), 15–32.

Howes, C., Phillips, D. A., & Whitebook, M. (1992). Thresholds of quality: Implications for social development of children in center-based child care. *Child Development, 63,* 449–460.

Katz, L. G. (1989). Afterword. In P. O. Olmstead & D. P. Weikart (Eds.), *How nations serve young children: Profiles of child care and education in 14 countries* (pp. 401–406). Ypsilanti, MI: High/Scope Foundation.

Love, J. M. (1993). "Does children's behavior reflect day care classroom quality?" Paper presented at the Society for Research in Child Development, New Orleans, March 1993.

National Association for the Education of Young Children. (1991a). Accreditation criteria and procedures of the National Academy of Early Childhood Programs. (Rev. Ed.). Washington, DC: Author.

National Association for the Education of Young Children. (1991b). *Guidelines for appropriate curriculum content and assessment in programs serving children ages 3 through 8*. Washington, DC: Author.

Phillips, D. (1987). *Quality in child care: What does research tell us?* Washington, DC: National Association for the Education of Young Children.

Spaggiari, S. (1993). The community-teacher partnership in the governance of the schools. In C. Edwards, L. Gandini, & G. Forman (Eds.), *The hundred languages of children. The Reggio Emilia approach to early childhood education.* Norwood, NJ.: Ablex.

Whitebook, M., Phillips, D., & Howes, C., (1993). *National child care staffing study revisited: Four years in the life of center-based child care.* Oakland, CA: Child Care Employee Project.

PART II

ISSUES IN TEACHING
YOUNG CHILDREN

9

TEACHERS IN PRESCHOOLS: PROBLEMS AND PROSPECTS*

The main ideas for this chapter arose from reflections during a visit to a model nursery school in Australia in 1976. In excellent and spacious facilities the staff offered the children warmth and friendliness and a traditional variety of play and creative activities, indoors and outdoors. The children moved easily from one activity to another and appeared to be enjoying their experiences. No signs of anguish or stress were observed.

Nevertheless, as I watched the children I was puzzled by a sense that in spite of the pleasure evident in the children's expressions and behavior, there seemed to be something missing. I tried to imagine what it might feel like to be a child in this comfortable environment. After some reflection it occured to me that if I were a child in this setting I might say to myself something like, "The adults here are all unfailingly kind, friendly and warm; they always say nice things to me, but inside of them is there anybody home?" Granted, young children are unlikely to ask themselves questions like the one that occurred to me. Granted also that the observed qualities of warmth and friendliness in the adults are desirable for teachers of young children. But what seemed to be missing in their interactions were responses to the children that could be characterized as serious, thoughtful, and informative. It seemed to me that the warmth and friendliness of the adults had a routine quality, and that perhaps that routinization is an occupational hazard to teachers of young children.

---

*This chapter was originally published as "Teachers in Preschools: Problems and Prospects," by Lilian G. Katz, 1977. *International Journal of Early Childhood*, 9(1), 111-124. Reprinted with permission.

This chapter was an effort to put the issues raised during observations in preschools in the larger context of developments in early childhood education during the 1970s and working conditions in the field.

In the period since the chapter was written, I have come to the view that the concept of intensity in the relationships between adults and children might be more accurately defined as contingency. When teachers respond invariably, though warmly, with kind and benign comments to whatever the children do, the adults' responses are not contingent upon the child's feelings, ideas, or behavior. Such noncontingent and low-intensity responses lack information for the children; they treat children kindly, but not seriously. My hypothesis is that children's intellectual development requires contingently informative responses from adults.

The remainder of the argument in the paper—that working conditions undermine the kind of alertness and sensitivity such contingent responsiveness requires—still seems to be valid in the 1990s. The full implications of the argument are captured in the recent position paper published by the National Association for the Education of Young Children called The Child Care Crisis *(Willer, 1987) and deserve our full and continuing attention.*

TEACHERS IN PRESCHOOLS: PROBLEMS AND PROSPECTS

The aim of this chapter is to explore some concerns about the special problems of adults who work with children in preschools, child care centers, kindergartens, and other early childhood settings. I shall attempt to make the case that some aspects of the nature of the work itself leads to types of programs that may undermine some of its central goals. The discussion is presented under four interrelated headings: (a) overall observations of current developments in the field of early childhood education; (b) issues in child-adult relationships; (c) problems in adult–child relationships; and (d) speculations about future prospects.

OVERALL OBSERVATIONS OF EARLY CHILDHOOD EDUCATION

It is well known that the field of early childhood education has greatly expanded during the last decade. This expansion is most marked in the United States but is certainly not limited to it. Increasing interest in development of young children, often reflected in the development of preschool programs, seems to be nearly worldwide.

Changes in Terminology

One of the interesting signs of the times is that the term *nursery school* has gradually dropped out of use in the United States and in some other countries as well, and has been replaced by the terms *preschool* and *early childhood education*. We can only speculate about the causes of such changes in terminology. Occasionally it seems that the change is due to the same root metaphor that results in such terms as precooked and preshrunk! Indeed, developments in the field over the last decade reflect much rationalization of today's pedagogy in terms of preparation for the next school or the next life!

A more serious examination of recent trends (in the United States, at least) suggests several factors at work. First, the term *nursery* seems to emphasize the nurturant functions of early education, whereas *preschool* stresses the preparatory and preventative goals of so-called intervention programs, of which Head Start is the best known. Second, the term *early childhood education* captures more fully than nursery education the variety of age groups served by programs for young children, the length of the program day, and the types of settings in which the programs occur. Early childhood education usually encompasses all types of programs and classes for children up to the age of eight. Nursery and preschool are terms usually used to describe programs for children before they reach the age of compulsory education.

Conceptions of the Teacher's Role

In addition to changes in program terminology, some reluctance to use the term *teacher* can also be observed, especially in discussions of day care center staffing. Instead, terms such as *child care worker* and *caregiver* are being used more frequently. The federally initiated program developed by the Office of Child Development (HEW) adopted the term Child Development Associate for adults working in Head Start and other preschool settings, and expressly eschewed the term teacher.

The causes of such reluctance to use the term teacher are not entirely clear. We can speculate that some believe that the term teacher implies the possession of official or state teaching credentials or diplomas—an implication that would be incongruent with the paraprofessional, aide, or assistant status of many adults working in early childhood programs. The reluctance may also reflect negative sentiments toward teachers in public schools among both workers and clients of programs such as Head Start and other community-based early childhood centers.

However, it may also be that to a large extent the reluctance to use the term teacher stems from some of the complexities involved in conceptualizing the adult's role and functions in programs for very young children. What proportion of the role is educational? How much is health-related? How much emphasis should be put on care?

It may be that before the large-scale expansion that began in the 1960s, people who worked with young children had a shared understanding of their role and functions. In a description of the ideal qualifications for nursery school teachers, Jessie Stanton stated:

> She should have a fair education . . . by this I mean she should have a doctor's degree in psychology and medicine. Sociology as a background is advisable. She should be an experienced carpenter, mason, mechanic, plumber and a thoroughly trained musician and poet . . . Now at 83, she is ready! (Beyer, 1968)

A more contemporary version of the ideal qualifications for preschool teachers would most likely add special education, linguistics, ethnic studies, anthropology, and ecology, at least. Such all-encompassing qualifications reflect the broad range of functions assumed by adults working with young children.

The terms used today—child care worker and Child Development Associate—may heighten awareness among the clients of early childhood practitioners, the general public as well as government officials, whose frame of reference is traditional elementary school teaching, of the complex responsibilities of adults who work with young children. In addition, the new names may, in a sense, be rewordings of the concept of the whole child, which outsiders often ridicule as a cliché. However, as Millie Almy has pointed out, whatever we are doing with a child, we are always affecting the whole person (1975, p. 50).

Another way to state the problem of "wholeness," or the range and variety of the preschool teacher's responsibilities, is that *the younger the child, the greater is the range of his or her functioning for which adults must assume responsibility.* And it is precisely this formulation of the adults' role that causes grave concern about the lives of teachers, child care workers, and others who work daily with the young. These concerns are discussed in two parts: first, in terms of *child–adult* relationships, and then in terms of *adult–child* relationships, although, as can be readily seen, the two parts are not easily separated.

ISSUES IN CHILD–ADULT RELATIONSHIPS

My concerns about specific aspects of child–adult relationships stem from impressions drawn from observing preschool programs around the United States, the United Kingdom, Australia, and other countries. In general the programs observed fall into two types, which I shall call Type C and Type D. (Types A and B are discussed later.) I shall present somewhat exaggerated characterizations of the two types in order to communicate my concerns as fully as possible. But keep in mind that there are no "pure type" programs in the real world!

Typology of Early Childhood Programs

Many programs fit into the category I have called Type C. These are the well-equipped, amply spaced programs with attractive play areas and an abundance of apparatus. These programs display the full range of traditional materials and activities. Whether Type C is seen in Illinois, California, or Cleveland; or in Canberra, Gloucestershire, or the West Indies the observer finds a housekeeping corner, dress-up clothes, puzzles, blocks, easels, swings, and so on. The children in Type C programs seem to be having fun in a pleasant environment and a congenial atmosphere. All of these qualities seem highly desirable and do not evoke concern. Beyond reasonable doubt, the children in Type C programs must see the adults as warm, friendly, helpful, and supportive—all qualities emphasized in traditional nursery and kindergarten literature and teacher training. My concern stems from an uneasy hunch that if I were a child in such a program I might say to myself (so to speak), "These adults are nice and pleasant, but (inside them) there is nobody home!" In other words, I wonder if the children can perceive these warm and friendly adults as thinking, responsive, real, and self-respecting persons.

No doubt you have all observed Type C-like programs. One teacher in such a program reported to me that at clean-up time she habitually spurred the children on by singing a song to the effect that "we are galloping horses" engaged in clean-up. The business of clean-up was softened and sweetened with this chant. I hasten to add that the reporter pointed out that she had learned this approach to clean-up time in the laboratory nursery classes at her training institution. Surely you are familiar with such kind but empty phrases pronounced in unvaried sweet tones, usually with the nonspecific pronoun "we," as in "we don't throw sand," when, in fact, "we" just did! Why do we seem to think that such soft, weak ambiguity is necessary? When we use these pat-

Warmth of Relationships

		high	low
Intensity of Relationships	high	**Type A** Optimum Preschool Environment	**Type B** "Military Academy" Model
	low	**Type C** "Traditional" Preschool Programs	**Type D** "Preacademic" Preschool Programs

FIGURE 9–1   Location of Preschool Programs on Two Levels of Warmth and Two Levels of Intensity of Relationship

terns of communication can we be perceived by children as real, thinking adults? Can we be seen as models of those intellectual qualities we wish to encourage and support in them? Some possible explanations for these patterns of teacher–child interactions are explored below.

I have classified as Type D programs the kind one sees more and more frequently, especially in the United States, in which children are engaged in routine instructional tasks, sometimes called "structured activities" or misleadingly labeled as "cognitive" activities. In Type D programs, children are engaged in academic or preacademic routines, learning to identify and classify circles, squares, sets of animals, vehicles, and so on. They fill out workbooks and worksheets, and engage in other prescribed "lessons" on phonics and the like. The type D programs, of which the curriculum materials are a central feature, are typically designed to be teacher-proof. To the extent that Type D program and curriculum developers succeed in designing teacher-proof curricula, one can assume, with little doubt, that the children could also look at the adults and ask "Is there anybody home?" The more teacher proof, the more likely the answer would seem to be "No."

Granted that the two types are somewhat overdrawn, they both concern me for some reasons that are obvious, and other reasons about which I am as yet unclear. Parenthetically, we should keep in mind that there is no reliable evidence that either Type C or Type D programs are harmful to children. A report of the results of Project Follow Through suggests that each type may be producing different and worthwhile outcomes (Stallings, 1975). Nevertheless, I have two major reservations about both types of curriculum models related to the hypothesized "nobody home" phenomenon.

Development of the Intellect

At this point I would like to emphasize a distinction between *academic* (or preacademic) activities and *intellectual* activities. The former involve routine instructional tasks in which children acquire a prespecified vocabulary, conventional concepts, and some rudimentary pupil role behaviors and skills that typically are sampled in standardized tests of academic skills or achievement. In contrast, intellectual activities involve exploration, experimentation, imagination, and the engagement of the mind in thinking, analyzing, recording, representing, and in a variety of ways extending, deepening, refining, and improving children's understandings of their experiences and environments.

My first concern is that neither of the two types of programs described above pays sufficient attention to the life of the mind or to the development of the intellect. Children in Type C programs seem to be having fun, and in a sense to be amused. In Type D programs, children seem to be acquiring some of the social skills associated with academic life and schooling, but the instructional tasks seem mindless and are frequently irrelevant to their own experiences and environments.

Nevertheless, each of these two extremes overlooks, in its own way, what seems to be a primary goal of education: to engage the learner's mind and to help that mind as it attempts to improve and develop understandings of its experiences. I believe that when educators make the engagement of the learner's mind their primary goal, and succeed in doing so, then learners find their education enjoyable. But the enjoyment is a side effect, not a main effect of such education. If enjoyment were our main goal, then we would not have to know very much, we would not have to study and think, to observe, to worry about our knowledge and skills as teachers. For young children, an assortment of birthday parties, musical chairs, and cartoon shows would provide enjoyment. But when engagement of the learners' minds and the refinement of their understanding constitute main goals, then alert, responsive, thoughtful, and knowledgeable adults are required.

Another concern is that both Type C and D programs may be neglecting the development of children's capacities to be interested in worthwhile aspects of their own environments; they seems to ignore, if not jeopardize, the development of the disposition to become intrigued and absorbed by the outer as well as the inner world (see Chapters 3 and 7).

To return to my second major concern about these two types of programs—my hunch that perhaps children view adults as though there is "nobody home" inside them—it is obvious that children are not likely to phrase the problem in just that way. Young children are unlikely to be analytical with respect to adult functioning, and probably accept their perceptions at face value. Thus it is more likely that the young do not know what they are missing, so to speak. My concerns about the hypothesized "nobody home" phenomenon stems from a hunch that if our programs are to have a real and enduring impact on children's intellectual development, the relationships between children and adults must be characterized by greater intensity than they typically appear to be—at least in the two types of programs just described.

Warmth and Intensity

In this section of the discussion I shall try to sketch first some ideas about how the development of the intellect and the attendant capacity to be absorbed, intrigued, and interested in the environment may be related to the intensity of the relationships between children and adults in our preschool programs. Secondly, I shall try to outline what characteristics of adult–child relationships seem to contribute to optimal intensity, and finally to show that the typical working conditions of adults in preschool programs may make optimal intensity of child–adult relationships difficult to achieve.

As early childhood educators we have traditionally and persistently emphasized children's need for warm and nurturant adults to support their psychosocial development. As far as I know, no one is advocating the contrary. However, I would like to suggest that warmth and intensity may be thought of as separate and independent dimensions of the relationships between children and adults.

Perhaps we can agree, at least for the purpose of discussion, that when we use the term *warmth* we mean the extent to which children experience the adults as friendly, supportive, accepting, affectionate, and positive toward them. I am not sure how to define *intensity*.[1] Rutter (1972; 1975) uses the term *intensity* in discussions of attachment, but offers no definition. He seems to use the term in contrast to apathy (1972, pp. 18-19).

Perhaps intensity is implied in the terms *connectedness*, *bonding*, or *attachment*. Ainsworth, Bell, and Stayton (1974) defined attachment as "an affectional tie that one person or animal forms between himself and another specific one—a tie that binds them together in space and endures over time" (p. 100).

---

[1] It has been suggested to me since this paper was first published that a more appropriate term for what I have called *intensity* here may be *contingency*; that is, that children perceive adults' responses to them as contingent upon their own actions, and that adults' responses are therefore differentiated rather than undifferentiatedly warm and positive, as in the "nobody home" pattern.

However, this definition of attachment includes affection and warmth. For the sake of this discussion, the term intensity is used to refer to the child's feeling or sensing that what he does or does not do, what he is or is not, *really matters to a specific other*. I want to emphasize, at least for the sake of exposition, that warmth and intensity could be thought of as independent attributes of adult-child relationships.

To illustrate the possible distinctions between warmth and intensity, let us imagine a very young child who might vary his behavior—for instance, engage in a variety of charming tricks—just to keep someone to whom he is warmly and strongly attached in his company. In such a case the child experiences the adult intensely and as someone warm. Wishing to maintain contact implies attachment as in Ainsworth et al.'s definition cited above.

But consider also that a young child could vary her behavior in order to avoid, reduce, or otherwise minimize the contact with a specific other. In this case, the other is not experienced as warm, but is nevertheless experienced intensely. The child feels or senses that what she does or does not do, what she is or is not, really matters to that other; the child is not indifferent to the other's responses, but does not experience the other as warm. Rutter (1972) has suggested that under some conditions, children may actually develop attachments to people or objects that cause them distress. In such cases there may be an intense relationship, but not a warm or affectionate one.

I am not, of course, advocating such intense but hostile or fear-laden relationships. I simply want to make the point that children may be able to experience adults more or less intensely, perhaps as more or less powerful, independently of their warmth or coldness. In Figure 9–1, the two variables, warmth and intensity, are combined into a typology in order to show where the two types of preschool programs I have described might fit. Given this hypothesized independence of warmth and intensity, I now focus on the way this particular aspect of child–adult relationships may help to inform us about aspects of teaching in preschool programs.

Intensity and Intentionality

A central thesis here is that our traditional emphasis on warmth, and our *under*emphasis on intensity, indicated in

Figure 9–1 as Type C programs, may help to account for the general observation that such programs have had a weaker impact on intellectual development than we had hoped. (It should be noted, however, that statements about the intellectual developmental outcomes of programs are at best impressionistic since they are not usually evaluated. Rather, evaluations typically assess academic outcomes.) The low emphasis on warmth and intensity of the Type D programs may have positive effects on children's academic development, at least in the short term, but may similarly fail to stimulate and strengthen intellectual development.

Some academic or preacademic preschool programs (such as the Engelmann-Becker Model from the University of Oregon) seem to fit into the Type B combination of the two variables. In pure form, Type B resembles a military academy. In such programs of low warmth and high intensity, academic progress is likely to be satisfactory (Smith, 1975), at least in the short term. The effects of Type B programs upon intellectual development have not been reported since intellectual development is not usually assessed. However, the typology presented here suggests that Type A programs, characterized by both high warmth and high intensity, may provide an optimal preschool environment that fosters both intellectual and psychosocial development.

A central thesis of this chapter is that optimal intensity of relationships between children and specific adults helps young children to develop their capacities for intentional behavior. A related hypothesis is that the exercise of the capacity for intentionality helps children to organize their own behavior, to set, pursue, realize, and achieve their own purposes.

Let us look again at the simple example of the young child who wants to keep a loved one in his or her company. When we say "wants" in this example, we are implying that the child has intentions. Escalona suggested that, when they are as young as 8 months, babies can and do "direct responses toward other persons as a means of obtaining an effect . . . "(1973, p. 56). Thus, during the first year, the capacity for intentional behavior emerges. The same capacity for intentional behavior is also at work when a baby wants to avoid another. It is reasonable to assume that it is not only in the case of warm bonds or relationships that the capacity for intentional behavior is developed. There is probably some kind of optimal intensity (and warmth) in the responses of adults to young children, such that either extremely weak or strong intensity of response to a child might equally, though via different mechanisms, disturb the development of the child's capacity for intentional behavior.

I am suggesting, then, that intense (and, I hope, warm) relationships between young children and specific adults may provide the contexts in which their ultimate capacities for purposeful living are shaped, strengthened, and cultivated. What seems especially relevant to our field, however, is the possibility that the very young child's emerging and developing capacity for intentional behavior also serves as the rudimentary form of hypothesis formulating and testing that characterizes the life of the mind. The very young child who intends to cause an effect (such as "stay with me" or "stay away from me" in our earlier example) engages in an early form of *if–then* thinking, or perhaps *this-behavior-is-related-to-that-effect* thinking. These possibilities seem to be supported by recent reports of research on mother-infant attachment. (Remember, however, that in definitions of attachment both intensity and affection—warmth—are usually combined.)

Ainsworth reported differences in the quality of mother's behavior for those infants in their first year whose attachments were what she labeled "secure" (n.d.). Among the differences Ainsworth reported were greater frequency of face-to-face vocalization and greater intensity of response in the mothers of securely attached infants than for less securely attached infants. Ainsworth indicated that the quality of maternal behavior she called "sensitivity" involved a highly differentiated tailoring of responses to match the baby's signals (Ainsworth, n.d.). These findings are hardly surprising. The picture of adult–child relationships given by this research is that in the case of the securely attached child there is an adult who is "home," someone who responds, who follows through, who engages the young child in sequences of connected interactions, and who also is warm. M. P. M. Richards captured this quality in "First Steps in Becoming Social."

> One of the first things that is required . . . is for you to be sure that your partner is actually attending to you and is involved in communication with you . . . within weeks of birth. . . . There are long sequences of interaction where the first fumbling links of intersubjectivity are made. The infant looks at the caretaker's face. The caretaker looks back into the eyes of the infant. A smile moves on the infant's face. The adult responds with a vocal greeting and a

smile. There is mutual acknowledgment. The "meaning" of this exchange does not simply depend on the action patterns employed by the two participants. Each must fit his sequence of actions with that of the other; if this is not done, the exchange may well become meaningless. An important means of knowing that a message is intended for you is that it follows an alternating sequence with yours. (1974, p. 92)

The significant aspect of the child–caretaker relationship here is that a sequence of responses is involved in which one party responds to the other in a sustained flow of behavioral responses that is similar to a conversation. These behavior "conversations," in which each party responds after taking into account information embedded in the other's response, seem to be early experiences in child–adult relationships essential to the development of the intellect, and ultimately to the capacity to think for oneself as well as to be able to organize one's own purposes and behavior.

Many programs for very young children have implemented the research on early deprivation and stimulation by dangling colorful and varied objects in front of babies. Certainly such adult activities can be stimulating. I am suggesting that mere stimulation is not enough for the intellect to grow on, but that sequences of meaningful interactions—"behavioral conversations"—may be required.

I have a hunch that the latter concern with interaction outlined above is in some way connected to the development of a child's disposition to be interested in relevant and worthwhile phenomena. Getzels (1969) defined interest as a characteristic disposition that impels an individual to seek out particular objects, activities, skills, understandings, or goals for attention and acquisition. As I look at the research on infants, it seems that the earliest form of the capacity for interest is what was called the *orienting response* (Cohen, 1973) or *attentional responsivity* (Porges, 1974) and later was called *attention* (see Chapter 6). The research of Porges and Cohen suggests that very early in life infants have the capacity for two different kinds of responses to stimulation: one is an alarm/flight response, characterized by cardiac acceleration; the other response seems to be cardiac deceleration and stability during information processing or attending. Optimal development implies cultivating the capacities for both types of responses. I doubt whether it is necessary to deliberately foster the capacity for the alarm/flight response. But

I suggest that among many criteria, one to use to evaluate programs for young children is the extent to which the adults' responses and the activities provided encourage children's absorption, involvement, or interest (for example, attending without alarm) in a sustained way over increasingly large segments of time.

In summary, these concerns about warmth and intensity imply a heavy burden on preschool teachers and child care staff. A Type A program seems to require that teachers maintain optimal vigilance and concentration on the children's activities in order not to miss cues embedded in their behavior. These cues inform adults about children's intentions, meanings, and potential interests, and thus inform their conversations. Factors that might be related to such child–adult relationships yield the further concerns to which I now turn.

ADULT–CHILD RELATIONSHIPS

Before examining worrisome aspects of adult–child relationships, I would like to present the assumptions on which the implications for teachers' roles are drawn.

Reciprocity and Symmetry

The first assumption is that while relationships between adults and children may be reciprocal, they are not symmetrical in many important respects. Perhaps the easiest illustration of reciprocal but asymmetrical relationships are cases of unrequited love, as exemplified in the early stages of the relationship between Cyrano de Bergerac and Roxanne in Rostand's drama. Most of us are probably familiar with those cases in which young children in primary school "fall in love" with their teachers. In these illustrations, reciprocal relationships are asymmetrical on a dimension of a certain kind of love. The teacher may be fond of the child, warm and accepting of him or her, but does not return the quality of love the child has for her. Similarly, the extent to which a child is dependent upon an adult might be reciprocated by the adult being dependable. But the distribution of dependency is asymmetrical in that a child experiences greater dependency on the adult than vice versa. The concept of asymmetry is relevant here, since young children may feel very attached (have warm intense relationships) to adult caregivers and teachers, but the caregivers may not experience maternal attachment to each child in their care.

Particularism and Universalism

A second assumption is that symmetry in the attachments (that is, the warmth plus intensity) of caregivers and teachers to children may not be possible. Here I am using the Parsonian (Parsons, 1964) distinction between relationships that are *particularistic* versus those that are *universalistic*. According to this distinction, mothers are particularistic in the sense that they are deeply emotionally involved in the child's welfare—if necessary, at the expense of other children. This irrational (hopefully optimal) attachment, which gives rise to strong affection as well as impassioned anger, seems to be functional for parent–child relationships (see Chapter 10).

By contrast, teachers and child care workers are expected and duty bound to apply all their skills and resources universalistically to each client without bias. It would be dysfunctional for a caregiver or teacher to yield to parental pressures to give their child "a break." As McPherson (1972) points out, "Whatever the teacher's style, her universalistic relationship to the pupil is central to her role" (p. 122). McPherson also points out that even though the teacher seems to use love in her teaching, she still has the brakes on. If this were not so, according to Jules Henry (1963), "Children would have to be dragged shrieking from grade to grade and most teachers would flee teaching, for the mutual attachment would be so deep that its annual severing would be too much for either to bear." There is thus a necessary asymmetry in attachment such that children are more strongly attached to their teachers than the reverse.

Optimal Distance and Burn-out

While optimal attachment between mother and child seems essential to many aspects of early development, including early intellectual growth, the universalistic pattern for adults who work with the young in preschool settings implies that such adults must strive for an optimal distance between themselves and the children. Optimal distance is valuable in that it permits the adult to act on the basis of the principles and knowledge of the field; that is, to maximize the rational aspects of the profession. Optimal distance can also serve to protect the teacher or caregiver from what otherwise would be an excessive emotional burden as indicated in the quotation from Henry cited above.

I also implied that there may be situational and pragmatic reasons why deep involvement or minimum distance between teachers and caregivers and children might not be feasible for child care workers. If child care workers were to become as intensely involved with the children as the children's own parents should, they could be expected to be emotionally burned out within a few months. Perhaps the teacher behavior patterns characterized as Type C can be explained as teachers' efforts to cope with the potential threat of becoming burned out. The "nobody home" phenomenon observed among some teachers of young children may result from having to achieve some kind of distance between themselves and their charges. Perhaps it can be thought of as a routinization or ritualization of warmth and intensity.

Another aspect of the distinction between patterns of mothering and of teaching is the degree of deliberateness, intentionality, or cognitive control of behavior. It would seem wise to encourage parents to be spontaneous rather than clinical or analytical with their children. Excessive self-consciousness for parents may lead to "analysis paralysis." It may be that when parents act in terms of cerebral or logically-derived decision making, their best resolutions break down under the weight of what is and should be the emotionally loaded nature of the relationship. In other words, the cognitive controls would not hold for very long!

IMPLICATIONS FOR TEACHERS AND CAREGIVERS

In contrast to the nature of parent–child relationships, it seems essential for teachers and caregivers to be intentional and deliberate; to plan and think through their activities on the basis of their knowledge of the underlying principles of child development and learning. Furthermore, optimal distance permits the teacher or child care worker to evaluate the child's progress realistically and thus to be in a stronger position to think and plan subsequent actions.

Now we seem to have a paradox: children's intellectual and social development (Program Type A) seem to require that their relationships with adults be both warm and intense—that they be optimally attached. Conversely, teachers and child care workers seem to require optimum distance from the children, suggesting that asymmetry in attachment between teachers and children is desirable. Can intense relationships, so essentially particularistic, be universalized? Are we, in child care centers especially, trying to professionalize motherhood? Is not the latter an inherent contradiction? These may be moot questions. Children are entering preschool and child care centers in increasing numbers and at younger ages. The pressing question is: What is required to ensure that these settings provide the best possible quality of relationships, the optimal combination of warmth and intensity, for young children to grow on?

I have suggested that for optimal relationships between children and adults to develop, as in the Type A programs, the adults must be vigilant and attentive, and in general they must concentrate on the sequential flow of meanings of children's responses to them. The extent to which child care workers and teachers are able to do so seems to be undermined by various aspects of the working conditions that are generally characteristic of preschool and child care settings.

In the United States working conditions in many child care centers are scandalously poor. Keyserling (1972) summarized some findings on working conditions and stated:

> the pay is so low that we are asking thousands of nonprofessional workers to subsidize the care of children of other women. We are also excluding from the day care field many women of intelligence and competence who cannot afford to accept salaries as low as some of those described, no matter how rewarding is work with youngsters, in human terms. (p. 107)

The low pay is also related to high staff turnover which, in turn, may undermine the stability of the child–adult relationships as well as nullify in-service training efforts.

Arvin and Sassen (1974) reported an investigation of the working conditions in corporation-based daycare centers. Not only was the pay per hour low but " . . . teachers work through the day with no real break" (p. 15). During lunch they had staff meetings. The frequent absence of job security and of adequate benefits, plus the many extra hours of work without compensation that is common in the profit-making daycare centers, contribute to the generally dismal picture of the "profession." It should be noted also that often when teachers complain about low wages, they are accused of not caring about children!

Another aspect of working conditions in preschool settings, especially daycare centers, seems to be an apparently deep sense of isolation reported by many child care workers. Many report feeling overwhelmed by the children's obvious emotional needs. Others report experiencing frustration and anguish from the knowledge of individual client families' personal and economic distress, and of the way much modern urban life impinges upon the lives of the families they serve. A caring child care worker could easily and quickly be burned out from such intense involvement in client's troubles. My hunch is that many respond to their working situation by becoming depressed and sometimes indifferent, and perhaps too distant from the children.

Such psychological depression or burn-out may result in low concentration, low vigilance, and a generally low rate of responding to children. Certainly low staff morale can hardly be expected to support sensitivity in staff responses. Such conditions would seem to reduce the likelihood that adults would be alert enough to tailor their responses to children's signals and meanings. Often adults working in such situations seem to fall into the habit of talking to each other much of the time (Weir, 1973). Their occasional responses to the children may be warm and friendly but they are unlikely to be marked by the intensity I have suggested to be essential for intellectual development.

It seems to me that one fairly reliable and universal correlation describing preschool educators is that the younger the child one works with, the less training one will have received, the lower the pay, prestige and status one has, and often, the longer the working hours!

Future Prospects

I have a strong hunch that we cannot have optimal environments for children unless the working conditions for their caregivers and teachers are also optimal. Obviously, the interacting forces and factors that influence the ultimate quality of children's experiences in preschool settings must be tackled on many levels and in many areas simultaneously.

Some recommend accelerating the trend toward genuine professionalization of child care workers. But alongside this trend is some antiprofessional sentiment as well. Increasing professionalization seems somewhat unrealistic at present, particularly in light of the typical compensation of child care workers. Some advocate the unionization of early childhood workers. It is difficult to predict the outcomes of such a movement when, on the whole, the larger community seems to be more interested in the availability rather than the quality of child care services.

Efforts to reduce the isolation of child care workers might be helpful. The provision of advisory services and in-service support could be helpful (see Chapter 16). Small and regular on-site workshops for groups of colleagues may also reduce the sense of isolation and strengthen mutual support among co-workers.

The development of parent cooperative daycare centers seems to merit further investigation and experimentation. Faragher, Garskof, and Hoffnung (1975) have shown how parent cooperative group care can have positive effects on staff morale.

Increasing our efforts and programs for working with adolescents may also help the situation in several ways. First, because today's adolescents are tomorrow's child-care and preschool clients, activities that improve their understanding of young children may contribute to later caregiving competence. But the transmission of information and knowledge alone may not have much impact. Secondly, it may be that many adolescents themselves lack sufficient direct experience with caring, thinking, responsive self-respecting adults.

Efforts to enhance public understanding of what early childhood educators try to accomplish may be timely. By this I am not suggesting pressure groups, conventional public relations, or other types of "propaganda." Rather, I propose that we share insights and understandings about children's development so as to encourage the public to ask what can be done to help our children, rather than to focus on finding out who is at fault or who can be blamed for the plight of many young families.

SUMMARY

In summary, I have tried to show that the development of young children's capacities to organize their own behavior and to think for themselves may require difficult modifications in the relationships between adults and children. The issues raised seem especially urgent in societies in which individuals must ultimately be able to make decisions and choices, to select from among wide varieties of alternative ideas, options, beliefs, values, and lifestyles. It may be that in order to function adequately in such complex societies it is necessary to have early experience with intense (as well as warm) relationships with one or more adult. At this point we do not know enough about the comparative effects of multiple caregivers who have homogeneous response patterns versus the single caregiver whose own pattern varies widely. The recent glowing reports of child care from visitors to the People's Republic of China may cause us to overlook the point that in collective societies the development of individual organization of behavior, ideas, and intentions may not seem urgent. On the contrary, in collective societies individual purposes and intentions may be nonfunctional. Perhaps in individualistic societies, the price many pay for individuality is loneliness.

Many years ago C. Wright Mills (1959) made a distinction between urgent public issues as they are officially formulated and insistent human troubles as they are privately felt: "The human meaning of public issues must be revealed by relating them to personal troubles—and to the problems of the individual life" (p. 226).

I have tried to show that the personal troubles of the young, as well as those of their caregivers and teachers in preschool settings, are embedded in larger public issues. We seem to be in need of an officially formulated public policy aimed at improving the working conditions of caregivers and ultimately improving the quality of the day-to-day lives of the children with whom they work.

REFERENCES

Ainsworth, M. D. (n.d.). The development of infant–mother attachment. *A final report to the Office of Child Development.* Urbana, IL: ERIC Clearinghouse on Early Childhood Education. (ED 122 924).

Ainsworth, M. D., Bell, S., & Stayton, D. (1974). Infant–mother attachment and social development: 'Socialization' as a product of reciprocal responsiveness to signals. In M. P. M. Richards (Ed.), *The integration of a child into a social world.* New York: Cambridge University Press.

Almy, M. (1975). *The early childhood educator at work.* New York: McGraw-Hill.

Arvin, C., & Sassen, G. (1974). *Corporations and child care: Profit-making day care, workplace day care and a look at the alternatives.* Cambridge, MA: Women's Research Action Project.

Beyer, E. (1968). *Teaching young children.* New York: Pegasus.

Cohen, L. B. (1973). A two process model of infant visual attention. *Merrill-Palmer Quarterly, 19*(3), 157–180.

Escalona, S. K. (1973). Overview of hypotheses and inference. In L. J.. Stone, H. T. Smith, & L. B. Murphy (Eds.), *The competent infant.* New York: Basic Books.

Faragher, J., Garskof, B., & Hoffnung, M. (1975). *Parent cooperative group child care.* Urbana, IL: ERIC Clearinghouse on Early Childhood Education.

Getzels, M. J. (1969). A social psychology of education. In G. Lindzey & E. Aronson (Eds.), *Handbook of Social Psychology: Vol. 5.* (2nd ed.). Reading, MA: Addison-Wesley.

Henry, J. (1963, Spring). American schoolrooms: Learning the nightmare. *Columbia University Forum, 6,* 24–30.

Keyserling, M. D. (1972). *Windows on day care.* New York: National Council of Jewish Women.

McPherson, G. (1972). *Small town teacher.* Cambridge, MA: Harvard University Press.

Mills, C. W. (1959). *The sociological imagination.* New York: Grove Press.

Parsons, T. (1964). *The social system.* New York: Free Press of Glencoe.

Porges, S. W. (1974). Heart rate indices of newborn attentional responsivity. *Merrill-Palmer Quarterly, 20*(4), 231–254.

Richards, M. P. M. (1974). First steps in becoming social. In M. P. M. Richards (Ed.), *The integration of a child into a social world.* New York: Cambridge University Press.

Rutter, M. (1972). *Maternal deprivation reassessed.* Middlesex, England: Penguin Books.

Rutter, M. (1975). *Helping troubled children.* New York: Plenum Press.

Smith, M. S. (1975). Evaluation findings in Head Start planned variation. In A. Rivlin & P.M. Timpane (Eds.), *Planned variation in education.* Washington, DC: Brookings Institution.

Stallings, J. (1975). *Implementation and child effects of teaching practices in Follow Through classrooms.* Monographs of the Society for Research and Child Development 40, nos. 7–8, serial no. 1632.

Weir, M. K. (1973). An observational study of language behavior of caregivers toward infants enrolled in day care centers. Unpublished doctoral dissertation, University of Illinois.

Willer, B. (1987). *The child care crisis.* Washington, DC: The National Association for the Education of Young Children.

10

MOTHERING AND TEACHING: SOME SIGNIFICANT DISTINCTIONS*

My concern with the topic of this chapter was stimulated by conference presentations, magazine articles, pamphlets, and brochures that featured slogans to the effect that a parent is the child's first teacher—sometimes the child's best teacher. At the same time I was working with many teachers—especially in child care programs—who seemed on the verge of burnout caused, in part, by their commitment to many of their charges who seemed to be in need of mothering.

If I were writing this paper today, I would surely cast the ideas in terms of distinctions between parenting and teaching rather than just mothering and teaching! A slow but inevitably steady trend toward fathers taking more direct participation in childrearing than in previous generations is indeed apparent.

In other respects, I doubt whether I would change the main ideas in the paper in any way if I were preparing it today. There are many parent education and parent involvement programs that use variations of the slogan "parents as teachers" and "parents as first teachers" in their literature and even in their official titles; it is even included in our list of national goals, now known as Goals 2000: Educate America. Nevertheless, it seems more realistic and appropriate to see the roles of parents and teachers as complementary but distinctive, as explained in the chapter that follows.

---

* This chapter was originally published as "Mothering and Teaching—Some Significant Distinctions," by Lilian G. Katz, 1980. In L. G. Katz (Ed.), *Current Topics in Early Childhood Education: Vol. III* (pp. 47–64). Norwood, NJ: Ablex. Reprinted with permission.

DISTINCTIONS BETWEEN MOTHERING[1] AND TEACHING

The problems facing American families have received widespread attention in recent years. Newspapers and magazines have capitalized on and perhaps contributed to a mounting sense of alarm over the imminent disappearance of "the family." The 1980 White House Conference on the Family was reported to have been the occasion of bitter factional disputes over fundamental views on the family and the extent to which public agencies can be expected to support beleaguered families and unconventional living arrangements.

Much of the talk in conferences and panel discussions and many reports in the media betray a belief that in the "good old days" families were wonderful, warm, comfortable and benign—always ready to provide the young with a harmonious and affectionate environment in which to grow. It is of some interest to note that the nostalgia in such discussions occurs at a time when the literature on the history of childhood and family life has been growing very rapidly.[2] The chances are that in the 1970s more has been written on the history of women, children, and families than in all the centuries before.

In general, the historical accounts of families and childhood now available suggest that the "good old days" were awful, especially for children (Langer, 1974; Stone, 1975, 1977; Wishy, 1972). In the not-so-distant past, at least in the Western world, adults were enjoined to save children from certain damnation, to break their wills, and to engage in other forms of what we would now call child abuse, mostly of a psychological type (see Wishy, 1972). For the majority of children, the history of childhood suggests a record of almost uninterrupted hunger, disease, psychological and physical abuse, and other miseries. On the average, the qual-

---

[1] The teacher-parent distinction discussed here may apply just as well to fathers as to mothers. There appears to be no biological or other *a priori* reason why the behaviors and feelings attributed to mothers in this discussion could not also be ascribed to fathers. Current research indicates that fathers do have a powerful impact upon their young children's development; however, though it is equally important, the nature of the father's influence is different from the mother's (Zigler & Cascione, 1980).

[2] A review of history indicates persuasively that although "child abuse" may be a modern term, the phenomenon is not a modern one (Langer, 1974; Stone 1977). It may be that the standards by which we define child abuse are constantly revised upwards so that today's norm is tomorrow's abuse. Perhaps this tendency is in the nature of the development and history of civilization.

ity of life for children is most likely much better, by absolute standards, than it has ever been before.

In the United States, we sometimes forget that the Fair Labor Standards Act, which protected children from unfair labor practices, was not enacted until 1939. It has been widely acknowledged that even then, the Act was passed because children were occupying jobs badly needed by unemployed adults during the 1930s.

We often attribute our family and childrearing problems to a vague phenomenon we refer to as "change." Change has always been with us, and ideally it always will be. Perhaps the rate at which social and economic patterns change has accelerated so greatly that they occur within generations rather than simply between them. Perhaps another source of upheaval is that changes affecting families and educators are not sufficiently synchronized—some parts of our lives change faster than other parts. One of the most vivid examples of poor synchronization of changes is that of increasing numbers of young mothers entering the labor force without corresponding increases in the provision of sufficient child care provisions and facilities of good quality.

The widespread feeling of frustration currently reported by parents and educators of young children cannot be alleviated by romanticizing the past, which, it turns out, was nothing to shout about for most of our ancestors. Since we constantly change the standards by which we define the "good life," some sense of failure, of falling below our ideals, is always likely to stalk us.

A contemporary view of family life indicates that although most children still live in families rather than institutions, specific family arrangements are changing. Families are smaller, and many more of them are headed by single parents. It may be helpful to keep in mind that the particular family arrangement a child grows up with is not as important to the child's psychosocial development as are the meanings he or she gives to that arrangement. Thus, for example, if one grows up without a father, the significance of such paternal deprivation will vary depending upon the meaning given to the deprivation. If the father is absent because he has gone off to war to save the country and preserve our freedom, the meaning of the absence will take a particular form. If nearly all the fathers of most peers have also gone off to war, father absence may be a shared, ennobling hardship. Indeed, in such a case, father presence might be insufferable to youngsters at certain ages.

If, on the other hand, the deprivation is due to the father's desertion of the family, it may have a different meaning. If the father is in prison for a heinous crime, then again the absence will very likely have another meaning to the child. If all one's peers' fathers are present, the meaning of the absence of one's own may cause painful feelings. If the separation or divorce of parents—a frequent cause of father deprivation—alleviates pre-separation disharmony and stress, father absence may take on a different meaning than it would have in other cases. The point is that deprivation itself cannot determine the outcome of a child's development, but the meaning the young child gives to that deprivation and the feelings those meanings engender may have significant effects on his or her development. One of the major responsibilities of caregivers is to help children give appropriate meaning to their experiences and cope with their feelings.

We seem to be at a point in social history when parents have great responsibility (although perhaps not enough authority) for helping their children to develop personalities capable of early self-sufficiency and autonomy (LeVine, 1980), to acquire complex motivational patterns that will enable them to make long-term occupational and career commitments, and to make choices from among a variety of possible lifestyles. Many of the stresses of parenting stem from the wide range of choices, alternatives, and options available to modern Americans in virtually every aspect of life. It is not difficult to imagine how many fewer arguments, heated discussions, and reductions in demanding behavior on the part of children would follow from having to live with minimal or even no choices in such things as food, television shows, toys, clothes, and so forth!

To some extent, parental stress is exacerbated by the shrinking size of the family. In times when families included seven or eight children, anxiety about the growth and accomplishments could be spread over the group. If one or two did well, three or four got by, and the rest were not much to brag about, the parents might still have been able to walk in the neighborhood with their heads held up. Fifty years ago, the offspring at the bottom of the pile could be accounted for by their resemblance to an uncle or great aunt from a particular branch or "the other side" of the family! However, the progress of social and behavioral sciences has heightened awareness of the centrality of parental influences on the outcome of development. Few today would buy the excuse of a "bad seed" occasionally showing up in descendants. A family with only one or two children may be putting too many eggs in the proverbial basket for it to be carried safely.

Because the family is potentially the source of the greatest good, it is also, in equal proportion, potentially the source of the greatest damage and pain. Ideally, the family is the major provider of support, warmth, comfort, protection, identity, and so forth. But when the family falls short in these provisions, suffering can be acute, and disturbances in development may result.

It is unlikely that parents were more devoted to their children in bygone days than they are today. The task of parenting has become more complex, and the impact of parental failure more serious. It is important to note that in every social class there are many children whose psychological lives are destroyed by their families. I should add that some of those children may be saved by one or two teachers who give them the support, recognition, and encouragement that is missing from other sources.

In fact, there is increasing pressure (often self-imposed) on teachers in child care centers, preschools, and primary classes to respond to the apparent needs of children, needs that are assumed to be unmet by their busy, working, and in many cases single parents. At the same time, there is growing enthusiasm for parent training and education and parent involvement in schooling. Among the outcomes of research on young children is the welcome acknowledgment that parents' behavior plays a central role in their youngsters' intellectual development.

The influence of parents on their children's personalities has long been recognized, if not exaggerated. But recent research findings, exemplified by the well-known works of Levenstein (1970), Schaefer (1979), White, Kaban, and Attanucci (1979), and others are reflected in such catchphrases as "Parents are the child's first teacher" or even "Parents are the child's best teacher." New optimism about the potential educational role of parents has given rise to numerous programs designed to help parents become more effective teachers of their young children. The objectives of many of these programs go beyond strengthening specific parenting skills to include training in tutorial and instructional skills as well.

In summary, pressures seem to mount on mothers to instruct their children in ways that will render them more responsive to schooling, perhaps in part due to a lack of confidence in teachers and schools and a sense of urgency in getting children started on the academic treadmill early. On the other hand, it is not unusual to hear teachers of young children complain that they must supply the nurturance and affection children seem to need before instruction can be effective. While mothers often believe that their children might better attain academic success if teachers were more competent, teachers often believe that their own efforts would be more successful if mothers only attended properly to their children's psychosocial needs. So long as such recriminatory attitudes persist, parent–teacher relationships can be characterized as missed opportunities for mutual support.

DIMENSIONS OF DISTINCTION BETWEEN PARENTS AND TEACHERS

It is obvious that teachers do many of the same things with young children that mothers do, and vice versa. It is in the nature of young children that from time to time they require of their teachers in preschool and kindergarten some of the same tending, caring, and guiding given them by their mothers at home. Similarly, mothers frequently help their children to acquire knowledge and skills that teachers do. Although the behavior of the two role-takers is likely to overlap on each of the seven dimensions discussed below, the central tendencies of each can be expected to yield the distinctions indicated in Table 10–1. In the service of exploration of the issues, distinctions between the two roles are somewhat exaggerated; no role-takers occur as the pure types described here. Furthermore, it should be understood that although the dimensions on which the roles of mothers and teachers are distinguished interact with each other, these dimensions are enumerated separately in order to highlight potential problems arising from confusion between them.

Scope of Functions

In a discussion of some of the discontinuities between families and schools, Getzels (1974) points out that the two institutions are discontinuous in at least two ways: specifically, in the scope and the affectivity characterizing relationships in the two settings.

TABLE 10-1   DISTINCTIONS BETWEEN MOTHERING AND TEACHING
IN THEIR CENTRAL TENDENCIES ON SEVEN DIMENSIONS

Role Dimension	Mothering	Teaching
1. Scope of Functions	Diffuse and Limitless	Specific and Limited
2. Intensity of Affect	High	Low
3. Attachment	Optimum Attachment	Optimum Detachment
4. Rationality	Optimum Irrationality	Optimum Rationality
5. Spontaneity	Optimum Spontaneity	Optimum Intentionality
6. Partiality	Partial	Impartial
7. Scope of Responsibility	Individual	Whole Group

Under the rubric of scope, Getzels points out that the functions to be fulfilled by the family are diffused and limitless, in contradistinction to those of the school, which are specific and limited. The all-encompassing scope of the responsibilities, duties, and potential content of the relationships within families is taken for granted. There is, according to Getzels, nothing about the young child that is not the parents' business. Thus, it is unnecessary to prove that any aspect of the child's life is within the purview of the family.

However, in the case of the school, relationships between teachers and children are specific in scope, function, and content in that the legitimate area of interaction "is limited to a particular technically defined sphere, and what is not conceded to the school because of its special competence remains the private affair of the participants" (Getzels, 1974, p. 48).

Similarly, Newson and Newson (1976) point out that the responsibility society "enjoins on parents to their young children is quite different from that which it expects from teachers, nurses and other professionals . . . for one thing it has no fixed hours . . . parents of preschool children never go off duty" (p. 400).

Hess (1980) also points out that the "relationship between child and parent is different in several ways from the relationship between child and caregiver. The mother-child relationship calls for and justifies more direct, intimate interaction, including anger and discipline as well as love and support" (p. 149).

The distinctions in scope of functions proposed by Getzels (1974), by Newson and Newson (1976), and by Hess (1980) appear to become greater and sharper as the pupil grows older. To teachers in preschools and primary schools, the distinctions are problematic precisely because of the age of the child: the younger the child, the wider the range of functioning for which adults must assume responsibility. Thus, age—and the level of maturity associated with it—in and of itself gives rise to confusion between the two roles. To expect child care or preschool and primary school teachers to accept as wide a scope of functions as mothers do serves to exacerbate the longstanding problems of unclear role boundaries.

Intensity of Affect

It seem reasonable to assume that both the intensity of affect (of all kinds) and the frequency with which behavior is marked by intense affect would also distinguish the two sets of role-takers. That is to say that on the average, when the central tendencies of mothers are compared with those of teachers, we should find more frequent and greater affective intensity in the behavior of mothers toward their children than the behavior of teachers in interaction with their pupils. As Rubenstein and Howes (1979) have pointed out, the role of day care teachers is "both more specified and limited than the role of mother at home . . . the mother's emotional investment may enhance the likelihood of high-intensity affective response" (p. 3).

Newson and Newson (1976) address this dimension by calling it "involvement" and suggest that quality makes parents different from other more "professional" caretakers. Specifically, they point out that

a good parent–child relationship is in fact very unlike a good teacher-child relationship; yet because the roles have certain ingredients in common, though in different proportions (nurturance, discipline, information-giving, for example), they are sometimes confused by the participants themselves, to the misunderstanding of all concerned. (pp. 401–402)

Pressure on parents to take on more instructional functions can lead to a variety of difficulties, one of which is exemplified in the case of a mother of a child with learning disabilities. The mother reported that she and her child were enrolled in a special home intervention program designed to teach mothers to give their learning-disabled children regular rigorous instruction and skill training at home. Although unintended by the program leaders, one effect was that the mother became so anxious about helping her son to meet the specified learning objectives set for them both that their relationship deteriorated. With each lesson in which he fell behind, she became disappointed and tense, and the child became nervous and recalcitrant, which, in turn, increased her own disappointment and tension, and so forth until, as she reported, she realized that "the boy had no mother." She withdrew from the lessons and asked the professionals to continue to teach him while she supported his struggle to learn by being the relatively soft, understanding, encouraging, and nondemanding adult in his life.

In some ways, this story reminds us of common problems encountered when trying to teach a close friend or relative to drive a car. We become aware of how much easier it is to be patient and understanding of a stranger than of someone close to us. Very often, the stress encountered in trying to teach someone very close to us places a heavy burden on the relationship.

In sum, one would expect the average level of affective intensity of the two role-takers to be distinguished from each other as indicated in Table 10–1. The affectivity dimension is closely related to the attachment dimension, which is discussed in the following section.

Attachment

Although the term *attachment* is widely used in professional as well as popular literature on child development and child rearing, it is a difficult one to define. In the literature on infant development, attachment refers to an underlying variable inferred from infants' reactions to strangers and to separations and reunions with primary caretakers (Cohen, 1974). Rutter (1979) indicates that attachment is a construct involving several features, noting that the concept should be distinguished from *bonding* to adults. The available definitions focus almost exclusively on the attachment of the child to adults. What is required for this discussion is a way of defining the attachment of the adults to their children. Ramey and Farran (1978) offer a broad definition of adult–child attachment, using the term *functional maternal attachment* to mean "simply those caregiving functions that must be performed for infants to sustain a normal development" (p. 2). The set of functions includes "at a minimum a refrain from physical and verbal abuse, the provision of information and affection, and direct personal involvement with the infant" (p. 2).

Research on the reciprocity and rhythmicity that characterizes normal mother–infant relationships brings us closer to a way of defining attachment so that the adult's attachment to the child is included. For the purposes of this discussion, attachment is defined as the capacity to be aroused to a wide range of behaviors and intense feelings by the status and behavior of the child. If the attachment is a mutual one, then one would expect the behavior and feelings of either member of the pair to activate strong feelings and/or reactions in the other. This definition is intended to include such feelings on the part of the adult as anxiety, alarm, fear, anger, and rage, as well as the proverbial "pride and joy" and other tender, loving, and caring emotions. Common usage of the term tends to refer primarily to the nurturant side of the spectrum of feelings and behaviors of adults and to overlook the point that intense rage or terror in the face of impending danger to the child are also manifestations of what we call attachment. The definition proposed here implies that the opposite of attachment is not rejection or anger, but indifference.

The entry in Table 10–1 called *optimum attachment* is intended to reflect the notion that whereas development could be jeopardized by mother–child attachment that is too weak, it could also be undermined by excessive attachment, commonly called "smother love."[3]

The optimum attachment recommended here as an ideal feature of mother-child relationships is distinguished from the optimum detachment that should mark teacher–child relationships. The latter is sometimes referred to as "detached concern" (Maslach & Pines, 1977). The term *detachment* is used not only to

---

[3] What constitutes an optimum level of attachment for any given mother–child pair would be difficult to predict or prespecify since we only know whether the attachment is optimum if the child is observed to be thriving; however, failure to thrive may not always be attributable to disturbances in attachment.

characterize the distinctions in the functions of the two role-takers, but to suggest also that it is appropriate for professionals to make self-conscious or deliberate efforts to distance themselves *optimally* from their clients. As Maslach and Pines (1977) have suggested, people who work intensively and intimately with other people for extended periods of time inevitably suffer stresses associated with strong emotional arousal. As they point out, one of the ways of coping with such potential stress is to adopt techniques of detachment, which vary in their effectiveness as well as in their relationship to the conduct of work: "By treating one's clients or patients in a more objective, detached way, it becomes easier to perform the necessary interviews, tests, or operations without suffering from strong psychological discomfort" (p. 100). The authors go on to suggest that "detached concern" is a term that conveys "the difficult (and almost paradoxical) position of having to distance oneself from people in order to cure them" (p. 100).

Teachers who are unable to detach themselves optimally from their pupils and thus become too close to them are likely to suffer emotional burnout, a syndrome typically accompanied by a loss of the capacity to feel anything at all for the client. Certainly, those who are too detached, for whatever reason, are unlikely to be effective in their work with children because such extreme detachment is also accompanied by low responsiveness to client needs and demands.

One of the advantages mothers have over teachers in dealing with the stresses of attachment, in addition to intense affect, is their tacit knowledge that their child's psychological and physical dependency upon them will slowly but surely be outgrown. Teachers of day care, preschool, and kindergarten children, on the other hand, must cope with dependent children year in and year out. They must protect themselves from potential burnout by developing an optimum level of detached concern—optimum in terms of their own emotional stability and effective functioning.

It should be noted also that teachers who are suspected of cultivating close attachments to their pupils in order to "meet their own personal needs," as the saying goes, are subject to substantial derision from colleagues and other professionals. Occasionally, such teachers come to perceive themselves as protecting children from their own parents, and occasionally the child's responsiveness to such teacher closeness gives rise to parental jealousy. As Anna Freud (1952) pointed out long ago, a teacher is neither mother nor therapist. A teacher with objective attitudes "can respond warmly enough to satisfy children without getting herself involved to a dangerous extent" (p. 232). She added that a teacher must not think of herself as a "mother-substitute." If, as teachers, "we play the part of a mother, we get from the child the reactions which are appropriate for the mother–child relationship" (p. 231). All of this could result in rivalry with mothers and other undesirable consequences, making teacher–mother mutual support and complementarity difficult to develop.

Optimum detachment is also desirable for teachers because it can free them to make realistic evaluations of their pupils' development and learning—a major component of their work. Mothers, on the other hand, may not have to make realistic or so-called objective evaluations of their children's growth very often, although their lack of realism is a frequent source of frustration to teachers! In the long run, a mother's optimism about her child's progress, even if it seems excessive, is probably in the child's best interest. Such optimism in and of itself may contribute to the child's growth and development. Maternal pessimism, on the other hand, may be more damaging than any teacher's realism. Many children seem to think that their mothers, being omniscient and knowing them more fully and completely than their teachers, are in possession of the "real truth" and that when there is a discrepancy between the mother's and the teacher's evaluation, the former is more accurate. Experience suggests that individuals caught between their mother's pessimism concerning their potential for achievement and a teacher's optimism devote considerable energy to the problem of how to keep the "real truth" from the teacher, having no choice but to accept their mother's view as the true one. Such a discrepancy may account for some people's lifelong doubts about their true abilities.

Differences in the assessment of the child by the two role-takers may be related to the differences in the baselines to which the child in question is being compared. A mother may be comparing her four-year-old to about a dozen other children whom she has observed casually; a teacher may be comparing the same child to one hundred and fifty she has observed closely. They may also be due to dramatic differences in the child's behavior in the home and at school. It is not uncommon to hear both mothers and teachers comment on how strikingly different the child seems in the setting other than the one in which he or she is commonly observed. Frequently, a mother will report that the teacher's description of her child is difficult to reconcile with her own experiences with the child. Studies of this phenomenon and the ways children cope with discrepant evaluations have not been found.

Another consideration leading to the recommendation of optimum detachment for teachers is the importance of minimizing the likelihood of incidents we might call "invasions of privacy" or other forms of encroachment upon aspects of children's socialization that are the legitimate domain of the family. Similarly, optimum detachment is recommended in order to help teachers avoid the ever-present temptation to engage in favoritism. Since it is unlikely that one can be strongly attached to more than one or two pupils, the risk of favoritism increases with increasing closeness to any one pupil. The optimum-detachment approach should help to reduce those dangers.

Many early childhood workers reject the value of optimum detachment because of their deep concern for children's need to feel closeness and attachment to adults. It is not clear how the proposed detachment would affect such "needy" children. But it is useful to keep in mind that whereas the relationships between adults and children in child care, preschool, and primary classes are reciprocal, they are not necessarily symmetrical. In particular, it may be possible for young children to feel very attached to their teachers, even to worship and adore them, without the teachers' responding at the same level of intensity. Such "unrequited love" during the early years may help the child to gratify needs for cathexis without placing severe emotional burdens on teachers. Research on such asymmetrical attachment might help to clarify the potential effects on such children of the detachment of their teachers.

Rationality

It is hypothesized here that effective mothering is associated, at least in part, with optimum irrationality, and that either extreme rationality or extreme irrationality may be equally damaging to the growing child. On the one hand, extreme rationality in a mother might be perceived by the child as cool, calculating unresponsiveness. Such a perception could lead to a variety of emotional disturbances. Extreme irrationality, on the other hand, may present the growing child with a range of problems stemming from insufficient predictability of the interpersonal environment.

By using the term *optimum irrationality* I do not intend to propose chaotic, scatterbrained mindlessness! Rather, the emphasis is upon adequate depth and strength of what we sometimes call *ego-involvement*—similar in nature to attachment as defined above.

The optimum irrationality suggested here is, in a sense, a matter of the mind, or the rational aspects of functioning, employed "in the service of the heart," so to speak. On the other hand, much literature is prepared for and presented to teachers to remind them to bring their hearts to bear upon the rational aspects of their work and their professional minds.

The element of ego-involvement may also be illustrated by the notion that if a mother perceives herself as a failure at mothering, she is likely to experience strong feelings of inadequacy, painful guilt, and deep regret, perhaps for a lifetime. If, on the other hand, a teacher perceives himself or herself to have failed at teaching, he or she can leave the occupation in a fairly orderly fashion (for example, at the end of an academic year), and such residual emotions as guilt and feelings of failure, regret, and defeat are likely to subside and disappear within a few months.

A different aspect of third dimension is captured in the expression "No one in her right mind would be a mother!" As Bronfenbrenner (1978, pp. 773–774) has put it, "in order to develop, a child needs the enduring, irrational involvement of one or more adults," by which he means, "Somebody has to be crazy about that kid!" For modern, well-educated mothers, however, this may appear to be something of an overstatement.

A rational analysis of the pros and cons of motherhood would be unlikely to lead to a decision to undertake it. Indeed, it is difficult to find reasons for having children today! Offspring are not useful as a hedge against economic dependency in old age. Rather than being considered potential members of the family labor force and contributors to the family income, they can be expected to become substantial drains on the family finances for a long time. Indeed, it is suggested by Stone (1975) that as the economic value of children has decreased, the importance of affectional bonds has increased. Thus, even more than their forebears, modern parents have children just because they "have to"—irrationally, so to speak.

Teachers, on the other hand, should be optimally rational in that they should bring to bear upon their work careful reasoning concerning what is to be done or not done. Teaching calls for rational analysis of how to proceed in the education of young children on the basis of accumulated knowledge of how children develop and learn, and with an understanding of what is appropriate pedagogy for children of a given age range and experiential background. Presumably, the value of teacher training is precisely that it equips the future teacher with information and knowledge from the relevant "supply" disciplines and from pedagogy, all of which become resources for proceeding rationally in the work of teaching. It seems reasonable to assume that teachers' possession of relevant knowledge would serve to increase their confidence in their own behavior and in their general role competence. However, increased knowledge for mothers may have the opposite effect—and may serve to undermine what is often rather fragile confidence when facing "experts" who may appear comparatively cool and confident in their own advice and procedures.

Spontaneity

Along very similar lines, parents should strive to be optimally spontaneous in dealing with their children. Many programs of parent education run the risk of encouraging parents to become excessively cerebral and self-conscious in responding to their children. Extreme pressure to modify their behavior may lead parents to a condition called "analysis paralysis." This inability to act with adequate confidence could be damaging to the mother–child relationship. The resolve to respond to one's child according to certain steps and procedures arrived at cerebrally (intellectually, as it were) may work well on the first or even the second occasion. But very often, even the strongest resolutions break down under the weight of what is (and should be) an emotionally loaded relationship. Such breakdowns are related to the fact that the child's behavior/status really matters to the parent, a situation that comes with attachment as defined above. The cool, calculating, ever-reasoning or reasonable parent might be perceived by the child as indifferent and uncaring.

Another aspect of spontaneity is that it is precisely spontaneity that gives a mother's day-to-day behavior the variation and contrast growing children can use as a basis for hypothesis formulation and testing in their quest to make sense of experiences. Indeed, it may well be that what gives play its reputed high value in children's learning derives from the spontaneous, casual, and often random variations produced in many types of play (Newson & Newson, 1979). These variations provide information that the child operates on and transforms into meaningful contents of the mind—for example, concepts, schemata, and so on. The opportunity to observe such spontaneous variation, and to obtain parental help in making logical inferences from them, may be the very thing to which slogans such as "Mother is the best teacher" refer.

By contrast, instruction can be defined as nonrandom, prespecified sets of stimuli or information intended to cause specific constructs and skills to be acquired. This contrast between spontaneous play and instruction may also help to account for some of the dissension concerning appropriate programming for infant day care. On the one hand, there is pressure to rise above the custodial functions of day care and to provide "developmental" programs. On the other hand, formal lessons, instruction, or structured activities are thought to be inappropriate for the young. If the staff must await spontaneous "teachable moments," they may feel as though they are not earning their keep, not really "working," and role ambiguity may intensify.

Whereas mothers should be optimally spontaneous with their children, teachers should strive to be optimally intentional about their work. Teachers' activities should be largely predetermined and premeditated in terms of aims, goals, and broad objectives that are more-or-less explicit and that are responsive to parents (the primary clients) as well as to pupils. With training and experience, teachers' intentional behavior takes on a spontaneous quality as well.

Spontaneity in the mother is important also in that it may contribute to the widest possible range of information becoming potentially available to the child. The availability of a wide range of information increases the probability that children will be able to locate information that matches adequately or optimally what they are ready to operate upon and/or assimilate. Furthermore, if the child's location of appropriate information is followed by the mother's focusing on the selected events or information, then the child's environment becomes a highly informative and responsive one. In studies of mother–infant interaction, researchers have suggested that adults exaggerate their facial and vocal expressions in order to provide "behavioral contrasts" in response to infants' "limited information processing capacities" (Tronick, Als, & Brazelton, 1980, p. 20). Thus, spontaneous variations in behavior ideally serve to increase the likelihood that matches between the child's readiness to process information and the adult's provision of information will be maximized. This assertion is supported indirectly by the findings of Hatano, Miyake, and Tiajina (1980). In a study of children's acquisition of numbers, the investigators, after having observed mother–child interaction two years earlier, showed that "the mother's directiveness was correlated negatively with the child's number conservation score" (p. 383).

As suggested above, instruction and pedagogy are concerned with narrowing the variations presented to the child so that specific information and child operations upon it can be maximized. However, if the narrow range of information presented by the pedagogue misses the mark for a particular child, the child's alternatives are fewer than they might be at home, and the result may be a sense of failure or inadequacy, which in turn may have deleterious effects upon the child's receptivity to instruction. Questions concerning what sets of variations, stimuli, or information should be made available to young children in preschool classes have occupied curriculum developers for many years, and definitive answers have not yet been formulated.

Perhaps it is this very degree of intentionality that most clearly distinguishes mothering from teaching and child rearing from education. This is not to say that parents have no intentions! It is likely, however, that parents' intentions are less specific and explicit to parents themselves, as well as to others, than are teachers'—and are less formal, more global, and more personalized in that they are held for their own individual offspring rather than for a group. Research on the degree and specificity of intentions among the two sets of role-takers might help to sharpen understanding of these role distinctions.

Early childhood educators often speak appreciatively of the great amount children learn from the hidden curriculum, from incidental learning, or from unintended or unplanned events. However, by definition, such unintended learning cannot be intended—one cannot intend something to happen unintentionally! Presumably, the purpose of training in pedagogy is to bring the consequences of one's pedagogical methods into closer and closer agreement with the intentions underlying one's pedagogy. Similarly, the virtue of instruction would seem to lie in the deliberate minimization of spontaneous or random variations in activities and responses, maximizing the likelihood that specific stimuli will be presented to the learner and that intended or predicted learning outcomes will most likely be assured.

Partiality

Along lines very similar to those already discussed above, it may be noted that mother–child relationships are not only charged with highly intense emotions but that "children in the family are treated as special categories" (Lightfoot, 1978, p. 22). Generally, parents do not merely want their children to be normal; they want them to be excellent! As Green (1983) points out, the aim of parents is "to secure the best they can get . . . they seek not simply the best that is possible on the whole, but the best that is possible for their own children" (p. 320). It is thus in the nature of things that parents are partial towards their own children; biased in their favor; champions of their children's needs; and exaggerators of their virtues, gifts, and assets. This *particularism* stands in sharp contrast to the universalism expected of teachers. Thus, it appropriate for parents to ask teachers to make special allowances and provisions for their own children, and that is precisely what a teacher usually cannot do since the teacher must treat the children impartially. Teacher impartiality means that, as needed, the teacher makes equally available to every child (whether the child is liked or not) whatever skills, knowledge, insights, or techniques the teacher has at his or her disposal. Indeed, it is the very capacity to make all of one's pedagogical know-how available to a child one does not especially like that marks the teacher as a genuine professional.

Scope of Responsibility

The great emphasis placed by early childhood educators on the importance of meeting the "individual needs" of their pupils may have obscured yet another distinction between the roles of mothering and teaching—namely, the mothers are typically concerned about the welfare of one rather than all of the teachers' pupils. Parents have a right to protect their own child's cultural/ethnic uniqueness and to ask of the teacher that special consideration, as appropriate, be made for their child. The teacher is responsible not only for every individual in the group, but for the life of the group as a unit. However, the teacher has to balance the importance of responding to unique individual needs against the responsibility for establishing and maintaining the ethos of the group through which the norms of behavior, expected levels of achievement, and even many feelings are learned.

Summary of Dimensions

The seven dimensions outlined here reflect a common underlying variable that is difficult to name. As Lightfoot (1978) has
put it:

> The universalistic relationships encouraged by teachers are
> supportive of a more rational, predictable, and stable social
> system with visible and explicit criteria for achievement
> and failure. [The teacher–child relationship] does not suffer
> the chaotic fluctuation of emotions, indulgence, and impul-
> siveness that are found in the intimate association of par-
> ents and children. . . . Even the teachers who speak of "lov-
> ing" their children do not really mean the boundless, all-
> encompassing love of mothers and fathers but rather a very
> measured and time-limited love that allows for withdrawal.
> (p. 23)

Newson and Newson (1976), in a study of 700 elementary school
children and their relationships to their families and schools,
also underscore this point:

> Parents have an involvement with their own children
> which nobody else can simulate. . . . The crucial characteris-
> tic of the parental role is its partiality for the individual
> child. . . . The best that community care can offer is impar-
> tiality—to be fair to every child in its care. But a developing
> personality needs more than that: it needs to know that to
> someone it matters more than other children; that someone
> will go to unreasonable lengths, not just reasonable ones,
> for its sake. (p. 405)

Our understanding of the potential problems arising from confusing the two roles might be helped by studies of those women
who occupy both roles simultaneously. Informal observation
and experience suggest that teachers who are also mothers of
young children may have elevated expectations of their own
children as well as of themselves. It has been reported that such
mothers are sometimes ashamed and embarrassed by their emotionality with their own children, expecting themselves to be as
level-headed at home as they are in the classroom. Similarly,
some expect their own children to exemplify perfection to enhance their credibility as teachers. But such emotionality at

home and detachment on the job at school are appropriate distinctions in role performance.

To the extent that such role fusion does occur and produces these kinds of expectations, clarification of the distinction between the mothering and teaching roles may help to alleviate some of the strains for those who occupy both roles at the same time. In addition, some research on the ways such dual role-takers define the two roles and what sources of role fusion, confusion, and strain they identify would be helpful.

IMPLICATIONS FOR PARENT EDUCATION

One of the major functions of parent education programs should be to help parents think through their own goals for their own children, to develop and clarify what kind of lifestyle they want to construct for the family, and to identify what they themselves perceive to be the major issues deserving attention. The program should offer parents insights and various kinds of information while encouraging them to accept only what makes sense to them and what is consistent with their own preferences.

Parent education programs should also encourage and support parents' confidence in their own impulses and in their own competence. It is hypothesized that in the long run, efforts to support impulses already in place and available to the mother will result in greater change and improvement in parental functioning than would efforts to change or replace those impulses directly. This hypothesis rests on the assumption that parental confidence, in and of itself, leads to greater effectiveness (particularly in matters relating to the assertion of authority in parent–child interaction) and that greater effectiveness, in and of itself, leads to greater confidence. This "looping" or "circularity," in which the effects of behavior become in turn the causes of effects, would seem to be especially powerful in relationships marked by high intensity of affect—that is, in relationships in which effects really matter to the actors. The hypothesis is also related to the assumption that greater parental confidence is more likely to lead to openness to new information than is parental embarrassment, shame, or low self-confidence.

As indicated earlier in this discussion, parent education that is excessively technique-based or technique-oriented may yield positive effects in the short run but greater feelings of inadequacy and/or guilt in the long run. This hypothesis is based on the assumption that parenting is not primarily technical but is more dispositional and ideally largely unselfconscious. Furthermore, consistency in the application of techniques tends to subside after a few weeks, and this inconsistency may be followed by heightened feelings of incompetence or guilt. A related point here is that children respond not so much to the specific behavior of their parents as to the meanings they themselves assign to that behavior. But the meanings children attribute to any given episode are a function of the larger pattern, of which they perceive a specific episode to be a part. Children may have difficulty giving the meanings their mothers hope for to technique-bound episodes. Thus, for example, parental reliance on specific techniques, phrases, or other maneuvers may confound the problems issuing from faulty patterns of behavior or from characteristic parental dispositions. The latter take time to change and reshape, and may perhaps be more effectively modified in parents who have more, rather than less, confidence (see Hess, 1980).

Parent educators often report that the spontaneous impulses of some of the parents they work with put children in jeopardy, usually in relation to their psychosocial rather than their intellectual development. To what extent such judgments are matters of taste, preference, and/or value differences between parent educators and their clients is not yet clear. In fact, it may be in the nature of things that parent educators have to work in the absence of sufficient certainty concerning the potential benefit or damage of a given maternal pattern. One way to cope with such uncertainty is to scrutinize as carefully as possible each case of potential jeopardy with regard to the certainty of risk or danger to the child. When, in the educator's best judgment at a given time, the potential for danger seems reasonably clear, then referral to specialized agencies should be made. It would be unethical not to do so. However, when examination of the available information raises doubts about the potential danger to the child, then the next appropriate step seems to be to encourage and support the mother's own pattern of responding to the child. Differences in taste, philosophical positions, and/or values probably underlie many of the judgments that educators make concerning the mother's need to change her behavior. However, it may be useful to remember that parent educators as well as teachers of young children are bound to take firm stands on their beliefs and philosophical positions. The latter gives teachers the kind of certainty required for action in complex situations, in which reliable data cannot serve as a basis for decision making (see Chapter 13).

Powell (1980) suggests that when parents are given new information or are pressed into changing their patterns of behavior in ways that are discrepant with their own values, they minimize the discrepant stimuli to reduce their influence. Powell's analyses of the various parental strategies for coping with the pressures placed upon them to change serve to remind us that education in parenting is not an easy matter (see Durio & Hughes, 1982). It may be that trying to get mothers to instruct their children in pre-academic tasks is easier than helping them with deeper and more complex aspects of development (for example, self-reliance, moral development, social skills, motivation, and so on).

Implications for Teachers of Young Children

The discussion presented above suggests a number of points that may help teachers in their encounters with mothers, as well as in coping with the day-to-day problems of working with young children.

It seems obvious, even without detailed analyses of the two roles, that the special contributions of each role-taker to the ultimate socialization of the young child should be mutually understood, accepted, and respected. Parent educators, as well as those who write in the popular press for parents, might help by acknowledging the complementarity of these functions rather than by trying to fix blame on one or the other for whatever social disaster is capturing popular attention at a given moment. Expressions such as "Parents are the child's best teacher" seem to suggest that teachers are, if not the worst, then certainly a distant second best. The comparison itself is inappropriate. What should be emphasized are the functions and characteristics of each role and how the efforts of each role-taker might be supported by the other.

Another implication of the analyses attempted in this discussion is that teachers should take time periodically to consider whether they have achieved an optimum level of involvement or detachment in their relationships with children. The risk of teacher burnout is a real one, especially when the work is with children whose families are under stress. Teachers who work together as members of a teaching team might also help each other by developing a system for giving each other relief during those moments when the emotional load feels too heavy.

In addition, teachers may be helped by focusing on those aspects of the child's functioning they actually do control. A teacher cannot change the family into which a child is born or with whom he or she is living. Nor can the teacher generally change very much of the parents' behavior. But a teacher can take responsibility for the time a child is actually directly in his or her care and can focus on making that time as supportive, enriching, and educative as possible. The latter is a sufficiently big task by itself without adding to it the need to make up for a child's alleged missing parenting!

Teachers may also find it helpful in their relations with mothers to acknowledge and accept the mother's advocacy for and partiality toward her own child as normal components of motherhood. Similarly, as mothers approach teachers to request special dispensations for their own children, teachers' acknowledgment of the "naturalness" of such demands may help them to respond more patiently, less defensively, and more professionally than they often seem to do. Teachers might be mindful on such occasions that although they may practice impartiality within their own classrooms, they champion their own classes when representing them as a group in comparison with other teachers' classes! On such occasions, teachers also ask for special dispensations and also describe their own classes as having special or unique needs, gifts, and strengths—much the way mothers do for their individual children. Recognition of this phenomenon may help teachers respond to parents with greater respect and understanding and to see the adversarial aspects of their relationship as inherent in their roles rather than as personality conflicts.

CONCLUSION

Much of the present discussion is speculative, based on informal observations and reports of the experiences of teachers, parents, and parent educators. Research that would ascertain the validity of these speculations would be helpful. Of all of the potential research efforts on matters raised in this discussion, those that would advance our understanding of the stresses and coping skills of teachers and child care workers have the highest priority. Present social and economic developments suggest that more and more children and their parents will come to depend upon professional child care workers and preschool teachers and that more parents will stand to benefit from well-designed parent education programs. Much is yet to be learned about how such professional activities should be conducted and about what kind of working conditions are desirable. Certainly, mutual support by the people involved should help each to cope more effectively with the stresses encountered when living and working with young children every day.

References

Bronfenbrenner, V. (1978). Who needs parent education? *Teachers College Record, 79*(4), 767–787.

Cohen, L. J. (1974). The operational definition of human attachment. *Psychological Bulletin, 81*(4), 207–217.

Durio, H. F., & Hughes, R. (1982). Parent education: Understanding parents so that they can understand themselves and their children. In S. Hill & B. J. Barnes (Eds.), *Young children and their families.* New York: Lexington Books.

Freud, A. (1952). The role of the teacher. *Harvard Educational Review, 22*(4), 229–243.

Getzels, J. W. (1974). Socialization and education: A note on discontinuities. In H. Leichter (Ed.), *The family as educator.* New York: Teachers College Press.

Green, T. F. (1983). Excellence, equity, and equality. In L. Shulman & G. Sykes (Eds.), *Teaching and educational policy.* New York: Longmans.

Hatano, G., Miyake, K., & Tiajina, N. (1980). Mother behavior in an instructional situation and child's acquisition of number conservation. *Child Development, 51*(2), 379–385.

Hess, R. D. (1980). Experts and amateurs: Some unintended consequences of parent education. In M. D. Fantini & R. Cardenas (Eds.), *Parenting in a multicultural society.* New York: Longman.

Langer, W. L. (1974). Infanticide: A historical survey. *History of Childhood Quarterly, 1*(3), 353–365.

Levenstein, P. (1970). Cognitive growth in preschoolers through verbal interaction with mothers. *American Journal of Orthopsychiatry, 40*, 426–432.

LeVine, R. A. (1980). A cross-cultural perspective on parenting. In M.D. Fantini & R. Cardenas (Eds.), *Parenting in a multicultural society.* New York: Longman.

Lightfoot, S. L. (1978). *Worlds apart: Relationships between families and schools.* New York: Basic Books.

Maslach, C., & Pines, A. (1977). The burn-out syndrome in the day care setting. *Child Care Quarterly, 6*(2), 100–113.

Newson, J., & Newson, E. (1976). *Seven year olds in the home environment.* New York: Halstead Press.

Newson, J., & Newson E. (1979). *Toys and playthings.* Middlesex, England: Penguin Books.

Powell, D. R. (1980). Toward a socioecological perspective of relations between parents and child care programs. In S. Kilmer (Ed.), *Advances in early education and day care: Vol. 1.* New York: JAI Press.

Ramey, C. T., & Farran, D. C. (1978, August). The functional attachments of mothers and their infants. Paper presented at the annual meeting of the American Psychological Association, Toronto, Canada.

Rubenstein, J., & Howes, C. (1979). Caregiving and infant behavior in day care and in homes. *Developmental Psychology, 15*(1), 1–24.

Rutter, M. (1979). Maternal deprivation, 1972–1978: New findings, new concepts, new approaches. *Child Development, 50,* 283–305.

Schaefer, E. (1979). Perspective on the family. In the proceedings of the meeting "Professionals and Parents, Moving toward Partnership." Richmond, VA: Virginia Commonwealth University

Stone, L. (1975). The rise of the nuclear family in early modern England: The patriarchal stage. In C.E. Rosenburg (Ed.), *The family in history.* Philadelphia: University of Pennsylvania Press.

Stone, L. (1977). *The family, sex and marriage 1500 to 1800.* New York: Mayer and Row.

Tronick, E., Als, H., & Brazelton, T. B. (1980). Monadic phases: A structural descriptive analysis of infant–mother face to face interaction. *Merrill-Palmer Quarterly, 26*(1), 3–24.

White, B. L., Kaban, B. T., & Attanucci, J. S. (1979). *The origins of human competence.* Lexington, MA: D.C. Heath.

Wishy, B. (1972). *The child and the republic: The dawn of modern American child nurture.* Philadelphia: University of Pennsylvania Press.

Zigler, E., & Cascione, R. (1980). On being a parent. In *Parenthood in a changing society.* Urbana, IL: ERIC Clearinghouse on Elementary and Early Childhood Education.

11

THE PROFESSIONAL
PRESCHOOL TEACHER*

The ideas in this chapter were developed from a talk given to a group of child care teachers on the topic of professionalism. The specific challenge of the occasion was to make the distinctions between professional and nonprofessional behavior concrete and practical.

One of the major elements of professions is their commitment to standards of practice for which members are—at least theoretically—held accountable. These standards of practice address the standard predicaments every professional practitioner is expected to encounter frequently. One of the problems involved in developing standards of practice is the identification of those standard predicaments. The tricycle incident was chosen as a example of a typical predicament as a result of a recent observation in a preschool setting. If the field of early childhood professional practice is to progress toward greater professionalism many more standard predicaments will have to be identified and agreement will have to be developed on the standard procedures appropriate to their solution.

* This chapter was originally published as "The Professional Preschool Teacher," by Lilian G. Katz. In L. G. Katz, *More Talks with Teachers* (pp. 27–44). Urbana, IL: ERIC Clearinghouse on Elementary and Early Childhood Education. Reprinted with permission.

THE PROFESSIONAL PRESCHOOL TEACHER

The term "professional" means many things to many people (see Ade, 1982; Hoyle, 1982; Chapter 14). While not all of these meanings can be explored fruitfully here, for the purposes of this discussion the aspects of professionalism of chief concern are a professional's application of advanced knowledge to his or her work (Zumeta & Solomon, 1982), the use of judgment based on that advanced knowledge, and the adoption of standards of performance below which no professional's performance should be allowed to fall.

As defined here, the advanced knowledge applied to the professional preprimary teacher's work is derived from developmental psychology and is drawn largely from research on the development of young children's social cognition. However, a full description of the work of preschool teachers would surely show that it involves the application of advanced knowledge from many other fields as well.

The term *judgment* is used here to refer to such cognitive processes as diagnosing and analyzing events, weighing alternative courses of action, estimating the potential long-term consequences of momentary actions and decisions, and other information processing in which advanced knowledge comes into play.

In the matter of practices that meet accepted standards of performance, the distinction between a professional and an amateur may be useful: An amateur does what she does for the love of it, does it occasionally, perhaps when she feels like it, and does it without remuneration.[1] On occasion, the amateur may be very skillful indeed, even though not necessarily formally trained. However, a practicing professional is ideally committed to performing at the same high standards, day in and day out, on every occasion, whether she is in the mood or not, whether she feels like it or not. Indeed, one of the major functions of a professional organization is to set standards of performance and to remind members to employ them. These standards are established to offer guidelines for the typical situations all members of the profession can be expected to encounter. They are based on

---

[1] The increasing number of male teachers in the early childhood field is indeed welcome. However, since the majority of teachers in preprimary settings are females, the feminine pronouns have been used through this chapter.

the best available advanced knowledge that applies to typical problems encountered during practice.

Outlined below are some speculations concerning how a professional preschool teacher or child care worker might respond to a standard situation encountered during her work. The examples are intended to show what professional judgment might be like in a very ordinary and typical teaching situation. These responses are contrasted with those of a person without training, and a few points are also added concerning what might constitute unprofessional responses to the same situation.

PROFESSIONAL RESPONSES IN A STANDARD PREDICAMENT

In order to explore what professional judgment might include, let us take a situation that almost every teacher of young children is bound to encounter sooner or later—and probably often. To set the stage, imagine a teacher of a group of 20 4-year-olds in a setting in which the outdoor equipment includes only two tricycles. In a group of American 4-year-olds in such a situation, squabbles will inevitably arise concerning whose turn it is to use one of the tricycles.

Specifically, imagine that a child named Robin goes to the teacher and protests, saying, "Leslie won't let me have a turn!" There are probably scores of "right" as well as "wrong" ways to respond in this situation. The types of professional judgment processes a teacher might engage in are presented below under three interrelated headings: (a) what could be taught in the situation, (b) clinical questions relating to individuals in the incident, and (c) curriculum and management concerns.

WHAT COULD BE TAUGHT IN THE SITUATION?

Ideally, a trained teacher approaches the situation described by asking herself, What can I be teaching in this incident? In formulating answers to this question, the professionally trained teacher takes into account the most reliable knowledge about the development of children; the norms of the age group; and the goals of the parents, the school, and the community at large.

The teacher's answers to the question should involve some of the skills, knowledge, and dispositions outlined below. The specific content of these skills may vary with the "philosophy of education," "learning theory," and goals to which the individual teacher or preschool subscribes. Those listed below reflect the present author's own views of the kinds of learning and teaching that seem appropriate at the preprimary level.

The examples of professional responses presented here depict the kind of judgment that might be expected of a well-trained, experienced teacher at the developmental stage referred to as maturity (see Chapter 12). Needless to say, a mature and experienced teacher formulates her judgment of the situation very rapidly, in a manner sometimes thought of as intuitive (that is, she processes large amounts of information, concepts, and knowledge on many levels and at great speed). A professional judgment of the situation could lead the teacher to answer the question, What can I be teaching? along the following lines.

Social Skills

Certainly, the teacher may encourage the development of skills in the social realm. Some of these social skills concern turn-taking, negotiating, and coping with rebuffs.

1. Turn-taking   The teacher can assist in the complex processes children have to learn such as learning to read others' behaviors for signs of when a request for a turn is most likely to work, when it might be best to give up, and when to come back for another try. The child's sensitivity to cues embedded in another's behavior that help decide the next best move may also be encouraged. Such processes are analogous to those studied in discourse analysis, which describe how young children learn the turn-taking skills required for participation in conversation (see Frederiksen, 1981; Shields, 1979; Wells, 1981). Indeed, some behavioral scientists suggest that all social relations involve turn-taking behavior.

Thus, the teacher might suggest to Robin that he or she simply wait a few minutes, do something else for a little while, and then try asking Leslie again for a turn. She might also suggest to Robin that Leslie be observed for signs of weariness or boredom with the tricycle, indicating that a bid for a turn as soon as such signs appear is likely to be successful. In such a case, the teacher is helping Robin to strengthen observational skills that could aid and strengthen turn-taking behavior.

2. Negotiating The growing literature on social cognition and its development indicates that during the preschool period children can begin to have the skills involved in striking a bargain (including the ability to guess what will appeal to another child and being able to make a deal in which each participant's preferences and needs are considered) (Rubin & Everett, 1982).

In such a case, the teacher encourages Robin to consider what might appeal to Leslie. Specifically, the teacher might say to Robin something like, "Go to Leslie and say, 'I'll push you on the swing if you give me a turn on the tricycle. . . .'" In this way, the teacher offers a verbal model of how the negotiations might go.

3. Coping with Rebuffs A teacher has a role to play in helping children to cope with having their requests, pleas, and demands turned down or rejected. Children do not have to win every conflict or succeed at every confrontation, and the ability to accept defeat and rejection gracefully probably has to be learned. The teacher can help Robin to learn this social grace by responding to the complaint by saying (in a matter-of-fact tone) something like, "All right. Perhaps Leslie will give up the tricycle later. There are lots of other things to do in the meantime. . . ." Specific activities can then be suggested.

Verbal Skills

The tricycle situation is also a good one in which to teach children how to express their feelings and assert their wishes more clearly and effectively.

1. Assertive Phrases It might be that Robin has not stated the desire for a turn with the tricycle very clearly. Perhaps Robin simply tugged at the tricycle or even whined a bit. The teacher can respond to Robin's complaint by saying something like, "Go back to Leslie and say, 'I've been waiting a long time. I really want a turn. . . .'" In such a case, the teacher models a tone of moderate but firm assertiveness that the child can imitate and introduces a simple phrase that the child can use when the teacher is not there. The professional teacher is committed to helping children acquire competencies that can be used when she is not present, thereby aiding the child's development in the long term.

2. Conversational Phrases   It may be that the children involved in the incident have few appropriate phrases and are only just learning to engage in heated conversations. In a study of how young children become friends, Gottmann (1983) has shown that a factor in success at friendship formation is the ability to de-escalate conflict situations. Those children who could defuse conflict were able to state their reasons for disagreeing with each other. The professional preprimary teacher is in an ideal position to help children acquire some of the skills involved in verbalizing conflicting wishes and opinions. Teaching such verbal skills can be done through a technique called Speaking-for-Children (see Schachter & Strage, 1982), a process in which the adult speaks to each child on behalf of the other and keeps up the conversation between contentious parties by speaking for them. In this way, the teacher offers phrases and models a verbal approach to a conflict situation.

Using this technique, the teacher might say to Leslie, "Robin really wants a turn," to which Leslie might grunt a refusal. The teacher then might say to Robin something like, "Leslie does not want to give up the tricycle yet." Robin might respond to this with a whining protest, in which case the teacher can paraphrase to Leslie what Robin is feeling by saying, "Robin really would like a turn now," and so on. In short, the teacher keeps up the conversation, verbalizing to each child what she infers to be the feelings and wishes of the other.

Social Knowledge

This typical preschool incident also provides a good opportunity to teach social knowledge. Nucci and Turiel (1978) have shown that preschool children understand the distinction between social conventions and moral transgressions, and thus can be helped with simple moral and social insights. The preschool teacher is in an ideal position in situations like the one described to stimulate and strengthen children's knowledge of social concepts such as those outlined below.

1. Social Perspective A professionally trained teacher can help children to learn some distinctions between what is a tragedy and what is not. Not getting a turn to ride a tricycle on a given day is not a tragedy. The loss of a loved one, the suffering of others, or separation from a very favorite friend or pet might be tragic and worthy of feelings of sorrow and sadness. The teacher helps the child put desires and wishes into perspective by responding to the complaint with gentle, good-humored empathy, rather than with tragic tones or a great rush to a rescue the child from distress.

Thus, the teacher might say to Robin something like, "I know you're disappointed not to get a turn on the tricycle, but there are other things that you like to do. . . . " Once again, the tone should be matter-of-fact and pleasant, without hint of reprimand.

2. Rudiments of Justice There is reason to believe that preschoolers are ready to absorb some of the rudiments of justice (Johnson, 1982), particularly in the form of "ground rules" (the notion that the rules and restraints a child is asked to observe are asked of others too and protect him or her as well as the others). Thus, a professionally trained teacher's response in the present situation would not be merely "Leslie, I want you to give Robin a turn now." This statement would also be followed by the tag "And when you need help getting a turn with something, I will be glad to help you also."

Similarly, if the situation were to lead to combat, the teacher might say to the instigator," I won't let you hit X, and I won't let anyone hit you either." The last part of such a statement, the tag, is what reassures the aggressor that he or she is in a just environment in which everyone's rights are protected and everyone's needs are considered. One of the important elements of the professional behavior illustrated here is the teacher's acceptance of responsibility for the learning and development of both the victim *and the aggressor* (see Grusec & Arnason, 1982). Thus, when Leslie hogs the tricycle and refuses to give Robin a turn (and when other techniques have failed), the teacher might say to Leslie something like, "Five more minutes, Leslie, then I want you to let Robin have a turn, and when you need help getting a turn with something just let me know."

3. Observers' Understandings and Skills Professional judgment includes taking into account what the children observing the incident might be learning. Virtually all the teacher responses outlined above can provide indirect instruction for the uninvolved children watching the incident from the sidelines. These children might also learn techniques of negotiation, bargaining, and verbal strategies for use in confrontation. In addition, the observing children might be learning what techniques and strategies "work" with which children. If they have also had an opportunity to observe the teacher state the ground rules, they are likely to feel reassured that they are in a just environment and while they are prohibited from harming others, others are similarly constrained against harming them.

Dispositional Learning

In addition to teaching social skills and social knowledge, the professional teacher also considers which personal dispositions could be strengthened or weakened in this situation.

1. Empathic and Altruistic Dispositions A professionally trained teacher is aware of the accumulating evidence that young children are capable of empathic and altruistic dispositions and that adults can strengthen these dispositions in various ways (Grusec & Arnason, 1982). For example, if Leslie resists giving up the tricycle, the teacher might say something like, "Robin has been waiting for a long time, and you know how it feels to wait a long time," thereby stimulating or arousing empathic feelings and nurturing the disposition to be charitable as well. This should not be said in such a tone as to imply sin or hidden evil impulses, of course!

Sometimes a child refuses to accede to the request of another precisely because he or she does know what it feels like to be in the other's position (for example, to have to wait for a long time). In such cases, empathic capabilities are there, but charity is not. It is not very useful for the adults in such situations to say things like, "How would you like someone to do that to you?" What answer can a young child give to such a question? In cases in which charity toward another person is lacking, the teacher must exercise judgment concerning how to respond in the best and long term interests of both children. Of course, confrontations such as these may be inevitable and benign; their significance should not be exaggerated or overinterpreted.

2. Experimental Disposition The tricycle incident is a good example of the many situations arising with young children in which the teacher can strengthen children's dispositions to approach social interactions and confrontations experimentally, as problem-solving situations in which alternative solutions can be invented and tried out—and in which a few failures will not be debilitating.

Returning to the incident, then, when Robin complains that Leslie won't give up a turn, the teacher can respond by modeling a mildly assertive tone and saying something like, "Go back and say to Leslie, 'I really want a turn. I've been waiting a long time.' If that doesn't work, come back and we'll discuss something else to try." If the teacher suggests what action to take without adding the notion of coming back to try again, and if the one suggestion offered fails, Robin's frustration or sense of incompetence may be increased. The tag in the teacher's statement ("Come back and we'll discuss something else to try") strengthens the disposition to tackle social situations experimentally and can be of significant long-term value to children.

3. Complaining and Tattling Professional judgment may indicate that Robin has acquired a strong disposition to be a complainer and that this tendency should be weakened. The professionally trained teacher tries to assess the legitimacy of complaints and discriminate between those requiring action and those lodged by the child in order to secure something wanted rather than needed. If, in the teacher's best judgment, the complaint requires no real intervention, Robin may be sent back to the situation with some suggested strategies for coping with it, as outlined above. Complainers do not always have to win or succeed at their complaints; if they often do succeed, complaining can become a strong and persistent disposition.

The term "tattling" refers to behavior in one child that is intended to get another one into trouble. Very often, behavior that appears to be tattling on the part of the young child may simply reflect a childlike understanding of the seriousness of the teacher's demands. The teacher must assess whether the child is simply reporting what he or she thinks the teacher wants to know about or whether the intent is to get another child into trouble and the disposition to do so is growing. In the latter case, based on her professional judgment, the teacher may decide to weaken this disposition by sending the child back to cope with the conflict. When children are older, perhaps 6 or 7 years of age, the teacher can explain the conditions under which behavior that we ordinarily think of as tattling is warranted (for example, when the consequence of some activity unknown to the teacher may constitute a physical or psychological danger to someone).

CLINICAL JUDGMENTS

The term "clinical" as defined here indicates the processes of taking into account the meaning of the behavior of each individual child involved in a particular incident into the context of all other known behavior and history of the individuals involved. Thus, the teacher might ask herself some of the following kinds of questions:

1. Is this a typical day for Robin? If so, is Robin becoming a chronic attention seeker? Is the threshold[2] at which Robin feels he or she is getting attention too high? If so, how can the threshold be brought down?

2. How much experimentation can Robin take at this time? Perhaps his or her disposition to be self-assertive is not yet robust enough to risk failure or rejection right now, and the teacher judges that Robin requires intervention and/or support in this particular confrontation at this particular time.

3. Does Leslie's behavior reflect progress? Perhaps this is the first time Leslie has exhibited self-assertion, and the incident is a welcome sign that earlier shyness or submissiveness is being overcome.

4. Can the two individuals in this particular incident learn the "right" things if they are left to resolve the situation for themselves? Some children can learn more mature and effective ways to resolve problems when left to their own devices, while others cannot. Thus, the teacher might also

---

[2] The concept of *threshold* is used here to refer to individual differences in the level at which attention is perceived. Some children feel as though they are getting attention with occasional smiles and friendly interludes; others require high frequencies and intensitites of contact. Such differences in threshold are learned (in interaction with predisposing characteristics).

ask, When should I use a partial intervention? Should I keep completely out of the way? One of the important factors the professional teacher considers in this respect is that if one of the participating children is a bully, he or she may get better at bullying by being left to resolve the conflict alone. In the interests of the children's own long-term development, the teacher will try to minimize the success of the bully or bossy child.

5. Will the present pattern of behavior of either of the two children involved cause them trouble later on if it is left unmodified now?

6. Are either of these children the victim of "character definition?" That is to say, have these children's characters been defined (perhaps Leslie as a selfish bully or Robin as a whining weakling) so that they are bringing their behavior into line with the traits attributed to them (see Grusec & Arnason, 1982)? There is ample evidence from research stemming from attribution theory that even adults, in many situations, bring their behavior into line with the expectations of those with whom they interact. It is not surprising that children are likely to persist in patterns of behavior that fit adults' characterizations of them. Taking such knowledge into account, the professional teacher scrutinizes her own definitions of the children involved to make sure that she has not "boxed them in" to being bullies or complainers or any other undesirable character types (see also Katz and McClellan, 1990).

CURRICULUM AND MANAGEMENT CONSIDERATIONS

As well as considering the skills and dispositions that can be encouraged and the clinical judgments that may be made, the professionally trained teacher will take into account the implications of the situation for curriculum and management. Specifically, the teacher might take up some of the following questions:

1. Is the behavior in this incident "normal" for this age group? In this culture? In the culture of the particular children involved?

2.   Has the right kind and/or quantity of equipment been obtained for children of this age, background, culture, and so forth? Are there enough suitable alternative activities? Is the curriculum sufficiently appropriate and challenging for the two children in this incident or in other incidents of the same kind?

3.   Might the children benefit from being given examples of ways of dealing with problem situations? The trained teacher knows that heavy doses of preaching and moralizing are unlikely methods with which to treat the behavior of young children. However, the teacher may select certain kinds of stories to tell the children that carry a relevant moral at an appropriate level of complexity.

The professional teacher is likely to ask herself how often a particular kind of incident is occurring and whether its frequency signals a need for adjustment of the curriculum. If these kinds of run-ins occur several times every day, it suggests that the curriculum should be evaluated and some efforts should be made to provide activities to engage the children's minds more fully. In handling a typical situation, the teacher can thus address not only the individual children involved but also the program as a whole.

Such program decisions include bringing knowledge of development and learning to bear on formulating responses to children's behavior and in making teaching decisions. The professional also considers the long-term development of the children involved and not just the incident and behavior of the moment. In addition, the professional considers the growth, development, and learning of *all* the children involved in the incident: that of both participants—the apparent aggressor and the apparent victim—as well as that of the children observing.

NONPROFESSIONAL RESPONSES TO THE INCIDENT

Many people without professional education or training are involved with children in groups. In many preprimary settings, parents, foster grandparents, and volunteers contribute greatly to the quality of the program by their participation. The term *nonprofessional* implies no inferiority; rather, the designation is used in order to contrast the application of knowledge and professionally accrued experience and practices with common-sense responses and to focus attention on how professional education and judgment come into play in daily work with other people's children.

In order to explore this contrast, it may be helpful to imagine how the person without professional education and experience might respond when confronted with this hypothetical situation. In general, the untrained individual is likely to focus on what is happening rather than what is being learned. Similarly, she is likely to see the situation as calling for "putting out the fire," hoping that will be the end of it, rather than one that calls for teaching a variety of skills, knowledge, or dispositions. In other words, the nonprofessional may wish simply to put a stop to the incident without considering which of many possible interventions is most likely to stimulate long term development and learning. (If teachers took the same approach and saw teaching as periodic fire-extinguishing, they would be "smoke detectors" rather than teachers!)

Many people without the benefit of professional education and experience might see the preferred response to this incident to be to distract Robin from the present misery. The use of distraction makes "good common sense." Distraction very often does work and is therefore a favored technique by many adults. However, for 3- or 4-year-olds it is not a necessary or preferred technique. While distraction "works," it does not really teach alternative approaches to the situation. On the contrary, it may teach children that complaining, tattling, and so forth very frequently get adult attention.

Other nonprofessional responses in situations like the tricycle squabble include saying such things to the children as, "Cut it out!" "Don't be so selfish!" "Be nice!" "Don't be nasty!" "We take turns in this school!" (even though we just didn't), and so on. Such exclamations are unlikely to do any harm, but they are also unlikely to teach the participants alternative approaches to the situation. Some nonprofessionals also respond to squabbling over equipment by putting it away or locking it up. This strategy does work, of course, but it does not teach, and teaching is the professional's commitment.

Occasionally, a nonprofessional is heard to issue a threat in such situations, as in the statement "If you don't let Robin have a turn, you won't go to the zoo with us on Friday." There are several problems with such threats. One is that they are often empty. Will the threatener really keep Leslie away from the zoo? How does one make the threatened sanction match the seriousness of the unwanted behavior? Sometimes the threats are out of proportion to the transgression. Then, when a really serious transgression comes along, what threats are left? Perhaps most 4-year-olds cannot yet sense that threats indicate that the adult has lost or given up control over the situation. But some 4-year-olds may sense that threats are acts of desperation. If so, their testing behavior is apt to increase, and the content of the relationships in the class may become focused on the rules, on what happens when they are broken, and on who is really in charge. When the content of relationships is dominated by such matters, the atmosphere becomes a highly contentious one. Furthermore, threats do not teach the children alternative skills for solving the problem, nor do they encourage new knowledge or strengthen desirable dispositions.

Some adults resort to bribery in situations like the example provided. They may say something like, "If you give Robin a turn with the tricycle, I will let you hand out the cookies at snack time." The danger in using a bribe is that it tends to devalue the behavior in which one wishes the child to engage. In other words, generosity and charity are discounted as not being worthy acts for their own sakes. Bribery often works. The professional question is, however, What does it teach?

Some adults use so-called time-out procedures—the removal of the child from contact with the ongoing life of the group—when a child persists in refusing to cooperate with other children. Time-out procedures often seem to work. Indeed, many teachers are trained to use them. The main problem is that time-out procedures do not teach new skills or desirable dispositions, although they do change behavior. As long as the child's mental ability is reasonably normal for his or her age, it is not necessary to circumvent the mind by insisting on something like a time-out chair. Furthermore, the cognitive connection between placing one's seat on a particular chair and acceding to another child's request for a turn with a piece of equipment must be fairly obscure if not confusing to a 4-year-old (see Chapter 5).

A variant of the time-out procedure is instructing a child to sit aside and "think things over" and to come back when he or she is "ready to behave properly." Such techniques are not likely to be harmful unless used excessively or with hostility. But they are unlikely to solve persistent behavior problems. They also fail to teach alternative approaches to the situations at hand. Studies of what children actually do think or feel on such occasions would help us to understand the consequences of these techniques.

Many adults in such predicaments moralize about the virtues of "sharing," "kindness," and "generosity," preaching the evils of selfishness. Though such approaches are unlikely to do children harm, they are not likely to teach various strategies to use when adults are not present—especially if moralizing is used to the exclusion of all other methods. Another common response of adults without training is to become preoccupied with the feelings and needs of the "victim" and to neglect the feelings, needs, and development of the child who seems to be the aggressor. The professional, on the other hand, is committed to responding to the feelings, needs, and development of *all* the children in her charge.

Many nonprofessionals respond to situations like this one by asking questions about who had it first, who started it, and how a conflict situation arose. The intent of such responses seems to be to discover whose fault the problem situation is and where to assign blame. For preschoolers, this line of inquiry is not usually relevant or helpful. The emphasis is best placed on teaching the children strategies for resolving the problem.

It has been reported that some untrained adults, when confronting situations like the hypothetical tricycle squabble, would say to Leslie such things as, "Your behavior makes me sad" or "Your acting that way makes me feel bad." While such statements are unlikely to harm the children, they seem to draw attention to the adult's own internal states and perhaps add a layer of guilt to the child's feelings. Again, however, the basic problem with this response is that it fails to teach the participants ways of coping with the predicament.

Finally, the nonprofessional person in such a situation is apt to employ not only common sense but also impulse, custom, or erroneous folk wisdom. The danger also exists that this individual may occasionally use shaming comparisons with other children in order to intimidate a child so that he or she will give in to the adult's demand.

UNPROFESSIONAL RESPONSES TO THE INCIDENT

One of the characteristics of a fully developed profession is that its members subscribe to a code of ethics that serves as a guide to professional conduct (see Chapter 15). Conduct violating any part of the code is unethical and therefore unprofessional. Nonprofessional behavior is that which is determined by personal predilection or common-sense wisdom rather than by professionally accrued knowledge and practices; unprofessional behavior is that which contravenes agreed-upon standards for performance of the society of professional practitioners or the code of ethical conduct they have adopted.

In general, unprofessional or unethical behavior is the result of giving in to the temptations of the situation at hand. It could be, for instance, that Leslie's and/or Robin's behavior frequently puts the teacher into the kind of predicament described in this discussion. On a given occasion, the teacher might feel a bit weary of it and stand by and let the chips fall where they may. Once in a while, she might silently pray that an aggressive child in this kind of situation will "get what he or she deserves," hoping that another child will bring the offender down a peg or two. Not only is it unethical to let one's own feelings dictate the response to the situation, but the "school of hard knocks," although powerful, is likely to provide the wrong lessons to children. From the school of hard knocks, most children learn to be hard.

It should be kept in mind that the professionally trained teacher is not without feelings of the kind alluded to here; what is professional in this situation is to school one's feelings with the knowledge and insight that constitute professional judgment and to respond in terms of that judgment rather than in terms of the feelings or temptations of the moment. Occasionally, we are tempted to blame the children for creating the predicament or to blame their parents for not raising them properly. However, what is relevant is not whom to blame but what to teach in this situation.

CONCLUSION

I have used the example of a typical incident arising in groups of young children to illustrate professional and nonprofessional ways of responding to them. Professional responses include the use of judgment based on the most reliable knowledge and insight available. The professional teacher exercises judgment in the service of the long-term best interests of the children; the untrained person working with children is more likely to respond in terms of the immediate situation and to settle for what "works" well for the moment rather than act in terms what is most likely to enhance the children's long term development.

Only a very small sample of the potential uses of contemporary knowledge about children's development and learning has been discussed here. However, it is hoped that even this brief description of what mature professionalism in preschool teaching might be like will add weight to the proposition that the effective training and education of preprimary teachers can help to make a significant contribution to children's development and learning.

REFERENCES

Ade, W. (1982). Professionalism and its implications for the field of early childhood education. *Young Children, 37*(5), 25–32.

Frederiksen, C. H. (1981). Inference in preschool children's conversations—A cognitive language in educational settings. In J. Green & C. Wallat (Eds.), *Ethnography and language in educational settings.* Norwood, NJ: Ablex.

Gottman, J. M. (1983). How children become friends. *Monographs of the Society for Research in Child Development, 48*(3) (Serial No. 201).

Grusec, J. E., & Arnason, L. (1982). Consideration for others: Approaches to enhancing altruism. In S.G. Moore & C.R. Cooper (Eds.), *The young child: Reviews of Research: Vol. 3.* Washington, DC: National Association for the Education of Young Children.

Hoyle, E. (1982). The professionalism of teachers: A paradox. *British Journal of Educational Studies, 30*(2), 161–171.

Johnson, D. B. (1982). Altruistic behavior and the development of self in infants. *Merrill-Palmer Quarterly, 28*(3), 379–387.

Katz, L. G., McClellan, D. (1990). The teacher's role in the social development of young children. Urbana, IL: ERIC Clearinghouse on Elementary and Early Childhood Education.

Nucci, L. P., & Turiel, E. (1978). Social interactions and the development of social concepts in preschool children. *Child Development, 49,* 400–407.

Rubin, K. H., & Everett, B. (1982). Social perspective-taking in young children. In S.G. Moore & C.R. Cooper (Eds.), *The young child: Reviews of research: Vol. 3.* Washington, DC: National Association for the Education of Young Children.

Schachter, F. F., & Strage, A. A. (1982). Adults' talk and children's language development. In S.G. Moore & C.R. Cooper (Eds.), *The young child: Reviews of research: Vol. 3.* Washington, DC: National Association for the Education of Young Children.

Shields, M. M. (1979). Dialogues, monologue and egocentric speech by children in nursery schools. In O.K. Garnica & M. L. King (Eds.), Language, children and society. London: Pergamon Press.

Wells, G. (1981). Learning through interaction: The study of language development. London: Cambridge University Press.

Zumeta, W., & Solomon, L. C. (1982). Professions education. In *Encyclopedia of educational research: Vol. 3* (5th ed.). New York: Macmillan and Free Press.

12

THE DEVELOPMENTAL
STAGES OF TEACHERS*

The conception of the developmental stages of preschool teachers presented in this chapter began to take shape when I was preparing a presentation for an in-service workshop for a small midwestern school district in 1971. When the program chairperson of the workshop informed me that all of the district's preschool and elementary school teachers would be in attendance, I puzzled over what to say that could be useful and interesting to a group varying substantially in background and experience. The attendees were likely to range from neophytes to teachers with more than thirty years of experience.

In particular, it seemed very likely that experienced teachers would find the ideas that were useful and relevant to their inexperienced colleagues to be old hat. Similarly, fledgling teachers might find the issues relevant to experienced teachers to be of insufficient practical value. The new teachers might welcome specific practical suggestions. The veterans in the audience, on the other hand, might welcome a talk about recent research and development and challenging ideas about the role of education in society.

Frances Fuller's pioneering work on developmental changes in the concerns of student teachers were somewhat familiar to me, and gave me the idea to apply the concept of development to the in-service period. I therefore began my talk by suggesting that in principle no one can enter a new social role as veteran! Furthermore, it is very likely that the progress from neophyte to

---

* This chapter was originally published as "The Developmental Stages of Teachers," by Lilian G. Katz, 1977. In L. G. Katz, *Talks with Teachers*. Washington, DC: National Association for the Education of Young Children. Reprinted with permission.

veteran in any role or line of work can be thought of in terms of progressive stages in which concerns and understandings of what it is about shift as experience accrues. The teachers responded so positively to this view of their own in-service needs that I was encouraged to develop this principle in greater detail.

Since most of my work at that time was with Head Start teachers, who typically had little if any preservice training, the paper was addressed to the developmental stages of preschool teachers.

Since that time a substantial body of research of the developmental stages of teachers has been reported. Using a specially designed questionnaire, my students and I attempted to validate the sequence of stages outlined in the chapter. We found some support for the proposed "survival stage." But our data indicated that teachers who were likely to have reached the hypothesized "mature" stage seemed to move out of the classroom to nonclassroom roles such as curriculum coordinators, reading specialists, and the like. The data also suggested that many veteran teachers had experiences that caused them to revert to the concerns characteristic of the survival stage when their local contexts changed. For example, some veterans reported that they had felt confident and competent until district policy introduced a new curriculum, or the school neighborhood changed and the children were different from those to whom they were accustomed. Even though the data did not clearly validate the hypothesized stages, many colleagues around the country continue to cite this paper as one of their favorites!

Teachers can generally be counted on to talk about developmental needs and stages when they discuss children. It may be equally meaningful to think of teachers themselves as having developmental sequences in their professional growth patterns (Katz & Weir 1969). The purpose of the present discussion is to outline the tasks and associated training needs of each suggested developmental stage, and to consider the implications for the timing and location of training efforts. The developmental stages and their related training needs are shown in Figure 12–1.

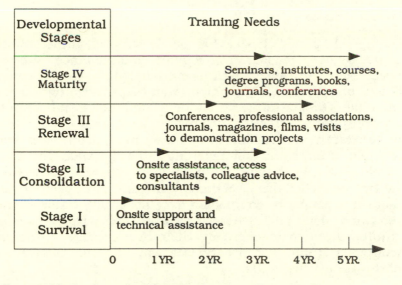

Developmental Stages	Training Needs
Stage IV Maturity	Seminars, institutes, courses, degree programs, books, journals, conferences
Stage III Renewal	Conferences, professional associations, journals, magazines, films, visits to demonstration projects
Stage II Consolidation	Onsite assistance, access to specialists, colleague advice, consultants
Stage I Survival	Onsite support and technical assistance

0   1 YR.   2 YR.   3 YR.   4 YR.   5 YR.

FIGURE 12–1   STAGES OF DEVELOPMENT AND TRAINING NEEDS OF PRESCHOOL TEACHERS

STAGE I-SURVIVAL

Developmental Tasks

During this stage, which may last throughout the first full year of teaching, the teacher's main concern is whether or not she can *survive*. This preoccupation with survival may be expressed in terms like these: "Can I get through the day in one piece? Without losing a child? Can I make it until the end of the week? To the next vacation? Can I really do this kind of work day after day? Will I be accepted by my colleagues?" Such questions are well expressed in Ryan's (1970) enlightening collection of accounts of first-year teaching experiences.

The first full impact of responsibility for a group of immature but vigorous young children (to say nothing of encounters with their parents) inevitably provokes teacher anxieties. The discrepancies between anticipated successes and classroom realities intensifies feelings of inadequacy and unpreparedness.

Training Needs

During this period the teacher needs support, understanding, encouragement, reassurance, comfort, and guidance. She needs direct help with specific skills and insight into the complex causes of behavior—all of which must be provided on the classroom site. On-site trainers may be senior staff members, advisers, consultants, directors, or program assistants. Training must be constantly and readily available from someone who knows both the trainee and her teaching situation well. The trainer should have enough time and flexibility to be on call as needed by the trainee. Schedules of periodic visits that have been arranged in advance cannot be counted on to coincide with trainees' crises. Cook and Mack (1971) describe the British pattern of on-site training given to teachers by their headmasters (principals). Armington (1969) also describes a way in which advisers can meet these teacher needs.

STAGE II-CONSOLIDATION

Developmental Tasks

By the end of the first year the teacher usually has come to see herself as capable of surviving immediate crises. She is now ready to consolidate the overall gains made during the first stage and to differentiate specific tasks and skills to be mastered next. During Stage II, teachers usually begin to focus on individual problem children and problem situations. This focus may take the form of looking for answers to such questions as: "How can I help a clinging child? How can I help a particular child who does not seem to be learning?"

During Stage I, the neophyte acquires a baseline of information about what young children are like and what to expect of them. By Stage II the teacher is beginning to identify individual children whose behavior departs from the pattern of most of the children she knows.

Training Needs

During this stage, on-site training continues to be valuable. A trainer can help the teacher through joint exploration of a problem. Take, for example, the case of a young preschool teacher eager to get help who expressed her problem in the question, "How should I deal with a clinging child?" An on-site trainer can, of course, observe the teacher and child *in situ* and arrive at suggestions and tentative solution strategies fairly quickly. However, without firsthand knowledge of the child and the context, an extended give-and-take conversation between teacher and trainer may be the best way for the trainer to help the teacher to interpret her experience and move toward a solution of the problems. The trainer might ask the teacher such questions as, "What have you done so far? Can you give an example of some experiences with this particular child during this week? When you did such and such, how did the child respond?" (See Chapter 5 for some examples of problem-treatment strategies.)

Also, in this stage the need for information about specific children or problem children suggests that learning to use a wider range of resources would be timely. Psychologists, social and health workers, and other specialists can strengthen the teacher's skills and knowledge at this time. Exchanges of information and ideas with more experienced colleagues may help teachers master their developmental tasks of this period. Opportunities to share feelings with other teachers in the same stage of development may help to reduce some of the teacher's sense of personal inadequacy and frustration.

STAGE III—RENEWAL

Developmental Tasks

Often, during the third or fourth year of teaching the teacher begins to tire of doing the same old things. She starts to ask more questions about new developments in the field: "What are some new approaches to helping children's language development? Who is doing what? Where? What are some of the new materials, techniques, approaches, and ideas?" It may be that what the teacher has been doing for each annual cohort of children has been quite adequate for them, but that she herself finds the recurrent Valentine cards, Easter bunnies, and pumpkin cut-outs insufficiently interesting! If it is true that a teacher's own interest or commitment to the projects and activities she provides for children contributes to their educational value, then her need for renewal and refreshment should be taken seriously.

Training Needs

During this stage, teachers find it especially rewarding to meet colleagues from different programs on both formal and informal occasions. Teachers in this developmental stage are particularly receptive to experiences in local, regional, and national conferences and workshops, and profit from membership in professional associations and participation in their meetings. Teachers are now widening the scope of their reading, scanning numerous magazines and journals, and viewing films and videotapes. Perhaps during this period they may be ready to take a close look at their own classroom teaching through videotaping. This is also a time when teachers welcome opportunities to visit other classes, programs, and demonstration projects.

Perhaps it is at this stage that the teacher center has the greatest potential value (Bailey 1971; Silberman 1971). Teacher centers are places where teachers can gather together to help each other learn or relearn skills, techniques, and methods, to exchange ideas, and to organize special workshops. From time to time specialists in curriculum, child growth, or any other area of concern identified by the teachers are invited to the center to meet with them.

STAGE IV—MATURITY

Developmental Tasks

Maturity may be reached by some teachers within three years, by others in five or more. The teacher at this stage has come to terms with herself as a teacher and has reached a comfortable level of confidence in her own competence. She now has enough perspective to begin to ask deeper and more abstract questions, such as: "What are my historical and philosophical roots? What is the nature of growth and learning? How are educational decisions made? Can schools change societies? Is teaching a profession?" Perhaps she has asked these questions before. But with the experience now behind her, the questions represent a more meaningful search for insight, perspective, and realism.

Training Needs

Throughout maturity, teachers need an opportunity to participate in conferences and seminars and perhaps to work toward a degree. Mature teachers welcome the chance to read widely and to interact with educators working on many problem areas on many different levels. Training sessions and conference events that Stage II teachers enjoy may be very tiresome to the Stage IV teacher. Similarly, introspective and searching discussion seminars enjoyed by Stage IV teachers may lead to restlessness and irritability among the beginners of Stage I.

SUMMARY

In the above outline, four dimensions of training for teaching have been suggested: (a) developmental stages of the teacher; (b) training needs of each stage; (c) location of the training; and (d) timing of training.

Developmental Stage of the Teacher It is useful to think of the growth of teachers as occurring in stages, linked very generally to experience gained over time.

Training Needs of Each Stage The training needs of teachers change as experience accrues. For example, the issues dealt with in the traditional social foundations courses do not seem to address themselves to the early survival problems that are critical to the inexperienced. However, for the maturing teacher, those same issues may help to deepen her understanding of the larger complex context in which she is trying to be effective.

Location of Training The location of training should be moved as the teacher develops. At the beginning of the new teacher's career, training resources must be taken *to* her so that training can be responsive to the particular (and possibly unique) developmental tasks and working situation she faces in her classroom and school. Later, as the teacher moves beyond the survival stage, training can move toward the teacher center and the college campus.

Timing of Training   The timing of training should be shifted so that more training is available to the teacher on the job than before she begins to work in the classroom. Many teachers say that their preservice education has had only a minor influence on what they do day-to-day in their classrooms, which suggests that strategies acquired before employment often will not be retrieved under the pressures of the actual classroom and school situation.

However, even though it is often said that experience is the best teacher, we cannot assume that experience teaches what the new trainee should learn. To guide this learning, and to make sure that the beginning teacher has *informed* and *interpreted* experience, should be one of the major roles of the teacher trainer.

REFERENCES

Armington, D. (1969). A plan for continuing growth. Mimeographed. Newton, MA: Educational Development Center. (ED 046 493)

Bailey, S. K. (1971). Teachers' centers: A British first. *Phi Delta Kappan 53*(3), 146–149

Cook, A., & Mack, M. (1971). *The headteacher's role.* New York: Citation.

Katz, L. G., & Weir, M. K. (1969). Help for preschool teachers: A proposal. Mimeographed. Urbana, Ill.: ERIC Clearinghouse on Early Childhood Education. (ED 031 308)

Ryan, K. (Ed.) (1970). *Don't smile until Christmas: Accounts of the first year of teaching.* Chicago: University of Chicago Press.

Silberman, A. (1971). A Santa's workshop for teachers. *American Education 7*(10), 3–8.

13

EARLY CHILDHOOD
PROGRAMS AND
IDEOLOGICAL DISPUTES*

I first began to think about the issues in this chapter when I was the only educator participating along with psychologists specializing in the measurement of intelligence in a panel discussion on contemporary trends. As the discussion proceeded I began to speculate on what would happen if we ranked every academic discipline on the large host university campus along two dimensions. On one dimension each discipline would be ranked according to the reliability of its data base. The second dimension would be a variable that combined the extent to which the field is dominated by charismatic leaders and is characterized by competing schools of thought or ideologies. Some of the comments by my fellow panelists led me to hypothesize that there is an inverse correlation between these two characteristics of academic disciplines. In other words, the more reliable the data base of a discipline, the less it is characterized by charismatic leaders and contending ideologies.

I then began to speculate about the implications of such a hypothesis for early childhood education. As far as I know, the hypothesis has not been tested, but the issues it raises still seem to be pertinent to our field.

---

* Originally published as "Early Childhood Programs and Ideological Disputes," by Lilian G. Katz (1975). *The Educational Forum, 39*(3), 267–271, and reprinted by permission in L. G. Katz (Ed.), (1977), *Talks with Teachers.* Washington, DC: National Association for the Education of Young Children, pp. 69–74.

As director of the ERIC Clearinghouse on Early Childhood Education for many years, I have had an opportunity to observe the flow of documents and inquiries, as well as to interact regularly with three of the groups of stakeholders in the field: the front-line workers in programs, child care centers, and classrooms; the research and development workers in laboratories, campuses, and industries; and government policy implementors at state, regional, and federal levels.

One of the most salient aspects of the field of early childhood education is the sharp divergence of views among workers and clients concerning what young children "need" as well as how and when these needs should be satisfied. (Franklin & Biber, 1977; Kohlberg & Mayer, 1972; Maccoby & Zellner, 1970). In the formal research and development literature, exchanges of these divergent views are typically couched in the languages of theory, methodology, and evaluation (Anderson, 1973; Stanley, 1973).

The ERIC Clearinghouse on Early Childhood Education[1] frequently receives requests to "send something that shows that model X does (or does not) work." Occasionally, a legislative assistant or a state official asks, "What do the experts say about teaching X to preschoolers?" Perhaps the most common case of conflicting views is expressed in questions about the effects of structured versus unstructured curriculum models. Inquirers are typically chagrined if not resentful when we inform them that "it depends on which expert you consult." Akers (1972) captures the national pattern when he says:

> The American public seems always to seek "the" way. . . .
> This pressure has contributed to competition among various
> . . . projects, leading to pronouncements of superiority or
> greater effectiveness of this approach over that. The worker
> in the field has been left either in a position of confusion
> and dilemma or of unyielding commitment to a particular
> program. (p. 7)

The main argument of this chapter is that the habitual argumentativeness in the field can be understood and appreciated when set within the framework of ideological rather than theoretical conflicts. I would like to discuss briefly some functions, conse-

---

[1] Renamed the ERIC Clearinghouse on Elementary and Early Childhood Education.

quences, and implications of the ideological conflicts in early childhood education.

PROBLEMS OF IDEOLOGY

The term ideology has many definitions (Naess, 1956). Tomkins (1965) takes ideology to mean:

> Any organization or set of ideas about which human beings are at once most articulate and most passionate, and for which there is no evidence and about which they are least certain.

In addition to these characteristics, ideologies seem to contain naive theories that attempt to establish or explain the relationships among events and phenomena. Such theories are typically related to an ideal conception of humanity and the good life (Naess, 1956). Although the term usually carries with it derogatory connotations, ideologies serve important functions and probably are indispensable.

FUNCTIONS OF IDEOLOGIES

A basic assumption here is that in any field in which the data base is unreliable—especially in terms of its validity—the vacuum generated by such data weakness is filled by ideologies. It is reasonable to assume that if scholarly disciplines were rank ordered in terms of their accessibility to reliable data, and ordered in terms of their freedom from ideological conflict, we could show a positive correlation between these two attributes. Early childhood education is a field especially susceptible to data weakness for several reasons.

First, the object of inquiry and investigation—the young child—is, by definition, immature. This immaturity has three consequences. One is that the organism is unstable. Mature organisms are relatively stable, if not rigid. But observed changes

in young children may signal instrument insufficiency, construct weakness, or growth, or all of the above in unspecifiable
proportions. Second, young children are undergoing development at a more rapid rate than at any other age, which makes
data about observed changes difficult to interpret. A third consequence of immaturity is that the organism is relatively powerless. The young child cannot get up and leave a child care center
when he or she does not like the quality of care. The child may
bite, vomit, wet, or "act out," but his or her power to modify
adults' responses is relatively small. It seems reasonable to
assume that the more powerless a client is, the more important
the worker's ethics—nested in an ideology—become.

A second reason for data weaknesses in early childhood education is that the definitive or critical experiments that might
settle important empirical questions cannot be performed. As
long as we have any reason to believe that something is good for
children, it would be unethical to withhold it from them just for
the sake of the advancement of science, or just to test techniques.
One example of such issues around which ideological disputes
revolve concerns the relative merits of placing young children in
child care centers (multiple caregivers) versus being cared for by
mothers or a mother-surrogate at home (single caregiver). The
accumulated research on relevant variables such as attachment,
loss, and separation anxiety (Bowlby 1973; Rutter 1971; Sears,
1974) is marked by the typical problems associated with heavy
reliance on clinical cases, clincal data, and insights.[2] Experimental research on relevant subvariables such as dependency
and nurturance (Maccoby & Masters, 1970) leaves many workers
with the typical doubts over the external validity of experimental
manipulations.

Taken together, these constraints on the development of reliable data, plus the pressure to protect the powerless through
commitments of sentiment (Katz, 1971), set an ideal stage for
ideological battles. In the absence of definitive experiments and
reliable data we can expect feminist groups to continue to press
for group care for the young and politicians to continue to claim
that group care threatens American family life. Scholars and
specialists in early childhood education similarly are caught in
the vacuum created by the unreliability of available data.

---

[2] See a recent acrimonious exchange on this very subject in a series of
commentaries by Fein, 1993; Walsh and King, 1993; Zimilies, 1993a, 1993b.

CONSEQUENCES OF IDEOLOGICAL CONFLICT

An apparent consequence of the ideological character of early childhood education is the development of encampments: Piagetians, behaviorists, neo-Freudians, open educators, and so on. Each camp seems to avoid the examination of counterevidence, primarily by rejecting each other's data as inadmissible. This state of affairs leads to statements such as those summarized in Rosenshine's (1972) law:

> There are some things tests cannot measure. These are among the most important of all. Our students did best on these.

Another apparent consequence of the ideological character of the field is its susceptibility to charismatic leaders. According to Nisbet (1966), charismatic authority in religion or politics

> is that wielded by an individual who is able to show through revelation, magical power or simply through boundless personal attraction . . . [or] . . . a unique force of command that overrides in popular estimation all that is bequeathed by either tradition or law.

Cohen (1969) has written persuasively to show Maria Montessori as a charismatic case in point in the field of early childhood education. As with ideological camps, charismatic leaders and their followers tend to avoid counterevidence as well as the kinds of cross-camp intellectual intercourse that might serve to advance the question-asking and problem-posing activities of the field.

Another consequence of early childhood education's reliance on ideology is its susceptibility to fads and bandwagons. As long as we are responding to powerful claims or persuasive personalities rather than to reliable evidence, programs and practices will fluctuate with the rise, fall, and resurrection of various "in" ideologies.

CONCLUSIONS

In frequent contacts with front-line workers in the field, I am often impressed by their lack of familiarity with what is known (with any reliability) about child growth, development, and learning. Similarly, in frequent contact with the knowledge producers in the field of child growth, development, and learning, I am impressed by how little they know and understand about what it is like to work day after day, in typically disheartening environments, with small and dependent children. This seems to me to constitute a serious two-way sophistication gap. A central role of our clearinghouse is to help each of these two groups understand the other and the contexts in which they work. It is no simple task; it requires having credibility in both groups and genuine respect and understanding of each group's needs and temptations (Katz, 1971). In addition, I sometimes find it my responsibility to help government policy formulators as well as implementors of innovative practices to understand each of these groups. Each group has its professional and occupational hazards and pressures. For the social scientist, skepticism toward data is functional, hence desirable; for the teacher, strong conviction about the rightness of what she is doing serves as a necessary motive for action; for the policymaker, a balance of skepticism and conviction seems to be required, although difficult to sustain against pressures for accountability.

Finally, if there is any single point I would like to convey to policy formulators concerning early childhood education, it is that policy decisions cannot—not even in the ideal case—be made soley on the basis of evidence. What we are willing to accept as evidence is also a function of our ideologies. The basic decisions in education are always moral decisions. Making these moral decisions is an activity in which there are no experts, but politically mobilized pressure and counterpressure groups, leaders and followers, and a large indifferent mass. No matter how carefully such policies may be developed, their implementations and evaluations occur in contexts of sometimes passionate and often bitter ideological controversies—a fact of life that the specialist and expert must learn to accept with understanding, insight, and forbearance.

REFERENCES

Akers, M. E. (1972). "Prologue: The way of early childhood education." In I. J. Gordon (Ed.), *Early Childhood Education, The Seventy-First Yearbook of the National Society for the Study of Education, Part II.* Chicago: University of Chicago Press.

Anderson, S. B. (1973). Educational compensation and evaluation: A critique. In J. C. Stanley (Ed.), *Compensatory education for children, ages 2 to 8.* Baltimore: Johns Hopkins University Press.

Bowlby, J. (1973). *Attachment and Loss: Separation, Anxiety and Anger: Vol. 2.* New York: Basic Books.

Cohen, S. (1969). Maria Montessori: Priestess or pedagogue? *Teachers College Record, 71,* 313–326.

Fein, G. (1993). In defense of data adoration and even fetishism. *Early Childhood Research Quarterly, 8*(3), 387–396.

Franklin, M. B., & Biber, B. (1977). Psychological perspectives and early childhood education: Some relations between theory and practice. In L. G. Katz (Ed.), *Current topics in early childhood education: Vol. I.* Norwood, NJ: Ablex.

Katz, L. G. (1971, January). Sentimentality in preschool teachers: Some possible interpretations. *Peabody Journal of Education, 48.*

Kohlberg, L., & Mayer, R. (1972, November). Development as the aim of education. *Harvard Educational Review, 42.*

Maccoby, E. E., & Masters, J. C. (1970). Attachment and dependency. In P. Mussen (Ed.), *Carmichael's manual of child psychology.* New York: Wiley.

Maccoby, E. E., & Zellner, M. (1970). *Experiments in primary education: Aspects of Project Follow-Through.* New York: Harcourt Brace.

Naess, A. (1956). *Democracy, ideology and objectivity.* Oslo, Norway: Oslo University Press.

Nisbet, R. A. (1966). *The sociological tradition.* New York: Basic Books.

Rosenshine, B. (1972). *"Memo number three." National Center for Really New Educational Ideas.* Champaign, IL: University of Illinois.

Rutter, M. (1971). Parent–child separation: Psychological effects on the children. *Journal of Child Psychology, 12,* 233–260.

Sears, R. R. (1974). Separation in apes and children. *Contemporary Psychology, 18.*

Stanley, J. C. (1973). Introduction and critique. In J. C. Stanley (Ed.), *Compensatory education for children ages 2 to 8.* Baltimore: Johns Hopkins University Press.

Tomkins, S. S. (1965). Affect and the psychology of knowledge. In S. S. Tomkins and C. E. Izard (Eds.), *Affect, cognition, and personality: Empirical studies.* New York: Springer.

Walsh, D. J., & King, G. (1993). Good research and bad research: Extending Zimilies's criticism. *Early Childhood Research Quarterly, 8*(3), 397–400.

Zimilies, H. (1993a). The adoration of hard data: A case study of data fetishism in the evaluation of infant care. *Early Childhood Research Quarterly, 8*(3), 369–386.

Zimilies, H. (1993b). In search of a realistic research perspective: A response to Fein, and Walsh and King. *Early Childhood Research Quarterly, 8*(3), 401–405.

14

THE NATURE
OF PROFESSIONS:
WHERE IS EARLY
CHILDHOOD EDUCATION?*

This chapter is an extension of the topic introduced in the previous one. In particular, it is an attempt to apply definitions of the concept of profession to the field of early childhood education and to explore its implications for next steps in the trend toward professionalization of the field.

The purpose of this chapter is to examine the nature of professions and to apply the main features of the concept of a profession to the current state of the art of early childhood education.

The nature of professions and professionalism has recently become a topic of discussion at early childhood meetings. Indeed, the theme of the 1985 annual conference of the National Association for the Education of Young Children (NAEYC) was "Early Childhood Education: A Proud Profession!" This theme might be a case of protesting too much! While early childhood workers may not be members of an "ashamed" profession, considering its public image, financial status, and intellectual standing (Silin, 1985), it can hardly be described as a "proud" one.

---

* This chapter is based on an address presented at the Early Childhood Organization Conference in honor of Miss E. Marianne Parry, O. B. E., Bristol Polytechnic, Bristol, England, September, 1985.

Mounting pressure to identify and acknowledge early childhood personnel as professionals is due in some measure to grave concerns over the very low pay, status, and prestige of those who work in preschool settings. My own concern about the social and occupational status of the early childhood practitioner is related to the assumption that we cannot have optimum environments for children unless the environments are also optimum for the adults who work with them. Taking this assumption as virtually axiomatic, for several years I have tried to describe the factors required to create optimum environments for teachers of young children (see Chapter 9). By focusing on the needs of teachers, I do not intend in any way to diminish the centrality of parents' roles in their children's welfare and development. On the contrary, it seems to me that it is in the best interests of parents to be concerned about the qualities, status, and working conditions of their children's teachers and caregivers.

In other words, improving the lot of teachers is in no way antithetical to the interests of parents. Indeed, there is persuasive evidence that young children are sensitive to the moods, emotional states, and morale of the adults around them (Cummings, Iannotti, & Zahn-Waxler, 1985). Thus, it seems useful to illuminate issues relating to those factors affecting the status and morale of teachers of young children. However, we must acknowledge that much of what is required to upgrade the conditions and wages of practitioners would place a heavy burden upon precisely that portion of the population that can least afford to accept it.

WHAT ARE THE CHARACTERISTICS OF A PROFESSION?

Early in this century, scholars began analyzing the nature of professions. Analyses continue apace today as more and more occupational groups strive to upgrade themselves to professional status (Forsyth & Danisiewicz, 1983; Goode, 1983). Many definitions of the term *professional* appear in the literature. While I have attempted to synthesize these various definitions, for the purpose of this discussion I am drawing most heavily on the work of H. S. Becker (1962) in his classic paper "The Nature of a Profession."

Becker distinguishes between two uses of the term professional: the scientific concept and the folk concept. The former refers to the way social scientists use the term, and the latter corresponds to meanings given to the term in everyday language.

Popular Uses of the Term "Profession"

According to Becker (1962), the folk conception of a profession is evaluative in that it is used as an honorific designation. In popular use, the term denotes a quality of spirit and an exceptional level of dedication to morally praiseworthy work. It is also associated with high social status and is often assumed to be correlated with a high income. As is apparent from the realities of the field of early childhood education, much of the drive toward professionalization is based on popular rather than the scientific connotations of the term.

With respect to achieving the goals implicit in the popular conception of professionalism, early childhood practitioners do not seem to be doing very well. It is my impression from extensive experience with colleagues in many parts of the world that the younger the child with whom the practitioner works, the less training is required, the less ability is expected, the lower the pay, the fewer the employment benefits, and the poorer the working conditions.

While it may seem to us that our moral praiseworthiness should be obvious to all, acknowledgment of this fact is not widespread. I think that this situation is due in part to the possibility that in many countries, people really believe that young children should be at home with their mothers enjoying what is sometimes referred to as a "Norman Rockwellian" version of family life. While the fact that young children participate in various kinds of preschool settings is not to be blamed on the workers who staff them, many laypeople believe that the work involved in caring for children is no more than minding babies whose mothers are otherwise engaged.

We ourselves have consistently and strongly asserted that young children learn through play. It is perhaps not surprising, then, to find policy makers and others suggesting that children might just as well be left to play at home or on the neighborhood playground. Such critics frequently assert that such learning experiences do not require the provision of highly trained personnel, specialized buildings, or equipment. However, contemporary research and scholarship concerning the role and effects of play on various aspects of development indicate that play is a very complex phenomenon (cf. Brown & Gottfried, 1985; Carpenter, 1983). We must be careful to indicate that some play experiences are more beneficial than others and to stress that adults have a major role in maximizing the benefits children may derive from them.

As to our status, good reason exists to believe that as the proportion of women in an occupation increases, its status decreases (Wolfle, 1978). As if that were not enough, there is also evidence that the status of a practitioner is correlated with the status of the client. If this is indeed the case, then teachers and nannies who work with the offspring of high status and high income families may enjoy greater status than those who work with the children of inner-city poor or unemployed parents. Such status diffusion, applicable to many fields of work, is unlikely to be altered much by the present drive toward professionalization.

Scientific Definitions of the Term *Profession*

Most scholars of the subject agree that eight criteria must be met before a field of endeavor may be termed a profession. In the absence of a formal or conceptual rationale for ordering the importance of these criteria, I shall order them by introducing those to be treated most briefly first and those most fully last.

Social Necessity Most scholars include as a criterion of a profession that its work be essential to the functioning of a society, suggesting that the absence of its knowledge and techniques would weaken the society in some way.

The evidence bearing on whether or not the work of early childhood educators is essential to society is mixed at best. While recent reports of the longitudinal effects of early childhood education (Consortium for Longitudinal Studies, 1983) are very encouraging, they are in need of large scale replication. We still have a long way to go to make a convincing case that teachers of the highest quality can provide services to young children without which society is at risk.

Given the power of experiences in later childhood and adolescence to offset the benefits of good early experiences, we must be very careful in the statements we make about what we can achieve. We can be no more sure that the effects of good early experiences cannot be reversed than that early bad experiences can be remediated. Haskins' (1985) recent report of a long-term follow-up study of primary school children who had been in day care has indicated that such children are more aggressive in their primary school years than children who were not in day care and that those who had been in "cognitive" programs were more aggressive than those in other types of settings. Since we do not know what Haskins meant by "cognitive," these results are highly susceptible to misinterpretation and abuse by policy makers. Nor is it likely that any of the subjects in his study were in programs of the quality to which most of us are committed.

Altruism The mission of a profession is said to be altruistic in that it is service-oriented rather than profit-oriented. Professionals are said to have clients rather than customers or consumers. Ideally, professionals are expected to perform their services with unselfish dedication, if necessary working beyond normal hours and giving up personal comforts in the interests of society. Professions identify the goals of their work with the good of humanity at large, placing strong emphasis on social ends in contrast to the more tangible or immediate ends served by tradespeople, merchants, or entertainers.

On this criterion, we ought to be doing very well. No one can claim that teachers of young children are busy amassing riches or engaged in work that is simply easy or glamorous! The service ideal and client-centeredness of professions seems clearly characteristic of teaching in general and early childhood teaching in particular.

Autonomy Most scholars in the sociology of professions agree that, ideally, a profession is an occupation that is autonomous in at least two ways (Forsyth & Danisiewicz, 1983). The practitioner is autonomous in that the client does not dictate to him or her what services are to be rendered or how they are to be received. Ideally, professionals who practice in large organizations or institutions are also autonomous with respect to their employer, who does not dictate the nature of practice but hires the professional to exercise judgment based on specialized knowledge, principles, and techniques. As Braude (cited in Forsyth & Danisiewicz, 1983) points out, "To the degree that a worker is constrained in the performance of his work by the controls and demands of others, that individual is less professional"(p. 42).

Issues concerning autonomy with respect to clients are complex for the early childhood educator. Our profession has at least three client groups: parents, children, and the larger society or posterity. All of us are challenged by the paradoxical situation of wanting to strengthen and increase parent involvement in children's education while at the same time wishing to exercise our best professional judgment as to what is in children's best interests. We still have much to learn about how to be more sensitive to parents without being intimidated by them. To laypeople, parent involvement seems so simple that our apparent resistance to it is difficult to understand. A large part of the parent involvement problem is that parents are not a monolithic aggregate. Understandably, parents do not all agree on what goals and methods are appropriate for early childhood education. Let us hope that we work in a country that prizes diversity of views, values, opinions, and cultures among the parents of the children we teach. However, the more diverse the client group, the less likely it is that all the parents of any one teacher's pupils will be equally satisfied. To which of the parents is the teacher to accede? All of them? The one with the loudest voice? The highest status? In the United States, schools have always been responsive to parents—but not to *all* parents—just to those few who have had power and status in the community. To develop as a profession requires that we learn how to respond to demands and desires on the part of clients that are sometimes strident and often incompatible and contradictory on the basis of our very best professional judgment, that is based on the best available knowledge and practices.

Although parents and society at large are served by our profession, most teachers think of children as their primary clients. A possible pitfall exists in this narrow view of the client group. Specifically, every school of thought, educational method, or approach in part argues its merits on the basis that "the children love it." Maybe so. But the fact that children "love" an activity is not sufficient justification for its inclusion in the curriculum. Children love candy, junk food, silly cartoons, and what are considered by many to be inappropriate television programs. Although children's preferences must be taken into consideration, decisions concerning curriculum should not be made solely on the basis of the enjoyment of one client group. Enjoyment, in and of itself, is not an appropriate goal for education. The appropriate goal for education—at every level—is to engage the learner's mind and to assist that mind in its efforts to make better and deeper sense of significant experiences. I should add here that when teachers accomplish this end, most children find their education enjoyable. In other words, enjoyment is a byproduct rather than a goal of good teaching.

In a sense, society or posterity is the educator's ultimate client. But societies such as ours often demand incompatible achievements. They want the young to learn to be both cooperative and competitive. They want conformity and initiative. It is no simple matter to help children learn where and when such different dispositions are appropriate. Our communities say that at the least, they want excellence, high standards of achievement, and equality of opportunity. What principles of learning, development, curriculum, evaluation, and testing can we apply to meet such multiple and often contradictory expectations (Green, 1983)?

Code of Ethics Consistent with client-centeredness, professional societies subscribe to a code of ethics intended to protect the best interests of clients and to minimize yielding to the temptations inherent in the practice of the profession (see Chapter 15). In addition, professional societies institute procedures for disciplining members in cases of violations of the code of ethics.

The development of a code of ethics for early childhood educators is not an easy task. The process involves identifying the major temptations confronted in the course of practice (Katz, 1984). The code should address ethical dilemmas inherent in relations with children, parents, colleagues, employers, and the general lay public. Many people are skeptical about the usefulness of such codes. However, it seems to me that the ethical norms of a group of colleagues, explicated in a code of ethics, can help give individual members the feeling that their colleagues will back them up when they have to take a risky but courageous stand on a controversial ethical issue. It is likely that when we believe our fellow practitioners will take the same stands as we would, or that they would censure us if we failed to live up to the code, our commitment to right action is strengthened.

The NAEYC has formed a special committee to work on the development of a code for its members. Several state branches of the association already have developed their own. Inasmuch as local values and cultural variations play a strong role in conceptions of ethical standards, it would seem wise for each country, region, or cultural unit to develop its own code.

Distance from Client   Since, by definition, the practice of a profession requires bringing to bear a body of knowledge and principles to the solution of problems and predicaments, the relationship between practitioner and client is marked by optimum emotional distance, disinterest, or "detached concern" (see Chapter 10). This distance from the client is reflected in the strong taboo against physicians treating members of their own families; in such situations, it is felt that emotional attachment and empathy might interfere with the exercise of reasoned judgment. This feature of professional practice does not preclude such feelings as empathy or compassion but is intended to place these feelings in appropriate perspective. Emphasis on such optimum distance is also expected to minimize the temptation to develop favorites among children and parents, and to inhibit the tendency to respond to clients in terms of personal predilection or impulses rather than on the basis of reasoned judgment.

I am aware that many specialists and teachers in early childhood education resist this aspect of professionalism—and not without reason. Among other things, they worry about meeting children's apparent need for closeness and affection. However, young children generally are capable of experiencing such feelings even when the teacher maintains an optimum distance. Though effective teaching requires intimate knowledge of pupils, this can be achieved by frequent contact, observation, and listening without the kind of emotionality required of family relationships. In addition, many early childhood educators associate optimum distance with a stereotypical view of a remote, unresponsive, and intimidating expert who is likely to breed resentment among parents. In fact, optimum distance serves to protect the teacher from the risks of emotional burnout that can endanger functioning as well as undermine effectiveness with children. I want to emphasize that the emotional distance should be an *optimum* one in that it should permit the teacher to be responsive, caring, and compassionate, as well as to exercise professional judgment and bring knowledge to bear on responses to children.

Standards of Practice   Most scholars also agree that a profession adopts standards of practice that are significant in three ways:

1. Standards are adopted below which it is expected no practitioner will fall. These standards are meant to ensure that

every practitioner applies the standard procedures in the course of exercising professional judgment. In some measure, these standards result in standardization of professional performance (for example, all physicians follow standard procedures in making diagnoses but exercise their own judgment in deciding what actions to take). In theory, at least, professional practice is distinguished from the work of artisans, tradespeople, technicians, or bureaucrats in that it does not simply implement fixed routines, rules of thumb, or regulations. Rather than following a set of recipes, the professional practitioner acts on the basis of accepted principles that are taken into account in the formulation of professional judgment.

2. The standards developed and adopted are addressed to the standard predicaments that every member can be expected to encounter fairly often in the course of practice. The standard procedures applied to the standard problems encountered in the course of practice are accumulated into the body of professional knowledge.

3. Standards of performance are universalistic rather than particularistic. Universalistic standards of performance imply that all the knowledge, skill, insight, ingenuity, and so on, possessed by the practitioner is available to every client, independent of such irrelevant personal attributes of the client as social and ethnic background, ability to pay, or personal appeal.

One of the major tasks ahead for us, as I see it, is to develop and articulate our perceptions of professional standards. One approach that we might consider is to enumerate and describe the standard predicaments that all early childhood educators confront in the course of their day-to-day work. One example of such attempt can be seen Chapter 11, which shows 4-year-olds quarrelling over whose turn it is to use a tricycle. In this examination, the responses of a professionally trained teacher are compared with the responses of an untrained person in order to highlight how professional judgment comes into play.

Much more work is needed to identify the predicaments considered most important and to explicate our understanding of the knowledge and practices professionally appropriate for resolving the predicament.

Prolonged Training Most scholars of the sociology of professions agree that a major defining attribute of a profession is that
it requires entrants to undergo prolonged training. Although
there are no standards by which to judge how long such training
should be, the training process itself is thought to have several
particular characteristics:

1. The training is specialized in order to ensure the acquisition
   of complex knowledge and techniques.
2. The training processes are difficult and impose cognitive
   strain. As a consequence of careful screening, some candidates can be expected to fail. Training should be marked by
   optimum stress and sacrifice, resulting in dedication and
   commitment to the profession (Katz & Raths, 1986).
3. In all professions, candidates are required to master more
   knowledge than is likely to be applied and more than the
   student perceives to be necessary. In all professions, candidates complain about these excesses and the apparent irrel-
   evance of much of the knowledge they are expected to
   master.
4. Institutions responsible for professional training must be
   accredited or licensed by processes monitored by practicing
   members of the profession. These institutions award certificates, diplomas, or degrees under the supervision of members of the profession.
5. All professional training institutions offer trainees a common core of knowledge and techniques so that the entire
   membership of the profession shares a common allusionary
   base.
6. Professional societies and training institutions, very often
   in concert, provide systematic and regular continuing education for members.

It is not clear what kind and amount of training is required for
high quality professional performance (see, for example, Katz,
1984). In general, I think that we should stop being defensive
about expecting candidates in teacher education to study theory,
research, history, and philosophy. My reasons for this stance
include the point made above that all professions expose their
candidates to more knowledge than they ever apply, expecting
not more than about a third of what is mastered to be retained.
(The more studied, the larger that third is.) Furthermore, evi-

dence exists to show that even though one forgets facts and concepts once they are mastered, such knowledge enables one to go on absorbing new facts and concepts more easily long after training has been completed (Broudy, 1983). In addition, I would like to suggest that there is a sense in which it is important for practitioners to be literate in their own fields: Though they may never use Montessori's ideas, all early childhood practitioners should know who she was and should comprehend the main ideas she espoused.

In many countries, there is cause for concern about the characteristics of entrants into training. Too often, young women are advised to enter early childhood education because their shyness makes them unsuitable for work with older pupils or because they are not academically strong enough to take up a more challenging or profitable occupation. Sadly, we have heard reports from several countries that preschool teachers have been urged to transfer into secondary teaching because they were judged "too good for infants."

Disheartening evidence exists to suggest that among graduates of teacher education degree programs, those with the greatest ability last the shortest length of time in the teaching service (Schlechty & Vance, 1981). As more alternatives and attractive opportunities for women become available, this "brain drain" is likely to continue. It can only be stemmed if working conditions and pay scales are dramatically improved and if the needs of young children are given higher social priority. To some extent, the field of early childhood education—especially child care and day nursery work—is caught in a vicious cycle. People enter it with few skills, and no one wants to pay good wages for workers with few skills. Because the pay is low, the likelihood is that those with little training and few skills will take up the work. How can we break this cycle? While we must acknowledge that there are poor teachers at work, even among those with extensive training, good in-service education can help. But what may be required for a real break in the cycle is public understanding and recognition of the potential benefits of high quality education in the early years and deeper public commitment to the welfare of young children.

It is not uncommon for laypeople to point out that they know of an outstanding teacher who has had no training. Perhaps all of us have encountered just such a gifted or "natural" teacher. This claim is, however, a dangerous one. Abraham Lincoln was a self-taught lawyer, but virtually everything about him was exceptional. Furthermore, there was a great deal less to be learned by lawyers in his time. The main point here is that a profession can never be designed on the basis of its exceptions. On the contrary, professional training is designed to provide *all* its practitioners with minimal standards to help them perform effectively. If all lawyers had Lincoln's remarkable qualities of mind and could teach themselves as thoroughly as he did, we might have no need for law schools.

Specialized Knowledge   Scholars seem to agree that a major defining attribute of a profession is that it is an occupation whose practices are based on specialized knowledge. This knowledge is thought to have several characteristics:

1. The knowledge is abstract rather than concrete (as in the case of crafts, sports, trades, or bureaucracies, in which the knowledge may consist of rules of thumb, rules, or regulations).
2. The knowledge consists of principles that are reasonably reliable generalizations to be considered in the course of practicing the profession. Some scholars insist that the knowledge underlying professional practice must be organized into a systematic body of principles.
3. The knowledge and principles are relevant to practical rather than metaphysical or academic concerns. They are intended to rationalize the techniques of the profession and, as such, are oriented to some kind of practical and socially useful end.
4. The body of knowledge is esoteric or exclusive in that it is known only to practitioners of the profession and is unknown to laypeople. In this sense, the profession has a monopoly on most of its relevant knowledge and techniques.
5. Practitioners belong to professional societies that take responsibility for disseminating new knowledge relevant to practice by producing scholarly journals and by providing conferences and workshops through which members are kept informed.

Can we identify the body of knowledge, specify the reliable principles, and develop a consensus as to the best available practices that will serve as a basis for professional practice in early childhood education? It is not clear what procedures are to be followed in finding answers to this question. We each might begin by listing those principles that we consider essential and worthy of inclusion and then examine the list in a systematic way. To what extent would we agree on our lists? Finding answers to these questions is one of the big tasks ahead of us.

Some principles I wish to nominate for inclusion in our professional body of specialized knowledge are outlined very briefly below. These assertions are derived from my own understanding of what constitutes the best practice and my interpretation of the literature on children's learning and development.

- Teaching strategies and curriculum decisions are best when they take into account both the potential value of immediate experiences and their long-term benefits. Teaching and curriculum practices that keep children busy and/or amused in the short term may or may not provide a solid foundation for the long course of learning and development.

- Young children's learning is optimized when children are engaged in interaction and in active rather than passive activities.

- Many of the experiences or factors that influence development and learning are likely to be most beneficial when they occur in optimum rather than extreme amounts, intensities, or frequencies. In terms of teaching strategies, for example, the help, attention, or stimulation given can be both too little or too great for the development of a given individual's self-reliance. Likewise, the extent to which the curriculum includes routines can also be excessive or insufficient for the management of the life of a group of children.

- The curriculum for young children is oriented toward helping them to make better sense of their own environment and experiences. As children grow, the concepts, ideas, and topics introduced are extended to include others' environments and experiences.

- Many aspects of development and learning have the characteristic of a recursive cycle in that once a child has a behavior pattern, the chances are that others will respond to him or her in such a way that the pattern will be strengthened. Thus, for example, a child who is unlikable is very likely to be responded to with rejection and to respond to rejection in such a way as to become more unlikable. A related principle of development is that a child cannot effect a change on his or her own; the adult must intervene to interrupt the recursive cycle.

- The more informal the learning environment, the more access the teacher has to information about where the child is in terms of development and learning. The more informed the teacher is, the more likely he or she is to be able to make appropriate decisions about what teaching strategies to use and what curriculum activities to introduce. A related principle is that the life of the group is likely to be enhanced by optimum rather than maximium informality.

- Appropriate teaching strategies and curricula are those that take into account the acquisition of knowledge, skills, *and* dispositions, especially the dispositions to go on learning and to apply the knowledge and skills acquired. Emphasis on the acquisition of knowledge and on practicing skills is excessive when it undermines such dispositions as curiosity, creativity, and other types of intrinsic motivation.

- The younger children are, the greater the variety of teaching strategies and the greater the flexibility of the curriculum required. The use of a single pedagogical method or narrow range of curriculum materials and activities increases the likelihood that a significant proportion of children will experience feelings of incompetence.

Many more principles can be added to this list, and I urge members of the early childhood community both as individuals and as members of a professional society to develop and share more.

WHAT LIES AHEAD?

It seems to me that the research on development and learning currently being reported in the journals is much more applicable to pedagogical practice than it was when I first entered the field 20 years ago. In Britain, the work of such scholars as Clark (Clark & Wade, 1983), Donaldson (1983), Dunn (Dunn & Dale, 1984), Karmiloff-Smith (1984), Rutter (Garmezy & Rutter, 1983), Wells (1983) and many others is rich in implications for principles of education in the early years. In the United States, the list of scholars whose work supports the informal, or intellectually rather than academically oriented, approach to early childhood education is also long. I commend the research of Brown (Brown & Campione, 1984), Carpenter (1983), Gottman (1983), Nelson (Nelson & Seidman, 1984), and Rogoff (1983), among many others. These investigators support the view that with the help of very skilled, observant, attentive, reflective, and thoughtful adults, children construct their own understandings and sharpen their skills through interaction with their environment. In this sense, it seems to me that contemporary developmental researchers are painstakingly rediscovering the insights of John Dewey.

I recently came across a copy of D. E. M. Gardner's *Testing Results in the Infant School,* a book published in England in 1941 and not widely known among early childhood educators in the United States. I was surprised to find that Gardner begins by describing two contrasting types of infant schools. Although she refers to the two types as School A and School B, we would most likely refer to one as formal and academic and the other as informal or child-centered. These descriptions can be used almost verbatim to characterize contrasting early childhood education settings today in many parts of the world. The basic arguments Gardner makes about appropriate learning environments for young children still have to be made today. Although current research on children's intellectual development reaffirms Gardner's views of how children learn, we have yet to marshal the kind of compelling evidence we need to establish that the methods advocated by Gardner and Marianne Parry are more effective than others, particularly in the long term.

There are several reasons why we cannot produce the kind of persuasive empirical evidence we need. First, it is difficult to conduct longitudinal studies of young children and their teachers that would take into account the accepted canons of social science research. It seems as though the more rigorous the research design, the less relevant or valid the data, and vice versa. Second, to conduct investigations that would satisfy standard scientific requirements would very likely be unethical: it is unethical to subject others to experiences one has reason to suspect may not be good for them for the sake of research—or for any other purpose.

Inevitably, then, we work in a field in which reliable data are difficult to obtain. In any field in which the database is slippery, the informational vacuum is filled by ideologies (see Chapter 13). Thus, our commitment to particular approaches even in the absence of compelling evidence that they are best or right is in the nature of the field. However, the risks attendant upon such conditions are that we tend to reject counterevidence and resist others' views. A professional code of ethics should remind us to keep an open mind, to look carefully at all the available evidence, to clearly identify to what extent the stands we take are based on evidence, on experience, and on ideology. Such reminders are among the important functions of professional societies. It may be that when we are clear about the bases of our views, we shall be better able to increase public understanding of them and thereby gain support in our efforts to improve provisions for young children.

REFERENCES

Becker, H. S. (1962). The nature of a profession. In N. B. Henry (Ed.), *Education for the professions* (pp. 27–46). National Society for the Study of Education Yearbook. Chicago: National Society for the Study of Education.

Broudy, H. S. (1983). The humanities and their uses: Proper claims and expectations. *Journal of Aesthetic Education, 17*(4), 125–148.

Brown, A. L., & Campione, J. C. (1984). Three faces of transfer: Implications for early competence, individual differences, and instruction. In M. E. Lamb, A. L. Brown, & B. Rogoff (Eds.), *Advances in developmental psychology: Vol. 3* (pp. 143–192). Hillsdale, NJ: Erlbaum.

Brown, C. C., & Gottfried, A. (1985). *Play interactions: The role of toys and parental involvement in children's development.* Pediatric Round Table 11. Skillman, NJ: Johnson & Johnson.

Carpenter, J. (1983). Activity structure and play: Implications for socialization. In M. B. Liss (Ed.), *Social and cognitive skills: Sex roles and children's play* (pp. 117–143). New York: Academic.

Clark, M. M., & Wade, B. (1983). Early childhood education [Special issue]. *Educational Review, 5*(2).

Consortium for Longitudinal Studies. (1983). *As the twig is bent.* Hillsdale, NJ: Erlbaum.

Cummings, E. M., Iannotti, R. J., & Zahn-Waxler, C. (1985). Influence of conflict between adults on the emotions and aggression of young children. *Developmental Psychology, 21*(3), 495–507.

Donaldson, M. (1983). Children's reasoning. In M. Donaldson, R. Grieve, & C. Pratt (Eds.), *Early childhood development and education* (pp. 231–236). London: Guilford.

Dunn, J., & Dale, N. (1984). Collaboration in joint pretend. In I. Brethertion (Ed.), *Symbolic play: The development of social understanding* (pp. 131–157). New York: Academic.

Forsyth, P. B., & Danisiewicz, T. J. (1983). Toward a theory of professionalization. In P. Silver (Ed.), *Professionalism in educational administration* (pp. 39–45). Victoria, Australia: Deakin University Press.

Gardner, D. E. M. (1941). *Testing results in the infant school.* London: Methuen.

Garmezy, N., & Rutter, M. (Eds.). (1983). *Stress, coping and development in children.* New York: McGraw Hill.

Goode, W. J. (1983). The theoretical limits of professionalization. In P. Silver (Ed.), *Professionalism in educational administration* (pp. 46–67). Victoria, Australia: Deakin University Press.

Gottman, J. M. (1983). How children become friends. *Monographs of the Society for Research in Child Development, 48*(3, Serial No. 201).

Green, T. F. (1983). Excellence, equity, and equality. In L. Shulman & G. Sykes (Eds.), *Handbook of teaching and policy* (pp. 318–341). New York: Longmans.

Haskins, R. (1985). Public school aggression in children with varying day-care experiences. *Child Development, 56,* 689–703.

Karmiloff-Smith, A. (1984). Children's problem solving. In M. Lamb, A. Brown, & B. Rogoff (Eds.), *Advances in developmental psychology: Vol. 3* (pp. 39–90). Hillsdale, NJ: Erlbaum.

Katz, L. G. (1984). The education of preprimary teachers. In L. G. Katz, P. J. Wagemaker, & K. Steiner (Eds.), *Current topics in early childhood education: Vol. 5* (pp. 209–227). Norwood, NJ: Ablex.

Katz, L. G., & Raths, J. D. (1986). A framework for research on teacher education programs. *Journal of Teacher Education, 26*(6), 9–15.

Nelson, K., & Seidman, S. (1984). Playing with scripts. In I. Bretherton (Ed.), *Symbolic play: The development of social understanding* (pp. 45–71). New York: Academic.

Rogoff, B. (1983). Integrating context and cognitive development. In M. E. Lamb & A. L. Brown (Eds.), *Advances in developmental psychology: Vol. 2* (pp. 125–170). Hillsdale, NJ: Erlbaum.

Schlechty, P.C., & Vance, V. S. (1981). Do academically able teachers leave education? The North Carolina case. *Phi Delta Kappan, 63*(2), 106–112.

Silin, J. (1985, March). Authority as knowledge: A problem of professionalization. *Young Children,* 41–46.

Wells, G. (1983). Talking with children: The complementary roles of parents and teachers. In M. Donaldson, R. Grieve, & C. Pratt (Eds.), *Early childhood development and education.* London: Guilford.

Wolfle, L. M. (1978). *Prestige in an American university.* Paper presented at the annual meeting of the American Educational Research Assocation, Toronto, Canada.

15

ETHICAL ISSUES
IN WORKING WITH
YOUNG CHILDREN*

The ideas in this chapter on the ethical issues involved in teaching young children grew from several encounters with preschool and child care teachers in which they raised questions that could not be settled on the basis of available regulations or evidence related to early childhood. As suggested in the chapter, many of the most important situations frequently faced by teachers involve moral dilemmas that cannot be settled on the basis of educational or developmental theory and research.

Since the original paper on which this chapter is based was published in 1977, the National Association for the Education of Young Children has published a code of ethics for teachers and a Statement of Commitment to accompany it that address most of the issues raised here (Feeney & Kipnis, 1992). Efforts by the National Association for the Education of Young Children to explicate types of ethical dilemmas encountered by teachers of young children are continuing and provide a basis for productive staff meetings and staff development.

---

* Originally published as *Ethical Issues in Working with Children*, by Lilian G. Katz, 1977. Urbana, IL: ERIC Clearinghouse on Elementary & Early Childhood Education. Reprinted with permission.

What should a teacher do when

> A parent demands that a method of discipline that goes against the teacher's own preferences be used?
>
> The owner of the day care center appears to be giving false information to the licensing authorities?
>
> A parent complains about the behavior of a colleague?
>
> A child tells a story about law-breaking behavior observed at home?
>
> A mother pours out all her personal troubles to her?

The list of questions of this kind is potentially very long. But answers to such questions cannot be drawn from research, from the accumulated knowledge of child development, or even from educational philosophy. The questions raised and their answers lie in the realm of professional ethics.

One of the characteristic features of a profession is that its practitioners share a code of ethics, usually developed, promoted, and monitored by a professional society or association. Agreement as to whether a given occupation is really a bona fide profession, and exactly when it becomes so, is difficult to obtain (Becker, 1962; see Chapter 14). In this discussion, the term *profession* is used in its general sense to refer to an occupation that is client- or service-centered as distinguished from occupations that are profit- or product-centered or bureaucratically organized. While day care and preschool personnel are not yet fully professionalized, their work frequently gives rise to the kinds of problems addressed by codes of ethics.

The purpose of this examination is to encourage discussion of the complex ethical problems encountered by day care and preschool workers. I shall attempt to suggest some of the central issues by addressing the following questions:

> What do we mean by a code of ethics?
>
> Why is a code of ethics important?
>
> What are some examples of ethical conflicts in day care and preschool work?
>
> What steps might be taken to help day care and preschool workers resolve these ethical conflicts?

WHAT DO WE MEAN BY A CODE OF ETHICS?

Of all the dictionary definitions of ethics available, the one most relevant to this discussion is from Webster's second edition, unabridged: "the system or code of morals of a particular philosopher, religion, group, profession, etc. . . . ." More specifically, Moore (1970) defines ethics as "private systems of law which are characteristic of all formally constituted organizations" (p. 116). He notes also that these codes "highlight proper relations with clients or others outside the organizations, rather than procedural rules for organizational behavior" (p. 116). Similarly, Bersoff (1975) says that ethical considerations "refer to the way a group of associates define their special responsibility to one another and the rest of the social order in which they work" (p. 359).

Maurice Levine (1972), in an examination of the complex ethical problems that arise in the practice of psychiatry, proposes that codes of ethics can be understood as one of the methods by which groups of workers cope with their temptations. He suggests also that ethics have the function of minimizing the distorting effects of wishful thinking and of limiting or inhibiting people's destructive impulses. In addition, Levine asserts that codes of ethics embody those principles or forces that stand in opposition to self-aggrandizement—especially when self-aggrandizement might be at the expense of others. Similarly, according to Levine, ethics provide guidelines for action in cases of potentially significant damage to others or potential harm to another's interest. In much the same spirit, Eisenberg (1975) suggests that the more powerful a change agent or given treatment and the riskier its application, the more important ethics become. Thus, as the risk to either the client or the practitioner increases, the necessity for ethical guidelines seems to increase.

From time to time, I have asked students in early childhood education to try to develop codes of ethics for themselves. Invariably, they produce sets of statements that are more appropriately defined as goals rather than ethics, although the distinctions between the two are not always easily made. The statement "I shall impart knowledge and skills" seems to belong to the category of goals. The statement "I shall respect the child's ethnic background" more readily seems to belong to the category of ethics. The major distinction between the two categories seems to be that goals are broad statements about the effects one intends to have. Ethics, on the other hand, seem to be statements about how to conduct oneself in the course of implementing goals. Codes of ethics are statements about right or good ways to conduct ourselves in the course of implementing our goals.

In summary, a code of ethics may be defined as a set of statements that help us to deal with the temptations inherent in our occupations. A code of ethics may also help us to act in terms of what we believe to be right rather than in terms of what is expedient—especially when doing what we believe is right carries risks. Situations in which doing what is right carries a high probability of getting an award or of being rewarded may not require a code of ethics as much as do situations rife with such risks as, perhaps, the loss of a job, a license to practice, the threat of professional blacklisting, or even harsher consequences. They are statements that encourage us—that literally give us the courage—to act in accordance with our professional judgment of what is best for the clients being served even when the clients themselves may not agree. Codes of ethics give us courage to act in terms of what we believe to be in the best interests of clients rather than in terms of what will make our clients like us. Ethical statements help us to choose between what is right versus what is, in a sense, more right; choices between right and wrong are not problematic. Needless to say, the ethical principles implied in the code reflect the group's position on what is valuable and worthwhile in society in general.

For purposes of this discussion, the main features of codes of ethics considered are the group's beliefs about (a) what is right rather than expedient; (b) what is good rather than simply practical; (c) what acts members must never engage in or condone even if those acts would "work" or if members could get away with them; and (d) acts to which members must never be accomplices, bystanders, or contributors.

WHY IS A CODE OF ETHICS IMPORTANT?

The specific aspects of working with preschool children that give rise to the ethical problems addressed here are the power and status of practitioners, the multiplicity of clients, the uncertainty of the empirical data base, and role ambiguity. Each aspect is discussed below.

Power and Status of Practitioners

It is taken as a general principle that in a profession, the more powerless the client is vis-à-vis the practitioner, the more important the practitioner's ethics become. That is to say, the greater the power of the practitioner over the client, the greater the necessity for internalized restraints against abusing that power.

Preschool practitioners have great power over young children, especially in child care centers and family day care homes. The superior physical power practitioners have over young children is obvious. In addition, practitioners have virtually total power over the psychological "goods and resources" of value to the youngsters in their care. The young child's power to modify a teacher's behavior is largely dependent on the extent to which a teacher yields that power. Whatever power children might have over their caregivers' behavior is unlikely to be under conscious control. Obviously, young children cannot effectively organize strikes or boycotts, or report malpractice to the authorities. Children may report to a parent what they perceive to be abusive caregiver behavior, but the validity of such reports is often questioned. Furthermore, parental reactions to these reports may be unreliable. In one case, a 5-year-old reported to his mother that he had been given only one slice of bread during the whole day at the child care center as punishment for misbehavior. His mother was reported to have responded by saying. "Then tomorrow, behave yourself."

It is neither possible nor desirable to monitor teachers constantly in order to ensure that such abuses do not occur. As Moore (1970) puts it, because there are often no other experts watching and the child's self-protective repertoire is limited, a code of ethics, internalized as commitment to right conduct, might help to strengthen resistance to occupational temptations and help practitioners to make ethical choices.

Another aspect of the work of preschool and day care practitioners related to ethical conduct is the relatively low status of practitioners in the early childhood field. Parents seem far more likely to make demands on practitioners for given kinds of practices in preschools, child care centers, and family day care homes than they are to demand specific medical procedures from pediatricians, for example.

A case in point is an incident concerning a young mother who brought her 4-year-old son to the child care center every morning at 7:30 and picked him up again every evening around 5:30 in the evening. She gave the staff strict instructions that under no circumstances was the child to nap during the day. She explained that when she took her son home in the evenings after her long tiring day of work she needed to be able to feed him and have him tucked away for the night as soon as possible. It is not difficult to picture the problems encountered by the staff of this proprietary child care center. By the middle of the afternoon, this child was unmanageable. The state regulations under which the center was licensed specified a daily rest period for all children. Sensitivity and responsiveness to parental references, however, were also main tenets of the center's philosophy. Although the staff attempted to talk to the mother about the child's fatigue and intractability, the mother had little regard for the staff's expertise and judgment, and a total disregard for state licensing standards.

In the situation described above, the staff was frustrated and angered by the mother and the child, and felt victimized by both. Could they put the child down for a nap and get away with it? A real temptation! Would that work? Would it be right? It might have been right to ask the mother to place her child in a different center. But such a suggestion has risks: A proprietary child care center is financially dependent on maintaining as full enrollment as possible. Also, in some communities alternative placements are simply not available.

Accumulated experience suggests that 4-year-olds thrive best with adequate rest periods during the day, and a state regulation requiring such a program provision is unlikely to be controversial. The problem outlined above could have been solved by invoking the state regulations. But state regulations are not uniformly observed. Why should this particular one be honored when others are overlooked?

Working daily with young and relatively powerless clients is likely to carry with it many temptations to abuse power. Practitioners may have been tempted at one time or another to regiment the children, to treat them all alike, to intimidate them into conformity to adult demands, to reject unattractive children, or to become deeply attached to a few of the children. Thus, the hortatory literature addressed to preschool practitioners reminds them to respect individual difference, to accept children, to use positive guidance, and to treat children with dignity. It seems reasonable to suggest that most such exhortations should be part of a code of ethics.

Multiplicity of Clients

A code of ethics may help practitioners to resolve issues arising from the fact that they serve a variety of client groups. Most preschool workers, when asked, "Who is your client?" usually respond without hesitation, "The child." But it is probably more realistic to order the client groups into a hierarchy so that parents are the prime group, children second, and the employing agency and the larger community third (Beker, 1976; Bersoff, 1975). Each group of clients in the hierarchy may be perceived as exerting pressures for practitioners to act in ways that may be against the best interests of another client group.

As a case in point, preschool practitioners often lament the fact that many parents want their preschoolers to learn to read, while they themselves consider such instruction premature for most preschoolers and therefore potentially harmful to them. At times, the best interests of both parents and children may be in conflict with agency interests and expectations, and so forth. A code of ethics should help to clarify the position of each client group in the hierarchy and should provide guidelines on how to resolve questions concerning which of the groups has the best claim to practitioners' consideration.

Uncertainty of the Empirical Base

Many differences of opinion about appropriate courses of action cannot be resolved by reference to either state or local regulations or a reliable body of empirical evidence. It is taken as a general proposition that weakness in the empirical base of a professional field often causes a vacuum likely to be filled by ideologies (see Chapter 13). The field of day care and preschool education is one that seems to qualify as ideology-bound, giving rise to a variety of temptations for practitioners.

The uncertainty and/or unavailability of reliable empirical findings about the long-term developmental consequences of early experience tempts practitioners (and their leaders) to develop orthodoxies and to become doctrinaire in their collective statements. Such orthodoxies and doctrines may be functional to the extent that they provide practitioners with a sense of conviction and the confidence necessary for effective action. Such conviction, however, may be accompanied by rejection of alternative methods and denial of some of the facts that may be available. A code of ethics could serve to remind practitioners to eschew orthodoxies, to strive to be well-informed and open-minded, and to keep abreast of new ideas and development.

Role Ambiguity

Research and development activities in recent years have resulted in increased emphasis on the importance of the developmental and stimulus functions of child care and preschool practitioners, as compared with more traditional custodial and guidance functions. In addition, recent policies related to early childhood education emphasize parental involvement at all levels of programming, concern for nutrition and health screening, and relevant social services. These pressures and policies add to and aggravate a long-standing problem of role ambiguity for preschool practitioners.

The central source of ambiguity stems from the general proposition that the younger the child served, the wider the range of the functioning for which adults must assume responsibility. Child care and preschool practitioners cannot limit their concerns only to children's academic progress and socialization. The immaturity of the client presses the practitioner into responding to almost all of the child's needs and behaviors. Responsibility for the whole child may lead to uncertainty over role boundaries in, for example, cases of disagreement with parents over methods of discipline, toilet training, sex-role socialization, and so on. Clarification of the boundaries of practitioner roles and/or the limits of their expertise could be reflected in a code of ethics.

SUMMARY

In brief, four aspects of the role of child care and preschool workers seem to imply the necessity for a code of ethics: high power and low status, multiplicity of client groups, uncertainty in the empirical database, and ambiguity of the role boundaries of practitioners. It seems reasonable to suggest that the actual problems encountered by practitioners in the course of daily situations typically reflect combinations of several of these aspects of the field.

WHAT ARE SOME EXAMPLES OF ETHICAL PROBLEMS?

Some examples of situations that seem to call upon preschool practitioners to make ethical choices are outlined below. Specifically, the examples are discussed in relationship to major client groups, such as parents, children, and colleagues and employers.

Ethical Issues Involving Parents

Perhaps the most persistent ethical problems faced by preschool practitioners are those they encounter in their relations with parents. One common source of problems is the fact that practitioners generally reflect and cherish so-called middle class values and tend to confuse conventional behavior with normal development. An increase in practitioners' self-consciousness about being middle class (in the last dozen years) seems to have increased their hesitancy to take a stand in controversies with parents.

Within any given group, preferences and values may vary widely according to parents' membership in particular cultural, ethnic, or socioeconomic groups. A practitioner may, for example, choose to reinforce children as they acquire conventional gender-role characteristics. But one or more parents in the client group may prefer what has come to be called an "alternative lifestyle" with respect to sex-role socialization. Or a parent may demand of her child's teacher that her son not be allowed to play with dolls, even though the teacher may prefer not to discourage such play. When practitioners are committed to respect and respond to parental values and input, they may be faced with having to choose between what is right and what is right. Similarly, the incident described earlier in this discussion of the mother who demanded that her child not nap during the day put the teachers in a choice between what was right and what was right. In a sense, it would have been right for the teachers to respect a parent's wishes, it would have been right to observe the state licensing regulations specifying daily periods of rest, and it would have right to encourage so young a child to take a rest during the day. What data or pedagogical principles can be brought to bear on such choices?

Similar types of parent–staff ethical conflicts arise from discrepancies between parental and practitioner preferences with respect to curriculum goals and methods. For example, practitioners often prefer informal, open, or so called "child-centered" curriculum goals and methods, while many parents opt for more academic approaches. If parents are the primary clients of the staff, what posture should the staff take when discrepancies in preferences occur? Specifically, suppose that a child in an informal setting produces a piece of artwork that appears to his parents to be nothing more than scribbles. The teacher respects the work as the child's attempt at self-expression and also values the kinds of fine motor skills exercised in this activity. However, what if the practitioner knows that the artwork might cause a parent to make demeaning remarks to or even scold the child? Suppose the same teacher also knows that if the child brings home work regarded by the parents as evidence of mastering the "Three Rs," the parents will offer compliments and rewards? How should the teacher resolve the conflict between his or her pedagogical and ideological preferences and the demands of the home on the child? What choice would be in the best interest of the child? It is unlikely that such issues can be settled on the basis of available evidence (Spodek, 1977).

Disagreements between practitioners and parents as to which child behaviors should be permitted, modified, or punished are legion. Some of these disagreements are a function of differences between the referent baselines of the two groups. Practitioners tend to assess and evaluate behavior against a baseline derived from experience with hundreds of children in the age groups concerned. Thus, their concepts of what is the normal or typical range of behavior for the age group are apt to be much wider than those of the parents. As a result, practitioners' tolerance for children's behavior (including such things as thumb-sucking, crying, masturbating, using dirty words, and displaying aggression and sexual and sex-role experimentation) is likely to be greater than that of the majority of parents. Sometimes the situation is reversed: the teacher's wider experience of children causes him or her to be concerned about a child's development although the parents, because of their limited exposure to the age group, accept it as normal. Parents do not universally accept the wisdom that comes from practitioners' experience; not infrequently, parents instruct caregivers and teachers to prohibit what practitioners themselves accept as normal behavior. How can practitioners respect parental preferences and their own expertise as well?

Yet another kind of problem between practitioners and parents is likely to affect the child very little. In the course of their daily work, preschool practitioners often encounter mothers who attempt to involve them too directly and intimately in their personal lives. For example, a mother may spill out all her problems to her child's preschool teacher. When this happens, the practitioner may find such information unwelcome. The parent in this case may be seeking advice on matters that lie outside of the practitioner's training and expertise. As a result, the practitioner may want to refer the parent to specialized counseling or treatment. Are there risks in making such referrals? What about the possibility that the unwanted information implies to the practitioner that the child might be in psychological danger, and the mother rejects the recommendation for specialized help? What is the practitioner's responsibility to the whole child? Such cases are common in many other occupational situations requiring confidentiality and sensitivity in handling information about clients' private lives. A code of ethics should address issues concerning the limits of expertise and the confidentiality of information.

Another ethical issue in practitioner–parent relations concerns the risks and limits of truthfulness in sharing information with parents and colleagues. For example, parents often ask preschool teachers about their children's behavior. In some cases, a parent wants to check up on his or her child in order to know whether the child is persisting in undesirable behavior. If the practitioner knows that a truthful report will lead to severe punishment of the child, how should a reply be formulated? Similarly, in filling out reports on children's progress for use by others, practitioners often worry as to whether a truthful portrayal of a given child will result in prejudicial and damaging treatment by practitioners receiving the report in the subsequent setting.

Withholding information is a type of "playing God" that generally causes considerable anxiety in teachers. In a similar way, let us suppose that a practitioner has good reason to believe that making a positive report to a parent about a child's behavior will improve relations between the child and his or her parents (even though the report might be exaggerated or untrue). Even if the ploy has a high probability of working, would it be ethically defensible?

In summary, day care and preschool practitioners face constant ethical dilemmas in their relations with parents. Contemporary emphasis on greater involvement and participation of parents in children's education and care is likely to increase and intensify these problems. A code of ethics cannot solve the problems encountered by preschool practitioners, but it can provide a basis upon which staff members and their clients might, together, confront and think through their common and separate responsibilities, concerns, and ideas about what they believe to be right.

Ethical Issues Involving Children

One of the sources of ethical conflicts for preschool workers stems from the fact that young children have not yet been socialized into the role of pupil. A 10-year-old has been socialized to know fairly well that some things are not discussed with teachers at school. The preschooler does not yet have a sense of the boundaries between home and school or of what he or she should or should not tell caretakers and teachers. Children often report parental activities that practitioners would rather not know about; sometimes such reports may be of private or even illegal things going on at home. One problem with this sort of information is that it is difficult to assess. It is important for the practitioner to realize that when he or she is presented with such a situation, asking leading follow-up questions may encourage a child to tell too much. What should a practitioner do with such information? Practitioners sometimes find themselves at a loss for words when this occurs (Rosenburg & Ehrgott, 1977).

Another type of problem related to program activities also seems to have ethical implications. Children's enjoyment of certain activities should of course be considered in program planning, but the enjoyability of an activity is not sufficient in and of itself to justify its inclusion in a particular program. For example, children like to watch television but are not adequate judges of what programs are worthwhile. This type of problem involves complex pedagogical, psychological, and ethical issues (Peters, 1966). Sometimes such problems are confounded by caregivers' tendencies to be motivated by a strong wish to be loved, accepted, or appreciated by the children. Children's affection and respect are useful indicators of the practitioner's effectiveness, but such positive responses should be the consequences of right actions rather than the motive underlying the practitioner's choices and decisions.

Preschool practitioners are increasingly under pressure to teach their children academic skills. On the whole, practitioners appear to resist such pressures, not only on the basis of the possible prematurity of such skill learning but also as part of a general rejection of so-called structured or didactic teaching. Occasionally, however, the pressure may be so great as to tempt practitioners into giving their charges crash courses on test items, thereby minimizing the likelihood of a poor showing on standardized tests. Even if practitioners can get away with such tactics, should they be ethically constrained against doing so? Should a code of ethics address questions of what stand to take on the uses and potential abuses of tests for assessing achievement, for screening, and for labeling children?

Ethical Issues Involving Colleagues and Employing Agencies

One of the most common sources of conflict between co-workers in preschool settings centers around divergent views on how to treat children. Staff meetings conducted by supervisors, or supervisory intervention and assistance on a one-to-one basis, seem to be the appropriate strategies and contexts for resolving such conflicts. But when a parent complains to one teacher about another, how should the recipient of the complaint respond? Such cases often constitute a real temptation to side with the complainant. But would that response be right? Perhaps one guideline that may be relevant to such interstaff conflicts would be for the individual practitioners involved to ask themselves (and other appropriate resource people) whether the objectionable practice is really harmful to children. If the answer, after serious reflection, is clearly "yes," then action by the appropriate authority must be taken to stop the harmful practice. But the state-of-the-art of child care and preschool education does not yet lend itself to definitive answers to all questions of clear and present danger to children. If the practices in question are objectionable merely on the grounds of taste, ideological persuasion, one's own culture, or orthodoxy, then practitioners should resist the temptation to indulge in feuds among themselves and to form alliances with parents against one another.

Examples of ethical dilemmas facing practitioners in their relations with employers include those in which practitioners are aware of violations of state or local regulations, misrepresentations of operating procedures in reports to licensing authorities, or instances of the owner's misrepresentations of the nature of the program and services offered to clients. To what extent should teachers contribute, even passively, to such violations? Most child care and preschool personnel work without contracts and thus risk losing their jobs if they give evidence or information that might threaten the operating license of their employing agency. Should employees be silent bystanders or accomplices in these kinds of situations? Silence would be practical, but would it be ethical?

Another type of dilemma confronts practitioners when agencies providing child care services require declarations of income from parents in order to determine their fees. One such case concerned a welfare mother who finally obtained a job and realized that the child care fees corresponding to her income would cause her actual income to amount to only a few more dollars than she had been receiving on welfare. Yet she really wanted to work. Her child's caregiver advised her not to tell the child care agency that she was employed and to wait for the authorities to bring up the matter first. It is easy to see that the practitioner in this situation was an active agent in violating agency and state regulations. But the practitioner also knew that alternative arrangements for child care were unavailable to this mother and that the child had just begun to feel at home and to thrive in the day care center. The practitioner judged the whole family's best interest to be undermined by the income-fee regulations. How would a code of ethics address such a predicament?

WHAT NEXT STEPS MIGHT BE TAKEN?

Some preliminary steps toward developing a code of ethics have already been taken. The Minnesota Association for the Education of Young Children (MnAEYC) adopted a code of ethical conduct responsibilities in 1976. The code enumerates a total of 34 principles divided into three categories: (a) general principles for all members; (b) additional principles for members who serve children in a specific capacity; and (c) principles for members who serve through ancillary services (such as training, licensing, and so on). Each category is further delineated into four subcategories for members who are trainers, licensing personnel, parents, and supervisors and administrators.

Many of the principles listed in the MnAEYC code correspond to suggestions made in this discussion. A number of the principles, however, might be more applicable to job descriptions than to a code of ethics (for example, Principle 29, which is for supervisors, states that the supervisor should provide regular in-service training to further staff development and to meet licensing requirements when appropriate). Three of the principles are addressed to members who are parents. Since parents are clients rather than practitioners, the appropriateness of including them in a practitioners' code of ethics is doubtful.

An initial code of ethics for early childhood education and development professionals has also been proposed by Ward (1977). Ward proposes 19 statements of commitments under three headings: (a) for the child, (b) for the parents and family members, and (c) for myself and the early childhood profession. These statements cover a wide range of aspects of working with young children, and together with the code adopted by MnAEYC could provide a useful basis for further discussion.

It seems advisable to begin at a local level to refine these codes or develop another code. Small groups of workers at a given day care or child development center or locale might constitute themselves into an ethics committee and thrash through issues to determine where they stand. Local efforts and problems could be shared with the ethics committees of statewide associations. The process of developing and refining a code of ethics will undoubtedly be slow and arduous.

Many practitioners are cynical about the value of such codes. but, as Levine (1972) points out, the work of developing a code involves self-scrutiny, which in and of itself may strengthen resistance to the many temptations encountered in practice. Furthermore, recent research on helping behavior suggests that individuals' responses to their own conflicting impulses are strongly influenced by their perceptions of the norms of the group with which they identify (Wilson, 1976). The norms of our group of colleagues, articulated in a code of ethics, may help to give us the feeling that colleagues will back us if we take a risky (but courageous) stand or censure us if we fail to live up to the code. The daily work of child care and preschool practitioners is fraught with ambiguities. A code of ethics may help practitioners to cope with greater courage and success.

REFERENCES

Becker, H. S. (1962). The nature of a profession. In N.B. Henry (Ed.), *Education for the professions*. The sixty-first yearbook of the National Society for the Study of Education. University of Chicago Press.

Beker, J. (1976). Editorial: On defining the child care profession: 1. *Child Care Quarterly, 5*(3), 165–166.

Bersoff, D. N. (1975). Professional ethics and legal responsibilities: On the horns of a dilemma. *Journal of School Psychology, 13*(4), 359–376.

Eisenberg, L. (1975). The ethics of intervention: Acting amidst ambiguity. *Journal of Child Psychiatry, 16*(2), 93–104.

Feeney, S., & Kipnis, K. (1992). *Code of ethical conduct and statement of commitment.* Washington, DC: National Association for the Education of Young Children.

Levine, M. (1972). *Psychiatry and ethics.* New York: George Braziller.

Minnesota Association for the Education of Young Children. (1976). *Code of ethical responsibilities.* Available from author, 1821 University Ave., Room 373, St. Paul, MN 55104.

Moore, W. E. (1970). *The professions: Roles and rules.* New York: Russell Sage Foundation.

Peters, R. S. (1966). *Ethics and education.* New York: Scott, Foresman.

Rosenburg, H., & Ehrgott, R. H. (1977). Games teachers play. *School Review, 85*(3), 433–437.

Spodek, B. (1977). Curriculum construction in early childhood education. In B. Spodek & H. J. Walberg (Eds.), *Early childhood education.* Berkeley, CA: McCutchan.

Ward, E. H. (1977). A code of ethics: The hallmark of a profession. In B. Spodek (Ed.), *Teaching practices: Reexamining assumptions.* Washington, DC: National Association for the Education of Young Children.

Wilson, J. P. (1976). Motivation, modeling, and altruism: A person x situation analysis. *Journal of Personality and Social Psychology, 34*(6), 1078–1086.

16

HELPING OTHERS
WITH THEIR TEACHING*

The basic ideas in this chapter originated from my experience as a UNESCO consultant in one of the Caribbean islands as I tried to understand and assist an education officer with the complex problems of helping others with their teaching. They were further elaborated upon when I worked with Project Head Start's Planned Variation Experiment in the early 1970s, as they became the basis for what was called The Enabler Model.

While the main focus of the chapter is on the role of those responsible for in-service education, it is hoped that the principles and techniques are relevant to the work of supervisors of student teaching as well.

Most programs for young children make provisions for the continuing education of staff members. Those who provide continuing education may be directors of Head Start programs or child care centers; they may be Child Development Associate (CDA) field trainers, supervisors of student teaching, consultants, curriculum specialists, or others. In the work of all individuals filling such roles aimed at helping others with their teaching, similar situations, issues, and problems arise, and similar decisions and choices have to be made.

The purpose of this discussion is to present some assumptions, principles, and techniques that might be useful for teacher educators, whether they work with in-service teachers or with care-

---

* An earlier version of this paper was originally published as "Helping Others Learn to Teach" in 1979 by the ERIC Clearinghouse on Elementary and Early Childhood Education, Urbana, IL.

givers in child care programs, CDAs, or even as prospective teachers. Typically the participant in in-service education is not in the traditional student role of working with an abstract or theoretical set of topics organized into formal lectures. Instead, the learner is usually an adult with strong involvement in the subject and object of the interaction—namely, his or her own teaching behavior.

Throughout this discussion, the term *principle* is used as defined by R. S. Peters (1970) to mean that which makes a consideration relevant. In other words, a principle is a generalization of sufficient reliability that it is worthy of being considered when making decisions. As such, principles are like decision rules, which help to guide choices among alternative courses of action. They are not ironclad, fail-safe rules to be applied mindlessly but are intended to be qualified by such phrases as "under some circumstances," or "as the situation warrants." Although these phrases are not mentioned repeatedly below, each principle outlined in the following discussion should be considered with appropriate qualifiers in mind.

PRINCIPLES FOR THE SELECTION OF FOCUS

All of us who teach, at whatever level, have to face the fact that we cannot offer our learners all the possible advice, suggestions, commentary, or information that might be helpful, useful, or instructive to them. When we work with people in any situation, we constantly make choices concerning the nature of the interactions we have. Like all teaching, the work involved in helping others with their teaching is embedded in relationships. It is useful to assume that relationships have to have content and that people cannot just "relate" without some content that is of mutual or shared interest or concern. In the case of professional relationships, the content is about something outside of the personal concerns of the two or more individuals in the relationship.

The potential contents of human relationships are so large and broad that some decisions must be made concerning which content is most relevant, appropriate, and useful at any given time in any given situation. Similarly, there are probably more than a dozen "right" or effective ways to respond in any given situation—and probably just as many ineffective ways. Since we cannot respond in all the ways that are possible, choices have to be made. Some choices of the content of interaction are made by invoking tradition (this is how we have always done it). Others are made on the basis of the assumption that teachers either want or expect them, or will attend carefully to them. Some choices reflect philosophical commitments. The principles outlined below are recommended for use when considering what content to focus on when we interact with the teachers and student teachers we want to help.

1. Focus on the Teacher's Understandings of the Situation The term *understandings* is used here to refer to teachers' ideas, thoughts, constructions, concepts, assumptions, or schemas about such things as how children learn, what "works," how they affect their pupils, what they expect of themselves, what others expect of them, their roles, duties, and so forth. Perhaps the most useful course of action available to in-service educators may be to focus on helping teachers develop understandings of their work that are more appropriate, more accurate, deeper, and more finely differentiated than they had previously been (see Katz, 1977).The rationale underlying this principle is that the focus on understandings helps the teacher acquire knowledge, ideas, insights, or information that he or she can keep and use after the in-service educator has left the scene.

Directives, prescriptions, instructions, or even "orders" might also address the problem the teacher is trying to cope with, but their value is likely to be of short duration. It seems reasonable to assume that modified understandings are more likely than prescriptions and directives to help teachers to generate appropriate new behaviors by themselves. To illustrate, one teacher complained that she had been unable to stop one of her kindergartners from persistently hitting several others in her class. When asked what approaches she had tried so far, she explained that she had already hit the boy as hard as she dared in order to "show him how much hitting hurts." In such a situation, the in-service educator might want simply to prohibit the teacher's hitting by citing a rule or regulation or a philosophical position.

However, the teacher's understanding of a kindergartner's ability to learn from being hit and feeling pain that it is important not to hit others seems inadequate. In this case, the teacher's understanding of the situation she is trying to cope with could be improved by suggesting to her that when adults hurt children (by hitting them) and provide a model for hurting others, they are unlikely to convince children not to do so as well. Such a principle concerning the adult as a model of desirable and undesirable conduct applies to many situations other than the specific one in question.

Other aspects of this teacher's understanding of children's responses to censure and her knowledge of alternative ways of handling the disruptive behavior of children might also be addressed by the in-service educator. While a directive or school district regulation might change the teacher's behavior in a particular incident, only modification of understandings is likely to have enduring value or to serve as a basis for more appropriate action in subsequent similar situations.

In-service educators often struggle with the question of how directive they should be. They frequently try to relate as "equals" to the teachers they are trying to help. While they are equal in most respects (they are equally adults, professionals, educators, citizens, and so on), it is taken to be a general principle that the role of any teacher—in this case the in-service educator—is legitimized by the fact that a teacher is someone whose understandings of the phenomenon of interest are better in certain ways than those of the learner. That is to say, an in-service educator is someone who has more useful, appropriate, accurate, or differentiated understandings than the teacher being helped. The tacit acknowledgment that such differences exist legitimizes the educator's right and authority to provide in-service training.

2. Focus on Strengthening Desirable Dispositions   Widespread enthusiasm for performance-based teacher education, and for competency-based education in general, seems to be associated with the risk of underemphasizing the development of learners' desirable dispositions. Dispositions, as defined here, include relatively stable "habits of mind" or tendencies to respond to experiences or to given situations in certain ways (see Chapter 3).

In deciding what responses to make to teachers, it is reasonable to choose those that are likely to strengthen enduring dispositions thought to be related to effective teaching. Such dispositions include openness to children's ideas and feelings, inventiveness or resourcefulness, patience (longer reaction times), friendliness, and enthusiasm. Dispositions that undermine effective teaching include tendencies to be impetuous, unfriendly, hypercritical, rejecting, racist, sexist, and so forth. Two suppositions provide the rationale for this principle. First, as already suggested, it seems obvious that we cannot teach all the knowledge, skills, methods, and techniques that are of potential use to teachers. This being the case, it seems advisable to teach teachers and caregivers in such a way as to strengthen their dispositions to go on learning, and to be inventive long after the in-service educator's work with them is over. Second, while we indeed want to help teachers with specific pedagogical skills and methods, it is important to do so without undermining their dispositions to be resourceful and "self-helpful." In short, we should guard against helping a teacher acquire competencies in a way that might engender or strengthen a disposition to be dependent or helpless.

3. Focus on Maintaining Competencies Already Acquired In our eagerness to be change agents, we may overlook the possibility that the teachers we work with may already have the competencies appropriate for, or required of, a given situation. Indeed, Gliessman (1984) has suggested that virtually all of the component skills of teaching are within the repertoires of most people, whether they have anything to do with teaching or not. People know how to listen, explain, give directions, state rules, and so on without professional training. Training is intended to mobilize already available skills into coherent and appropriate patterns for teaching.

Thus, the focus of in-service education should be on helping teachers use already available competencies more reliably, consistently, appropriately, or confidently. For example, a kindergarten teacher might be sufficiently skilled at guiding a discussion with pupils but may vary too greatly in his performance from one occasion to the next. If so, he probably does not require a training module on discussion skills, but would perhaps benefit more from a fuller or better understanding of the causes of his own performance fluctuations, or from assistance in becoming more alert to cues that cause him to perform in ways that (as the saying goes) he "knows better" than to do! He might be helped, at least temporarily, by the suggestion that he refrain from leading discussions except when classroom conditions are optimal. In that way, the teacher may be able to consolidate and strengthen mastery of a skill he already has before trying it out under less than optimal conditions. Similarly, teachers of young children are often exhorted to "listen" to the children. It is reasonable to assume that all teachers have such listening competencies in their repertoires, although they may employ them inappropriately and/or inconsistently.

In yet another case, a teacher may have the skills required to deal with a given situation but she may fail to use them with sufficient confidence to be effective. For example, if the teacher's actions betray a lack of confidence when she is setting limits or redirecting or stopping disruptive behavior, children may perceive mixed signals, challenge her, and thus exacerbate the situation, causing her already low confidence to decrease further. In such cases, the in-service educator's role becomes one of "shaping" and/or supporting the teacher's efforts to practice and strengthen already available behavior, rather than focusing on the acquisition of new competencies.

4. Focus on Building Long-term Relationships This principle refers to those situations in which an observation of a teacher prompts us to offer "corrections." Sometimes, in our eagerness to be helpful and to establish our own credibility, we may offer corrections too hastily. Although in certain situations it may be appropriate to make corrections, there is often the risk of losing the opportunity to go on helping that teacher over a longer period of time by alienating him or her through *premature* corrections. The principle of withholding correction is not a matter of the "rightness" of the advice but of allowing sufficient trust to develop between the in-service educator and the teacher so that the advice can be seen as an offer of help rather than as a criticism from an outside expert.

5. Focus on Providing Moderate Amounts of Inspiration Many of the teachers we are trying to help can cope admirably with the complex tasks and responsibilities they face. They may not require new techniques, modules, packages, or gimmicks, although they may believe them to be necessary. They may simply need occasional renewals of courage to enable them to sustain their efforts and to maintain enough enthusiasm to keep working at an unglamorous and often underappreciated job. Excessive sapping of courage or enthusiasm, at times approaching depression (that is, believing one's efforts have no effect), is a potential contributor to ineffectiveness, no matter how many competencies the teacher has. Such ineffectiveness may depress enthusiasm and courage even further, which in turn may again decrease effectiveness, initiating a downward spiral. The in-service educator may be able to intervene in the downward spiral by providing *moderate* inspiration, encouragement, and support.

It seems important that the inspirational message be specifically related to the work setting and its particular characteristics rather than a generalized message of goodwill. It is also suggested that supportive and encouraging messages contain real and useful information about the significance of the teacher's efforts. For example, it is likely to be more useful to say something like, "Those new activities really seemed to intrigue the older children in your class," than to say, "You're doing great." Furthermore, it may be wise to provide inspiration in optimum rather than maximum amounts so that teachers neither become "hooked" or dependent on it, thus undermining their dispositions to be self-helpful in the long run, nor feel really let down when the "high" wears off.

GENERAL TECHNIQUES FOR WORKING WITH TEACHERS

The principles outlined above are intended as overall guides or decision-making rules to help in-service educators select appropriate responses to in-service teaching situations. The general techniques described briefly below are intended to help the in-service educator to further the goals implied by those principles.

1. Maintain an Optimum Distance   Many educators consider closeness, warmth, and supportiveness essential and valuable attributes of their relationships with learners. Research seems to support the contention that warmth, for example, is related to teacher effectiveness, whether at the school or the in-service level. However, in-service educators may be tempted to make the error of being too close to the teachers for whom they are responsible. An optimum rather than maximum or minimum distance is recommended for several reasons. First, excessive closeness may inhibit or limit the teacher educator's ability to evaluate the teacher's progress realistically. Indeed, in such cases the teacher educator may be unable to help the teacher confront serious weaknesses or may fail to perceive the weaknesses at all. Second, if the teacher educator becomes too close to the teacher, he or she may unintentionally impinge on the teacher's right to privacy, a right deserving protection.

Third, there is some danger that if the teacher educator becomes too close to one of the teachers in a group, the tendency inadvertently to make a disparaging remark about another teacher in the group may be great, and credibility and effectiveness may thus be undermined. Fourth, if the relationships between teacher educators and teachers become too close or involved, emotional "burnout" for the teacher educator may result within a few months (Maslach & Pines, 1977). Not only may excessive personal stress be the result, but effectiveness on the job may also suffer. Minimum (versus optimum) closeness occurs when the educator's distance from the teacher or student teacher is too great. This would be manifested by coldness or aloofness, and is unlikely to provide a relationship in which growth and development can occur.

2. Cultivate the Habit of Suspending Judgment There is a strong tendency among those of us who are teachers to pass judgment on what we see in the classroom. We tend to judge not only the rightness or goodness of what we see, but also to assess whether the teacher is doing things "my way" or not. Such judgments seem to come naturally! However, if the intention is to stimulate and support someone's development, then instead of passing judgment, it may be more to the point to ask oneself questions such as the following: How can I account for what I am observing? Why is the teacher responding to the situation in this way? and, Why is this happening? In seeking answers to such questions, rather than judging the events observed, we are much more likely to learn those things that will increase our capacity to help the teacher. Answering such questions allows teacher educators to discover possible causes of a teacher's observed behavior. Each possible cause can be examined for plausibility, and when a reasonably plausible guess or answer has been identified, an appropriate method for helping the teacher can be selected and tried.

This technique is recommended for several reasons. First, it includes two features: It can help us resist the temptation to pass judgment, and at the same time it can encourage us to inspect our observations more closely. This in turn can help to slow down our responses to the situation, thereby reducing any tendency to overreact. Second, asking how the observed behavior might be accounted for is likely to lead to learning more about the people we are trying to help, and thus to increase insight into how the teacher defines the situation.

Obviously, there are many possible reasons why teachers do what they do. Sometimes the teacher's reason for a given action is that it appears to work, or perhaps a given action is all the teacher knows how to do in a particular situation. Often, teachers take certain actions because they think that the director or the principal wants them to behave in this way, even though that may not necessarily be the case. Some teachers do what they do because they think that others, such as parents, evaluators, colleagues, or visitors, want them to do it; or because their own teachers did these particular things; or because these things are simply traditional, and so forth.

In-service educators' attempts to account for the observed behavior of a teacher should help them to make more informed decisions about what to do next to help the teacher. The technique of suspending judgment is related to the more general principle of timing (Katz, 1977)—that the longer the latency before a teacher responds to the learner, the more information the teacher has and the more likely he or she is to make better decisions about the next steps. This latency principle seems especially relevant to in-service educators because they often enter classrooms cold, so to speak, with little if any prior information concerning the antecedents of the situation observed. The temptation to pass judgment rapidly may lead to important errors in assessing teacher needs and competencies.

3. Phrase Suggestions in Experimental Form Most teaching involves occasions when the most appropriate response to the learner is to make a suggestion. When giving suggestions to teachers, it is helpful to phrase them in the following form: "Next time X comes up, try Y, and see if it helps." Depending on the situation, it might be good to add something such as "X helps some teachers in this kind of situation—but if you find it doesn't seem to help, we can talk about something else to try."

This technique is recommended for several reasons. First, it can be expected to strengthen the teacher's dispositions to be experimental and resourceful. Furthermore, when a suggestion is offered with the implication that it is the one solution or the only answer to the problem, and if attempts to use it subsequently fail, the teacher's sense of frustration and defeat may be intensified rather than diminished. Similarly, it is advisable to make suggestions that the teacher to whom they are offered can be expected to try successfully. If suggestions require much greater sophistication than the teacher has, then the consequences are very likely to be feelings of failure and a greater sense of help-lessness or incompetence. Suggestions should be offered in such a way that in those instances—which will inevitably occur—in which the suggestion is not successful, the teacher can under-stand the reasons why failure resulted.

Another reason for recommending this technique is that when suggestions are made in terms of what to try "next time," the likelihood of humiliating or embarrassing the teacher about the incident just observed is minimized. Some in-service educators are so eager to get teachers to analyze their own "mistakes" following an unsuccessful teaching episode that they might inadvertently embarrass them, which in turn could undermine the teachers' dispositions to go on learning, trying, inventing, and seeking the best methods for themselves.

4. Avoid the Temptation to Stop Pattern Behavior From time to time we observe teacher behavior that we think should be stopped cold. While the teacher educator's position may indeed be right, a two-step approach toward such situations may be helpful. First, we can ask in such situations whether the behavior observed really endangers any child. If the answer is a clear "yes," then we must use all the resources at our disposal to bring the behavior to a halt. If the answer is ambiguous ("maybe") or if it is "no," then the next step is to help the teacher to try out and practice alternative strategies with which to replace or supple-ment the old patterns.

If we succeed in stopping a teacher's behavior in advance of sufficient mastery of a new pattern, he or she may be left without alternative methods of coping with the situation. This situation may cause the children's behavior to become more unacceptable and increase the teacher's own feelings of frustration and failure. Occasionally, this sequence of events is followed by a type of backlash—a strengthened conviction that the old pattern was really the right one after all.

5. Help the Teachers Define Their Jobs so that Their Objectives are Achievable From time to time, inservice educators work with teachers who have defined their jobs so that they have to achieve every possible objective, or to achieve objectives that are almost humanly impossible to achieve. For example, many teachers of young children think their jobs require them to "love all the children" in their classrooms. It is reasonable to assume that they do not have to love or even like all the children they teach—though they do have to respect them all. The latter is not always easy, but is far more achievable than universal love!

The point is that when teachers define their jobs so that the probability or potential for achievement (and therefore satisfaction) is very low, they are likely to experience decreases in responsivity and sensitivity, which reduces effectiveness. Diminished effectiveness can, in turn, lead to feelings of depression, which further diminishes effort and hence achievement and satisfaction. Thus, a downward spiral seems inevitable (Seligman, 1975).

In such cases, the in-service educator can assist teachers by helping them to clarify their own purposes and to settle on some boundaries for their responsibilities and authority. Successful assistance along these lines should lead to the teacher's increased sense of effectiveness and satisfaction, which in turn should increase responsiveness and sensitivity. This increased responsiveness and sensitivity is then likely to foster heightened effort, effectiveness, and satisfaction.

6. Serve as a Neutralizer of Conflicts   Once in a while, in-service educators find themselves trying to help teachers in a situation marked by within-staff conflicts. In such situations, we are often tempted to align ourselves with one side or the other. If we give in to that temptation, we may lose our effectiveness in the long run. The technique that seems useful on such occasions is to remind the contentious parties as gracefully as possible of their superordinate and shared objectives, and to encourage them to keep their minds and energies focused on their long-range common responsibilities. Similarly, it seems useful to resist the temptation to follow up rumors or in any other way to transfer potentially inflammatory information. It is also helpful to avoid reinforcing complaining behavior. One has to sort out and determine which complaints are legitimate and deserve to be followed up and which ones simply reflect the possibility that complaining is, for some people, the only way they know to get others' attention.

7. Use Demonstrations of Skills Cautiously   The technique of cautiously modeling behavior or practices is a useful tool for in-service educators, and opportunities to demonstrate one's skills are often also opportunities to strengthen one's credibility as an educator. But modeling is not without some risks. For example, many in-service educators have had the experience of entering a child care center or preschool class in which (for whatever reason) the situation is out of control. Because we have worked with children for many years, we may know how to bring order to the scene in a flash. In addition, being a relative stranger may increase our power to obtain compliance from young children. But such a demonstration of skill may cause some teachers to look at the scene and say to themselves, "I'll never be that good," or "Why is it so easy for her or him?" and to become even more discouraged and insecure. Or, in the case of demonstrating our skill with older children, the risk occasionally exists that the demonstration will make the teacher look incompetent in the eyes of the pupils. Both of these potentially negative consequences of demonstration must be carefully weighed against the positive value of modeling good practices and enhancing credibility.

8. Share Your Understanding of How a Teacher Sees You Keep in mind that we do not always know how the teachers we work with perceive us. We know that we are kind and warm, sincere and helpful, generous and giving, and so forth! But we are unlikely to be perceived that way in all situations. Some teachers may be afraid of us or unnerved by our presence, even though we do not see ourselves as threatening in any way. If we sense that these kinds of feelings are generated by our presence, it is helpful to let the teacher know that we understand these feelings; that we have also experienced similar feelings; and that we realize teachers might look at us with apprehension, suspicion, or even fear. Acknowledging the potential for such perceptions may be a technique by which to diffuse the excessive stress teachers sometimes experience when they are observed. Furthermore, the shared insight might clear the way to selecting more useful and constructive content for the relationship between the teacher and the in-service educator.

9. Resist the Temptation to "Use" Teachers Some inservice educators are especially intent on getting something accomplished for the children and seem to construe the situation as "getting to the kids through the teachers." If we want to help children (and no doubt we do), then we should do so directly instead of trying to use teachers. The focus should be on helping the teachers as people worthy of our concern and caring in their own right. It is useful to define the role of teacher educator as someone who helps and works with teachers for their own sakes. When we do that wholeheartedly and well, the children will surely benefit also.

CONCLUSION

In the course of employing the principles and techniques enumerated here, several assumptions that underlie the application of these principles might be pointed out. First, it seems useful to assume that not all teachers can be helped by any one teacher educator. Occasionally, an assignment includes a teacher who constitutes a "chronic case" for a given teacher educator. Such a teacher drains large portions of energy, and somehow nothing really seems to help. While this teacher seems to be taking much time and thought, and making no progress, there are other teachers we are responsible for who are ready and waiting to respond to our help and to make developmental advances with relatively modest efforts on our part.

On such occasions, it is a good idea to take the time to think through very deliberately whether or not we see any potential for growth for this teacher under our guidance. We ask ourselves, Do I see any potential for development in this teacher through my efforts? If the assessment is ultimately a positive one, then we can make a "go" decision and mobilize all the professional resources available for the task at hand. If the assessment is ultimately negative, then we can make a "no-go" decision and make every effort to refer this teacher to other teacher educators, agents, or sources of assistance.

The usefulness of the assumption that none of us can teach everyone equally effectively resides mainly in the apparent effects of scrutinizing one's own thoughts and feelings about the case and making a clear choice or go/no-go decision. Once the decision has been made, then the energy drained in agonizing over the chronic case seems to become available for work with those teachers who are ready to respond to our help. Indeed, the content of a relationship that is chronically unsatisfying becomes focused on the pain and frustrations it engenders instead of on the problems of improving the teacher's effectiveness. Furthermore, it appears that when a go decision has been made, we begin to notice some positive attributes of the teacher in question. (Such positive attributes were there before, but we overlooked them by focusing on the chronic aspects of the relationship.) This awareness in turn tends to improve our responses, which in turn seems to lead to more positive responses on the teacher's part. Thus, a positive snowball can be set into motion by engaging in deliberate scrutiny of our own thinking about the difficult or chronic cases we encounter.

Furthermore, it seems useful always to hold to the assumption that every teacher we work with has an inner life of concerns and dreams and wishes and fantasies and hopes and aspirations and so forth, just like all of us. We do not have to know the content of that life. But if we respect the fact that it is there we are more likely to treat the teacher with dignity and with respect, an approach not only essential in teaching but also ethically sound.

Another useful assumption is that every teaching decision contains its own potential errors. If, as suggested above, we decide not to correct a teacher for the sake of building a long-term relationship, we may make the error of letting the teacher continue to perform incorrectly. If we correct the teacher immediately, we risk the error of undermining a relationship that could stimulate significant long-term development and affect a teacher's entire career. Similarly, if we demonstrate to a teacher our own skills in working with children, we may strengthen our credibility, but we may make the error of causing the teacher to feel ashamed or less confident of his or her own competence. On the other hand, if we pass by opportunities to demonstrate our skills, what we teach may be discounted as coming from an inadequate, high-minded, and impractical or naive source; therefore, our ideas and suggestions may be dismissed out of hand.

Until such time as we can devise approaches and techniques that are error free, we might accept the assumption that every choice or decision contains some errors. We can then think through what those errors might be and select the ones we prefer to make. This assumption should free us to make deliberate choices about the appropriate content of our relationships with the teachers we work with and to proceed with sufficient confidence to help them strengthen their own teaching abilities and self-confidence.

REFERENCES

Gliessman, D. (1984). Changing teacher performance. In L. G. Katz & J. D. Raths (Eds.), *Advances in teacher education.* Norwood, NJ: Ablex.

Katz, L. G. (1977). Challenges to early childhood educators. In L. G.. Katz, *Talks with teachers*. Washington, DC: National Association for the Education of Young Children.

Maslach, C., & Pines, A. (1977). The burn-out syndrome in the day care setting. *Child Care Quarterly, 6*(2), 100–113.

Peters, R. S. (1970). Concrete principles and the rational passion. In N. F. Sizer & T. R. Sizer (Eds.), *Moral education*. Cambridge, MA: Harvard University Press.

Seligman, M. E. (1975). *Helplessness: On depression, development, and death*. San Francisco: W.H. Freeman.

AUTHOR INDEX

SUBJECT INDEX